# FIRST WE TAKE
# MANHATTAN

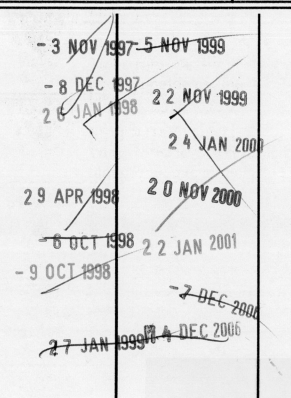

## Choreography and Dance Studies

A series of books edited by Robert P. Cohan, C.B.E.

**Please see the back of this book for other titles in the Choreography and Dance Studies series.**

# FIRST WE TAKE
# MANHATTAN

## FOUR AMERICAN WOMEN AND THE NEW YORK SCHOOL OF DANCE CRITICISM

### Diana Theodores
*Dartington College of Arts, Devon, UK*

**harwood academic publishers**
Australia • Canada • China • France • Germany • India • Japan
Luxembourg • Malaysia • The Netherlands • Russia • Singapore
Switzerland • Thailand • United Kingdom

Emmaplein 5
1075 AW Amsterdam
The Netherlands

---

**British Library Cataloguing in Publication Data**

Theodores, Diana
    First we take Manhattan: four American women and the New York
    School of Dance Criticism. – (Choreography and dance studies; v. 10)
    1. Dance criticism – New York (N.Y.)
    I. Title
    792.8'015

    ISBN   3-7186-5876-3 (Hardcover)
    ISBN   3-7186-5886-0 (Softcover)

Cover design by Gareth James, incorporating *Frontier* (1935) with choreography by Martha Graham: photo © 1941 by Barbara Morgan.

# CONTENTS

v

Contents

# INTRODUCTION TO THE SERIES

*Choreography and Dance Studies* is a book series of special interest to dancers, dance teachers and choreographers. Focusing on dance composition, its techniques and training, the series will also cover the relationship of choreography to other components of dance performance such as music, lighting and the training of dancers.

In addition, *Choreography and Dance Studies* will seek to publish new works and provide translations of works not previously published in English, as well as to publish reprints of currently unavailable books of outstanding value to the dance community.

Robert P. Cohan

# LIST OF PLATES

# ACKNOWLEDGEMENTS

Grateful acknowledgement is made to the following for permission to reprint previously published material: The Nation Company, Inc. for the selections from Nancy Goldner's reviews in *The Nation* magazine; Alfred A. Knopf for selections from Arlene Croce's reviews in *Afterimages, Going to the Dance, Sight Lines* and for selections from Edwin Denby's reviews in *Looking at the Dance* and *Dancers, Buildings and People in the Streets*; Marcel Dekker, Inc. for selections from Deborah Jowitt's reviews in *Dance Beat*; David R. Godine Publishers for selections from Deborah Jowitt's material in *The Dance in Mind*; Duke University Press for selections from Sally Bane's *Greenwich Village 1963: Avant-Garde Performance and the Effervescent Body*; Harwood Academic Publishers for selections from Roger Copeland's article "Backlash Against Balanchine" in *Choreography and Dance*, Vol. 3, Part 3, 1993; Little, Brown and Company for selections from Martin Esslin's *Anatomy of Drama*; Marcia B. Siegel for selections of material from *At the Vanishing Point, Watching the Dance Go By, The Shapes of Change*; and from reviews by Jill Johnston in *Marmalade Me*.

Photograph Permissions:
Research Division of The New York Public Library, Astor, Lenox and Tilden Foundations: permission to reproduce six photographs from The Dance Collection

The George Balanchine Trust

Martha Graham, *Frontier*, 1935 © 1941 Barbara Morgan: Willard & Barbara Morgan Archives
Martha Graham, *Primitive Mysteries*, 1935 © 1941 Barbara Morgan: Willard & Barbara Morgan Archives

Photographs:
Herbert Migdoll, James Klosty, Anne Bradley, Jack Mitchell, Barbara Morgan, Lois Greenfield, Jules Cohen, Hsü Pin, Costas, and Israel

# PREFACE

Two events in my life led indirectly to the writing of this book. The first occurred when I was fifteen. I had my heart set on being the dance critic for *The New York Times*. My father, very matter of factly, suggested I call Clive Barnes (who *was* the dance critic for *The New York Times* then) to seek advice on my career prospects. It took a lot of persuasion on my father's part for me to act on this advice. I think his clinching line was, "He's a human being just like you." To my astonishment Mr Barnes responded to my call and invited me to a "consultation." On the appointed day I nervously arrived at his apartment armed with a portfolio of my "reviews." He made me a sandwich (a BLT), patiently read every single one of my reviews, made encouraging sounds, and advised me to "keep at it" for another ten years. The second was when I read Marcia Siegel's *At The Vanishing Point* hot off the press while I was taking a summer course in dance criticism at The American University in Washington DC, taught by Alan Kriegsman of *The Washington Post*. I read it from cover to cover in a day with the same addiction that one reads an unputdownable novel. To me it was a revelation about dance writing.

Since my adolescent "career consultation" with Clive Barnes I have "kept at it" in one form or another, as a writer or teacher or dance practitioner. My most sustained work in journalistic dance writing was as dance critic for *The Sunday Tribune* in Ireland (from 1984 to 1992). My work there was spurred by having to relate a whole spectrum of dance encounters – from Irish dancing to the Bolshoi Ballet – to a traditionally literature and theatre-oriented readership. I was also in the unique position of having been the only dance critic in the country with a regular column. In my own immediate environment I was a pioneer and it was very hard work. The magnitude of effort of the pioneers who are the subject of this book was and remains an inspiration. For a long time, Marcia Siegel, Deborah Jowitt, Nancy Goldner and Arlene Croce influenced and even shaped my very perceptions about dance; and although my views, since living abroad, have re-formed considerably in the context of European choreography, their legacy remains unsurpassed for the clarity, intensity and identity of response to a particular dance culture in a particular time. Their collective literature – which I term here the New York School of dance criticism – creates an enduring model for mode, method and theory in "textualizing" dance.

The following people are gratefully acknowledged for helping me in this task: Dr George Jackson, whose dialogue, practical help and support was invaluable; the Dartington College of Arts Research Committee; Madeleine M. Nichols and Rita Waldron, Dance Collection, The New York Library for Performing Arts at Lincoln Center; Rita Felciano, The Dance Critics Association; Denise Theodores, picture research; Lloyd Morgan, Morgan Press, Inc.; David Vaughan, Cunningham Dance Foundation; Charles Woodford, Princeton Book Company Publishers; Stephanie Clemens, Executive Director of The Doris Humphrey Society; Nena Couch, The Jerome Lawrence and Robert E. Lee Theatre Research Institute at Ohio State University; Susan Scanella, Tharp Productions; Gail Perlberg, Feld Ballets New York; Jack Mitchell, James Klosty, Lois Greenfield, Costas, Israel, Jules Cohen; and Jo Woodcock, Tamsin Whitney and Robin Tay at Dartington College of Arts. I especially want to thank my publisher at Harwood Academic for his initial interest in this book and his continuing support, and Muriel Topaz, my editor, whose thorough responses and many exclamation marks in the margins helped so much to clarify and complete this manuscript. Gareth James, friend throughout, patiently let me "get on with it" while attending to countless tasks to make my life a little easier and designed the main concept for the bookcover. To Nancy Goldner, Arlene Croce, Deborah Jowitt and Marcia Siegel I extend my deepest appreciation for precious time out of impossibly busy schedules, for cooperation and generosity. I am also deeply grateful to Marcia Siegel for allowing me to reproduce some of her sketches here. This book is dedicated to my unfailingly supportive parents in Newport, my loved ones in Lafayette, and my wonderful sons, Justin and Toby, in Devon.

# 1

## FRONTIERS AND PIONEERS

Four American women, Marcia Siegel (1932-), Deborah Jowitt (1934-), Arlene Croce (1934-) and Nancy Goldner (1943-) are writers who became dance critics partly by accident and partly by design. They came of age during the "formalist heyday" in New York,[1] all had a mission to publish serious writing about dance, and consciously generated and promoted a distinct development in dance criticism through the profile of their work and their teaching. They created a new critical dance language, a new rigor of investigation in responding to dance, and an aesthetic sensibility so persuasive and influential that a whole generation of dance viewers and critics alike, from the late 1960's to the end of the 1980's, marveled at the prolific and profound nature of the *Golden Age of Dance* in New York. It is a generation that read, relished and imitated the critical parameters and sentiments of the articulate four. The championing of *the American classicists,* the *permission* to be passionate and majestically subjective in dance criticism, the prolonged attention to description and analysis — the virtual inhaling of dances, and the reading of dances for what they in themselves could offer up for meaning, for theory, for contextual considerations — these things were their legacy. Although they have rarely exchanged dialogue in public forums or aligned themselves in any formal way,[2] I nevertheless proceed cautiously but confidently with the notion that this *pas de quatre* of women writers form the New York School of dance criticism.

The image on the cover of this book serves as the starting point for my story. Barbara Morgan's classic photograph of Martha Graham in her 1935 solo, *Frontier* invites us in an instant to consider both the clarity of shape in this dance image and the scale of space witnessed in Graham's gaze at an imaginary vastness.

---

[1] Roger Copeland "Dance Criticism and the Descriptive Bias" *Dance Theatre Journal,* v. 10, No. 2, 1980, p. 27.

[2] Deborah Jowitt and Marcia Siegel share continuous dialogue about their work. Apart from this communication, all four critics emphasised in numerous discussions with me that they worked almost entirely in isolation from each other.

*She sits resolutely on her fence, gravely surveys and marks out her turf, salutes the space around her, and kicks up her heels at the pleasure of it all... The conquest of the land is analogous to the forging of her body, to the mastery of her art.*[3]

This is what Deborah Jowitt wrote about *Frontier* in her book, *Time and The Dancing Image*. As if giving a critical voice to Graham's frontierswoman described by Jowitt, the critic Jill Johnston articulated an equivalent pioneering vision of criticism in the *Village Voice* when she said

*I'll take a plot of level territory and stake out a claim to lie down on it and criticize the constellations if that's what I happen to be looking at... The future is upon us and the Art of Criticism has already come into its own in those public places where the critic is lying down on a soft piece of ground to enjoy a bit of blue and yellow scenery.*[4]

Johnston, a critical activist whose territory in print covered everything from literature to lesbian politics, and all arts and art-in-the-making, published the above essay in 1965, the starting point for Deborah Jowitt's career as a dance critic. Jowitt was inspired by Johnston's liberating colloquial style and her ready-to-look-at-anything critical stance.

Looking over Barbara Morgan's image and Jowitt's and Johnston's above texts, certain key words come into focus. *America, women, territory, claim, shape, clarity, scale* and *pleasure* are words that are actually present or implied in those sources. I believe these words are indicators of both the explorative and forthright nature of the journey the critics of the New York School have traveled. The clarity and scale described in the *Frontier* image is taken up in the merging Manhattan sky-line. This outline of architectural salutation to the sky contains within it a superabundance of stimuli that inhabits the space between, within and beneath those buildings, in a city that offered the New York critics a bounty of discovery in their most loved art. And in this dance-heightened environment these critics set about to clarify the shape of American dance, responding to a prolific generation of choreographers and influencing a prolific response to dance criticism as a new literature.

The time frame under examination for this New York School begins in 1965, when Marcia Siegel was editing *Dance Scope* (she founded the journal in 1964), Deborah Jowitt started airing her views on dance as part of Baird Searles' WBA New York radio program "The Critical People," Arlene Croce founded *Ballet Review*, and Nancy Goldner started coalescing her dance

---

[3] Deborah Jowitt, *Time and the Dancing Image*, New York: William Morris & Co. Inc., 1988, p. 177.

[4] Jill Johnston, *Village Voice*, September 16, 1965, p. 18.

training and publishing house experience into a critical voice, as yet unpublished but passionate and prolific. My cut off point is 1985, two years after George Balanchine's death, the end of the so-called dance boom in New York and the start of a fallow phase in the cycle of art in which retreat, reflection and recession (not entirely economically induced) are the pre-conditions for renewal and reformation. 1965–1985: such a recent history, such a confluent era. The aesthetics of virtuosity played opposite the aesthetics of denial,[5] theatre of chance opposite epic spectacle. The chaste and virtuoso metaphysics of Cunningham's balletic modernist events, Balanchine's pristine neo-classicism, the heroic pedestrianism of the Judson Movement, Tharp's popular aculturations, the shape- superlatives of Graham and Taylor, dance on Broadway and the ever-populating choreographic and technical "hybrids" all contributed to a dance culture in New York that, as Croce suggested, "achieved all it set out to do in the 20th century." In this twenty-year span these New York critics witnessed a "Golden Age" of choreography and their original chronicling of events in a unique time formed a body of literature, of dance texts, whose fresh historical significance it is vital to address as critical discourse and debate in dance intensifies.

The New York dance environment afforded the critics of this study access not only to an unprecedented volume of performance but also to changing casts, retrospectives of large bodies of choreographers' works, to revivals and reconstructions as much as to rebellions. In a sense these writers approached their task of criticism as a kind of political lobby. They addressed dance as a cultural phenomenon, communicating a meticulously examined subjective response to dance, collectively forging an attitude, an appetite and an activeness in their *seeing* with which to penetrate the subject of dance as deeply as possible in their reviews. They consciously pioneered notions of "serious writing" about dance in the intellectual/journalistic spheres.

All formed their critical careers and reputations in New York largely through their writings in *The New Yorker* (Croce), *The Christian Science Monitor* and *The Nation* (Goldner), *The Hudson Review* and the *Soho Weekly News* (Siegel), and *The Village Voice* (Jowitt). Many other publications have served as outlets for their writing and these, along with collections and books published are cited in later chapters and in the bibliography. A generation of critics such as Winer, Shapiro, Aloff, Banes, Greskovic, Zimmer, Supree, Macauley and others have felt their influence. A generation of dance

---

[5] Sally Banes "Yvonne Rainer: The Aesthetics of Denial" in *Terpsichore in Sneakers*, Boston: Houghton Mifflin Company, 1980, p. 43.

audiences have been ideologically persuaded by their vision and voice. It is arguable that other dance critics, writing with distinction and insight in high-profile publications in the same time and place might profitably be included in a discussion about a New York School. What sets my pas de quatre of critics apart is their conscious mission to teach dance criticism (predominant in the careers of Siegel, Jowitt and Goldner) and to *define* American dance. Implicit in so much of their writing is an acknowledgement of their vantage point at the watershed of American dance history. Always poised between heritage and vanguard, these four women wrote into their critic's job description a self-appointed guardianship of the *Americanness* of American dance. At the heart of their literature lies a kind of sacred sisterhood encoded in the practice of what I call the "three P's"— *preservation, possession and purification* — as modes of response to the art of dance. These responses will be discussed in later chapters.

The definition of school is fairly wide. In identifying a school I am examining the values and characteristics common to a group of critics who share a particular dance environment and who influence our perception of dance in a particular way. "Walk into a museum gallery for the first time" says George Jackson,

> *and before you can look at any of the art properly, chances are that you'll become aware of style... By style I mean the things that advertise authorship as well as a point of view, a hierarchy of values, the set of assumptions that define the universe of a work, or a corpus or an entire school... To differentiate between style and individuality may be tricky. The handwriting is not something seen right away, as soon as one enters the gallery. One must really look at the choreography to discover what the Petipa academics of Balanchine's* Grand Pas Glasnuv *have in common with the split atom classicism of* Agon *or the symphonism of the* Adagio Lamentoso *(Tchaikovsky's Symphony No. 6 Pathetique). Once one has looked, it may be simple to see but not at all easy to say.*[6]

Jackson's comments on what constitutes style, made in the context of discussing George Balanchine, are apt in the discussion of this school of individual but collectively identifiable critics.

My own discoveries about these critics were made through their words themselves. In the same way that these critics have advanced the notion of "reading dances" — allowing the dances to speak to them on their own terms about meaning, humanity, codes of behaviour and the inherent expressiveness of steps — so I have had, through their writings,

---

[6] George Jackson "Requirements for a Book about Balanchine" *Washington Dance Review*, Summer-Autumn, 1989, p. 8.

a more profoundly complete experience of dance. And, as the process of reading their criticism reveals their links, it also reveals the workings of the various influences and experiences they brought to their task of writing dance criticism.

Arlene Croce came to dance criticism via film criticism and a wide experience of writing for publications of the highest literary standards; Goldner arrived at the job having initially trained with the School of American Ballet and after having worked as an editor with several publishing houses; Siegel was first a news reporter and then studied Movement Analysis at the Laban/Bartenieff Institute; and Jowitt had a long standing career as a choreographer and performer in dance and theatre. Via all these routes and investigative processes, this pas de *quatre* of critics possesses signature characteristics in their response to dance. To be expediently glib one could say that Croce responds to "the power of the foot", Siegel to body shape and movement qualities, Jowitt to the kinesthetic sense of movement phrases, and Goldner to the mysteries of a dance's effects. Amongst these critics, the dance work is perceived as being a whole history of performances and not just the single performance event. While they may begrudge a revival for lacking stylistic clarity, or carefully monitor the changes and attitudes present in a work by its performances and by its audiences, these critics are united in their ability actively to describe the immediate look and impact of dances as well as analyse their distinguishing characteristics.

Technically the methods employed by these critics are unremarkable in themselves and idiosyncratic to each writer. Siegel describes her critical process as one of analysis, interpretation and subjective awareness. From the image of the dance, she first titles her piece to bring both this image and her ideas into focus. Next, she describes the central image or images and finds, through describing, that associations grow and meanings become clearer. Jowitt works with contrary ideas, addressing first what the dance is *not*. She then works on describing the dance with the non-viewer in mind. Croce separates the seeing process from the writing process through time, often letting the work she has viewed "become a part of her" for about a week before writing.[7] Goldner intuits the whole work, all at once, finding out what it is that moves her, then solving the mystery of why that is so.

For all of them dance resonates with value and meaning within the culture and time it reflects. At the heart of the matter is choreography.

---

[7] Interview with Arlene Croce, New York City, June 1985.

Goldner goes so far as to say that "the choreography of the time has taught us to see in a particular way."[8] This idea of choreography as *art object* is clarified, elucidated and morally protected throughout the writings of the New York School of dance critics. Croce, the former of tastes and opinions and standards often seems to want to "save" dance from its fans — those who enjoy dance as "undifferentiated sensation." Siegel pleads with dancers not to "muck around with their posterity." Jowitt would like audiences to get away from the idea of the immediate performance as the work and care more about the dance as an enduring entity. Goldner investigates the work for its permanent values, beyond cast changes and the erosions or alterations of time.

The "eyeless" critic, unable or unwilling to distinguish between the performance and the dance cheats us of posterity, of definition and clarification. The "eyeless" dancer who is unable to distinguish among the shapes of different choreographers, of different physical attitudes and philosophies also contributes to this "erosion" of dance history. In both cases the critic as historian and criticism as a tool for the historian are obliged to direct our attention to these problems and lead the way to rectification. These critics see their task partly as "aesthetic conscience" for the art of dance. In so doing they constantly clarify through seeing and through language an accurate, active and specific vocabulary of dance and dancers.

Perhaps these individualistic critics of such distinction will feel a little uncomfortable with the idea of being labelled as a "School." Martin Esslin gives me a little boost of courage. When discussing a similar objective in theatre criticism, he argues:

> *a descriptive term applied post factum may be useful even if the people to whom it is applied are unaware of its existence and meaning, provided that such a term is not taken as totally defining the works to which it is applied, but merely as descriptive of certain features which they have in common and which are basic to them. Neither a mouse nor an elephant has to know that they are both mammals, and the fact that they are both mammals certainly does not mean that they are identical. And yet the term is of considerable usefulness in understanding both these animals... in those 'movements' in which the practitioners are unaware, consciously, of any common endeavour, we often find very deep inner similarities and connections.*[9]

---

[8] Interview with Nancy Goldner, New York City, September 1985.

[9] Martin Esslin, *An Anatomy of Drama*, London: Sphere Books Ltd, Abacus edition, 1978, pp. 58–59.

I cannot help being fascinated with the parallel that exists between this group of contemporary American women writers who were the pioneers of a new dance criticism and the women choreographers who pioneered the American modern dance: Duncan, Humphrey, St. Denis, Graham. Both groups created new languages and approaches for grappling with their disciplines; each pushed the subject of dance into new and enduring dimensions. In describing these critics as pioneers, I am reminded of Arlene Croce's comments from "The Avant-Garde on Broadway" that "in American dance, the roll call, from Loie Fuller to Isadora and onward, is virtually all-women and all-pioneer..."[10] In her discussion of the Judson Dance Theater movement Sally Banes described women as "a dominant majority," who "emerged to create a space... where they could be leaders and creative artists," who "transformed that space from a marginal, lower-status art form to a central arena — where all the arts met — for avant-garde expression of the early Sixties."[11] I would argue that the critics of the New York School likewise transformed the status, space and "arena" of dance criticism from marginal to mainstream. With their conciousness of a pioneer inheritence — from Duncan to Graham, Rainer to Tharp — these critics pioneered a new criticism that expanded our notions and vocabulary of dance more persistently than any other dance criticism published during the period cited. They demanded we pay attention to dance as theatre art with the same willingness and imagination we might to other forms of literature. Their writings examined and re-examined dances so that detailed observations of casts, growth of individual performers, stylistic and technical changes in works, the preservation and understanding of new and renewed dance values, all became shared critical territory. There was amongst these critics a striking familiarity with the American dance scene, a kind of "in house" quality which, rather than being exclusive in tone, infected the reader with their enthusiasm and intimate knowledge of the "family tree" of American dance. They had the sheer volume of dance on their side. They had a willingness to look for and appreciate *the new*, and see new aspects of a tradition or heritage. They renewed their response to dance again and again, infusing their "critical repertory," as Croce coined it, in the same way that a dancer must find out something for the first time every time he performs. In the spirit of "historian" I am impressed by the shape and texture of an era

---

[10] Arlene Croce, "The Avant Garde on Broadway" in *Afterimages*, New York: Alfred A. Knopf, 1978, p. 340.

[11] Sally Banes, *Greenwich Village 1963* (Avant Garde Performance and the Effervescent Body) Durham and London: Duke University Press, 1993, p. 72.

through their writings, but I am also alerted to the historical significance of the writing itself in that it introduced and refined a revolution in dance. Siegel states in *The Shapes of Change* "When he (Balanchine) repeats an arabesque or a battement twelve different ways he's not exposing his own lack of ideas but the arabesque's plenitude of them,"[12] a comment which reflects the spirit of the New York "School."

While the contemporary historical span addressed here is 1965–1985 it is fully recognized that these four critics are ever-active, and that their most recent work signals new direction, insights and affiliations.[13] It is entirely within the historical context that I write about them here, at times, in the past tense.

At the start of this chapter I pointed out key words in an attempt to anchor my *instinctive* notions about these critics. It will be useful now to list the characteristics that identify them as a school. Each of these characteristics are addressed in the chapters that follow:

– the perspective they bring to writing on dance as *women*
– their collective construction of a "critical repertory"[14] along with their conscious drive to teach and influence the direction of dance criticism
– the predominant value of *choreography* in their work – that through choreography they were "taught how to look"
– the central aesthetic value of *classicism* and their pursuit of a specifically American classicism
– a formalist appreciation of *style-as-meaning* and of dance on its own terms
– the operation of a *preservation* mode – seeking to distinguish between styles, to define styles, to place style within historical and cultural contexts and promote a consciousness about dance heritage
– an alertness to innovation and an affirmation of a *tradition of the new* as an aesthetic value

---

[12] Marcia B. Siegel, *The Shapes of Change*, Boston: Houghton Mifflin Company, 1979, p. 221.

[13] Nancy Goldner is currently dance critic for the *Philadelphia Inquirer*. Arlene Croce is working on a critical study of George Balanchine. Marcia Siegel continues in her post as Associate Professor of Performance Studies at the Tisch School of the Arts, New York University, and has produced essays for several forthcoming publications on dance history and criticism. Deborah Jowitt continues to write for *The Village Voice*, is teaching on the faculty of the Dance Department at the Tisch School of the Arts, New York University, and has contributed essays to recently published and forthcoming dance books. In recent discussions all four of these critics articulated different reflections on their writing over the twenty year span cited as well as fresh insights on their writing in relation to the current dance they view.

[14] Arlene Croce, "Introduction," *Going to the Dance*, New York: Alfred A. Knopf, 1982.

- the use of *re-creative* description which is kinesthetically intuited, action-based and responsive to a choreographer's unique language
- the use of *poetic or sensual* description which uses imagery to offer up the essence of a dance and the sensation of its effects
- the use of *analytical* description which traces the effect of a dance to its factual sources in the choreography and performance

These last three facets of description, re-creative, sensual and analytical, always permeate these critics' writings simultaneously, creating a set of aesthetic values that is as implicit "as atomic physics is present in sunlight when you feel it."[15] In the chapter addressing description, the term itself will be assessed in relation to its employment in the writings of the New York School and in relation to debate on its relevance to dance theory.

The inventory of identifying characteristics listed above emerge in the first instance as the "afterimage"[16] of impressions, hunches, and phrases that I take away with me both immediately after reading these critics' texts and also over time, reading their writings again and again. Often, and much to my fascination, the process has reversed itself through chance. In a kind of *I Ching* procedure I have cast open the pages of their writings and encountered these characteristics like reliable and loyal friends with uncanny consistency. Through familiararity with the works they view, the critics have constructed a critical repertory of cross-references and links between dances and between their own reviews of these dances. Through familiarity with their writings in varying contexts, individually and collectively, over time and changes, in print and in dialogue, and after much scrutiny, a critical repertory of characteristics of the New York School is, likewise, constructed. When the afterimages of their writings have been analysed, the effects of their imagery, vocabulary, styles and sensibilities traced, tracked, logged or pondered in relation to the dance they viewed and the dance criticism of their time, these characteristics endure. Through repeated encounters with these characteristics their stature as useful organizing principles for defining a school of dance criticism, is affirmed.

---

[15] R. P. Blackmur, *The Double Agent*, New York: Arrow Editions 1935, p. 287.

[16] Arlene Croce, "Preface", *Afterimages*, New York: Alfred A. Knopf, 1978.

# 2

# UNDER THE INFLUENCE

## The Critic

Great art is disorienting. It changes your perception of the world, of ways of seeing. It forces you to make new kinds of observations. It questions. Sometimes it resolves. Chaos and resolution: The chaos that comes from *daring to recognize* new structures; the resolution that comes from the reconciliation of technique and expression. "The fusion," as Arlene Croce describes it, "is itself the complete experience one looks for."[1] In a generation replete with choreographic landmarks, the New York School critics fequently grappled with the task of finding a critical voice with which to respond to the insistent disorientations and resolutions of the works they viewed.

Seeing Merce Cunningham's *Winterbranch* for instance, Marcia Siegel addressed first her own process in saying *"When I learned how to look at it* it seemed to open the whole world of modern art to me......" (italics mine). Her response to the work, once 'seen', presented her with an equally rigorous critical task of ordering the chaos of "the new" while allowing the work to thrive in the tumult. "I think of *Winterbranch'"* confides Siegel, "as a latter day *Sacre du Printemps*. Scandalous, offensive, extreme, crucial. But its power lies in its ability to make you mad, to shake your equilibrium."[2]

These critics formulated a working manifesto which defined and re-defined itself in reaction to and in anticipation of the developments in dance they observed and experienced. They both chronicled *and* created their art histories. While it is true that the aesthetic assumptions and values evident in critics' writings are directly related to the art environment and culture they inhabit, this is only part of the picture. The active, creative response of a critic

---

[1] Arlene Croce, "Ballets Without Choreography", *Afterimages*, New York : Alfred A. Knopf, 1978, p. 322.

[2] Marcia B. Siegel, *Watching The Dance Go By*, Boston: Houghton Mifflin Company, 1977, p. 286.

**Plate 1** *Winterbranch*, choreography by Merce Cunningham (1964). Dancers: Meg Harper, Chris Komar, Brynar Mehl, Robert Kovich, Susanna Hayman-Chaffey. Photograph © Jack Mitchell. Courtesy of Cunningham Dance Foundation, Inc.

can show the viewer  values he might otherwise miss.[3] In so doing the critic achieves not only recognition for a work but defines the work and locates the values relevant for its aesthetic appreciation. This point can be illustrated by a comparative example, for instance, between the critics, Cyril Beaumont and Edwin Denby, both writing on the same ballet, Frederick Ashton's *Cinderella*. This is a classical, full length, narrative ballet in which sets, decor, costumes, lighting and music, and choreography formed a total theatre production. The ballet was discussed by Beaumont in *Ballet and Opera*, February 1949. The first *fourteen* pages of Beaumont's essay are dedicated entirely to a detailed moment-to-moment description of the production values — the sets, placement of props and dancers on the stage, colours, mood and overall activity. The first description of *movement* appears on page 10:

> *In the final solo there is a very interesting use of pirouettes to suggest an increasing exhilaration of spirit. Cinderella circles the stage, ending in a corner down-stage, travelling first by a sequence of three single turns, followed by a double then a series of one single, one double: the diagonal is crossed with a series of very quick single turns. The varying speed of the several turns admirably succeeds in conveying a sense of mounting ecstasy.[4]*

Denby's critique, from the same reference, establishes from the first page a description of the movement which at the same time penetrates something about its organization and perceptual outcome:

> *As dance choreographer his great moments are a set of classic variations for girls representing the Four Seasons (the good Fairy calls each in turn to attend Cinderella), and a number of entrances for the Jester during the ball...... The part is Alexander Grant's, the company's most interesting male dancer. Like a jet of force he darts forward in deep plié, in reverse, bent sideways, bent double, leaping down a flight of stairs, springing into the meagre dances of the Guests with a smiling threat. In the Jester's leaps Ashton has timed the rhythm to the leap's arrival (instead of to its departure from the ground) and because your ear anticipates the rhythm, the crouching dancer's downward course through the air keeps the beautiful suspense of an animal pounce. More delicately Ashton uses the same device in the feminine Season's variations and there too it gives the dancer an other than human presence....[5]*

For Beamont "A critic's first duty is to try and inform the reader what the ballet is about."[6] For Denby the essential task of the critic is "to produce a

[3] Laurel Quinlan, "A Way of Seeing: Edwin Denby's Ballet Criticism" *Masters Thesis*, York University, Toronto, 1982.

[4] Cyril Beaumont, *Ballet and Opera*, February 1949, p. 10.

[5] Edwin Denby, *Ballet and Opera*, February 1949, pp. 27–34.

[6] Cyril Beaumont, "The Practice of Ballet Criticism" in *Dancers and Critics*, ed. Cyril Swinson, London : Adam & Charles Black, 1950, p. 13.

hypothesis of what makes a dance hang together and communicate its images so they are remembered."[7] Clearly the above illustrations, the one re-creative, the other analytical, do just that. Beaumont is clearly concerned with a narrative order and logic, both choreographically and critically. His observations tend to break the work into parts, which should ideally add up to an expressive, meaningful whole. For Beaumont, themeless ballets are expressively impenetrable. This view leads him to the conclusion, in a review of Balanchine's *Ballet Imperial* "that where a ballet has no theme, the critic's manner of writing resembles an account of a combination of geometry and applied mechanics.... It is much easier to describe a ballet of incident like *The Rake's Progress* than *Symphonic Variations*."[8] For Denby, criticism is shaped by what the dancers do. The 'incident' is in the materials of movement. This is also the case in the criticism of the New York School. For instance, Deborah Jowitt, addressing Graham's *Primitive Mysteries* channels our attention to the *action* with a sense of vivid narrative. Gesture, sound, phrasing and image are all active agents in a creation of the *dance text* of the work.

> When the figure in white runs in tiny steps from one cluster of women to another, each group responds to her gesture with one of its own, and these terse gestures bloom out of stillness as icons suggesting crowning, praying, rocking a cradle, spreading a ritual meal.... The piano strikes single chords while the oboe sustains a high wail. On an abrupt chord the woman stretches out her arms and the others begin to circle her in huge, wracking leaps.... Even when the leaps accelerate and scale down into runs the effect is terrifying....[9]

It is with this *innovative process of seeing* that the critic can influence taste and sensitivity and create a climate of acceptance for an artist or a whole movement in art. We can look to Clement Greenberg's promotion of the Abstract Expressionists, to Frank O'Hara's championing of the New York School of Poetry, Martin Esslin's of Beckett, John Martin's of Graham, Edwin Denby's of Balanchine and so on for vivid examples of this process. "Clarity," says Roger Copeland, "the ability to see clearly, is what distinguishes critics like Denby, Jowitt and Croce from the rest of us." He says that they exemplify what John Martin must have meant when he wrote:

> The greatest thing a human soul ever does in this world is to see something and tell what it saw in a plain way. Hundreds of people can talk for one who can think, but few souls can think for one who can see. To see clearly is poetry, prophecy and religion — all in one.[10]

---

[7] Edwin Denby, *Looking at the Dance*, New York: Curtis Books, 1949, p. 15.

[8] Cyril Beaumont, "The Practice of Ballet Criticism" in *Dancers and Critics*, London: Adam & Charles Black, 1950.

[9] Deborah Jowitt, *The Village Voice*, May 30, 1977.

[10] Roger Copeland, "Seeing Clearly", *Ballet News*, February 1980, pp. 22–24, 42.

## The Environment

The New York School critics enjoyed, during the time span discussed, a more wide-ranging, active dance environment than any other dance critics in the world. The way in which this richly textured dance heritage plays upon their critical sensibilities and, at the same time, the way in which their perceptions have ordered and illuminated this heritage has resulted in a distinguished critical identity. The thrust of constant change, and the melting pot of styles and genres that has been an uniquely American dance experience have dictated an active, flexible response on the part of these critics. At the same time it is the very nature of that response, balanced between the sensuously physical and the rigorously analytical, that has defined the essence of American dance culture and created a vocabulary for its appreciation and recognition.

The women of the New York School of dance criticism have taught audiences how to look at a largely formalist dance genre, but they also, in the sweep of innovations that comprise the peak era of their dance viewing, have attempted to clarify the American ancestry of dance more rigorously than ever before. That task has certainly included a wide range of dance outside the purely formalist framework of leanness, purity of means and movement for its own sake. The extraordinary scope of their challenge is met first and foremost with love, echoing E. M. Forster's declaration that "in the case of criticism one has to start with love."[11] Love for their subject is surely one of the most influential forces contributing to the excitement of their writing. But this is no innocent love. It is knowledgeable love, or perhaps both. In her role as a literary critic, Virginia Woolf (included in Arlene Croce's "roll call" of "all women and all pioneers" in the making of American art) read all books twice, once with abandon and once with severity.[12] The New York critics seem to "read" all the dances they view in a similar fashion, with freshness and scrutiny, capturing as fast as they can the dance in a culture which sprang from "the classic modernist compulsion to make it new,"[13] while often paying homage to visionaries and traditionalists.

This tradition of *the new* was a heritage they shared with critics commenting on the Dada movement in New York in the Thirties, the New York School of Painting in the Forties, the New York School of Poetry in the Fifties, and the inter-disciplinary Avant Garde in New York in the Sixties.

---

[11] E. M. Forster, "The Raison d'Etre of Criticism in the Arts" in *Two Cheers for Democracy*, London: Edward Arnold, 1951, p. 114.

[12] Ibid, p. 126.

[13] Neill Baldwin, *Man Ray (American Artist)*, New York: Clarkson N. Potter, Inc., 1947.

As Sally Banes, in her richly informative work, 'Greenwich Village 1963' described the latter:

> The art of the early Sixties laid the groundwork — in content, style and technique — for the two distinct branches of vanguard art that would directly follow it: the medium oriented formalism of the Seventies and the deeply ambivalent, ironic, reflexive art of the Eighties and Nineties (that is, second generation postmodernism)... it was clear that the deep scrutiny of every medium that was part of the interdisciplinary flux of the Sixties led first, in the Seventies, to a rigorous and sober asceticism, a principle of minimalism and separation, oddly appropriate in the wake of Sixties excess.[14]

Sixties excess in the arts seemed to spring, innocently enough, from a national "official mood of optimism" inspired by the Kennedy administration's White House patronage for the arts and major political landmarks in the wake of the Cold War. Referring to Banes again:

> The American Dream of freedom, equality and abundance seemed as if it could come true... the arts seemed to hold a privileged place in that democratic vision, not merely a reflection of a vibrant, rejuvenated American Society, but an active register of contemporary consciousness.[15]

New York was the culture capital of America and it launched a proliferation of high art culture with the building of the arts complex, Lincoln Center, in the middle of Manhattan, housing the Avery Fisher Hall, the Metropolitan Opera House, the New York State Theatre, the Vivien Beaumont and Mitzi Newhouse Theatres, the Julliard School and the New York Public Library and Museum of the Performing Arts. In 1963 the Ford Foundation invested $8 million to "Americanize Ballet." As Marcia Siegel described in her "Introduction" to her critical collection, *Watching The Dance Go By*

> In one stroke Lincoln Center drastically altered several facts of dance life.... Lincoln Center and the subsequent rash of little Lincoln Centers that broke out all over America turned dance — that is ballet — into a full-fledged constituent of fashionable culture.[16]

Balanchine's School of American Ballet at Lincoln Center served as the central training ground and this "Americanization" of ballet was decidedly Russian schooled. While the ballet, theater, opera and music went into big budget profile, the Judson Movement and alternative arts scene downtown were at a parallel point of prolific activity.[17] Jill Johnston prophesied in *The*

---

[14] Sally Banes, *Greenwich Village 1963* (Avant Garde Performance and the Effervescent Body), Durham, London: Duke University Press, 1993, p. 7.

[15] Ibid, p. 3.

[16] Marcia B. Siegel, *At the Vanishing Point*, New York, Saturday Review Press, 1972, p. 3.

[17] Sally Banes, op. cit., p. 5.

*Village Voice* that the Judson Group would "galvanize a Renaissance in modern dance for the first time in twenty years."[18]

These two major movements of the Sixties — the high art, high profile, high-financed culture zone of Lincoln Center and subsequent Americanization of Russian ballet, and the Sixties avant-garde culture, produced a "juncture" of sensibilities. These sensibilities, in dance, were essentially those of classicism and formalism. They bridged the cultures of the elite and virtuoso, and the democratic and pedestrian. The notion of "purity of means" was the link between them and a fundamental force in the critical views of the New York School.

In "dance boom" New York there were several major ballet companies including: the New York City Ballet, whose repertory consists mainly of Balanchine's works and represents a neo-classical aesthetic; American Ballet Theatre which functions as a world repertory company, with special regard for the classics; the "smaller, swingier" Joffrey Ballet performing mostly the works of Joffrey and Arpino, along with some historical reconstructions and some experimental ballet; and Dance Theatre of Harlem, making its official debut in 1971, a company of black dancers performing a largely classical repertory. A few chamber ballet companies sprouted up in New York as well, and Modern Dance popularity rose dramatically obtaining increased funding and reaching wider audiences. Jowitt commented in *Dance Beat*

> *...I've been overwhelmed by the sheer numbers of choreographers and dance companies this country has accumulated since I started writing criticism. This is an astonishingly rich period in American dance. All forms and styles from the past co-exist with the newest experiments. And our own ways of seeing are changing...... and widening....*[19]

And Siegel commented in *Watching the Dance Go By* that "Perhaps 2,000 dance performances take place in a year."[20] Many other venues for presenting dance grew up as well. The Brooklyn Academy of Music, the New York Dance Festival at the Delacorte Theatre, spaces like Dance Theatre Workshop, Riverside Church, Cubiculo, the Kitchen, St. Mark's Church and many more galleries and museums offered viewing of everything from traditional to avant-garde dance, all keeping the immense level of dance activity at full charge. Occasionally there were the ambitious "Retrospectives" reviving repertory long unseen and re-awakening a curiosity and a pride

---

[18] Ibid, p. 67.

[19] Deborah Jowitt, *Dance Beat*, New York: Marcel Dekker Inc., 1971, p. 60.

[20] Marcia B. Siegel, "Introduction", *Watching the Dance Go By*, Boston: Houghton Mifflin, 1977, p. xvi.

about American Dance heritage. The whole world of Black Dance, diverse dance genres and the musical theater dance world are also major forces in the rich tapestry of dance seen in New York. New York is a CULTure. Movements rise and fall; there are constant innovations and inventions, fusing the new and the old, discarding, reasserting, alienating and popularizing.

The liveliness and range of the dance scene in New York over these last twenty years are reflected nowhere better than on the pages of these critics' writings who clearly love the challenge of taking it all in and making such readable sense out of it. The titles in their collections are a reflection of just how voluminous and diverse their dance environment is; Jowitt's *Dance Beat* refers to whole sections on new ballets, new looks in musicals, the pioneers and second generation of moderns; repertory of old works and the changing face of current work, the rebels of the post modern movement, including such novelties as dances on roof tops, epic spectacles, the minimalists to the super virtuosos and a host of international forms. Her second volume, *The Dance in Mind* reinforces many of those categories, expanding, elaborating, or seeing in a new way. This collection also selects some "master" choreographers such as Balanchine, Cunningham, Tharp and Taylor for detailed profiling.

Siegel's books too, *At the Vanishing Point* and *Watching the Dance Go By* divide reviews into similar categories of ballets, moderns, new experimental work and other dance forms. Croce's collections, *Afterimages*, *Going to the Dance*, and *Sight Lines* present the sweep of theatre dance forms, issues, themes and images featured in New York seasons and reflected in an array of review titles from "Swans" to "The Avant Garde on Broadway," "A Hundred Ways to Make a Dance" to "A New Old Giselle." Goldner's only published collection, *The Stravinsky Festival of the New York City Ballet* unabashedly chronicles an event which is "about the sheer abundance" of the choreography of Balanchine.

## Influences

The critical essays of E. M. Forster and the "strongly opinionated" music criticism of B. H. Haggin, are cited by Nancy Goldner as direct influences on her own critical psyche; Marcia Siegel claims John Martin's writings on the American modern dance as a strongly influential force in her own work; James Agee's and Pauline Kael's film criticism and Andrew Porter's music criticism which "set a certain scholarly example in the *New Yorker's* heretofore casual criticism"[21] were rich sources for Arlene Croce's early dance writings

---

[21] Arlene Croce, discussion, September 1994, New York City.

as was the "slangy" style of Jill Johnston's dance column in the *Village Voice* an inspiration for Deborah Jowitt's preliminary work. Many other writers and critics in all the arts were and still are sources of influence and inspiration for the New York School.

But the "spiritual" exemplar for this school of critics, overall, is Edwin Denby. This is not to say that Denby offered a vision of dance that they share in equally. But in the face of the severest critical problem — the ephemerality of dance — Denby radiated an optimism and a faith in dance's capacity to speak for itself. As the "New Statesman" for Balanchine, he suggested a *perception* and *conception* of dance that swayed the next generation of dance viewers. Especially in his response to Balanchine, Denby displayed a persuasive imagination and created a language, a means of responding to and interpreting a whole spectrum of dance in New York. Denby's appetite for seeing embraced alertness, subjectivity and imagination. The poetic and analytical descriptiveness of Denby is the most enduring and the most useful legacy in the "medium-oriented scrutiny" of New York's "formalist heyday."

> *Denby was never afraid to say exactly what he saw"* says Jowitt. *Seeing his type of concentration was as useful to me as his way of seeing Balanchine…. Watching Denby watch had a great impact on me. Once, at a particularly obscure and alienating Kenneth King concert at which many people walked out and were hostile, Edwin said "Once you get past anger or being sick you could watch this all night." It was his willingness to be absorbed that was so inspiring.*[22]

Writing about his introduction to Willem de Kooning's paintings in the 1970's Denby commented that:

> *To see something until it becomes beautiful is one of the tasks of a critic. If the work in question refuses to become beautiful, there may be a fault either in the observed or in the observer. Then again, there may simply be an incompatibility of tastes. To discover which, and understand why, becomes a second task.*[23]

Denby's comments reflect perhaps an ideal for criticism. Maintaining an "observing attitude" he commits allegiance to the work and accepts it on its own terms. This is not to suggest that criticism should be non-judgmental or non-evaluative. The valuing process and the evaluating process must be fuelled by an appetite for seeing. It is in this manner of seeing that the

---

[22] Interview with Deborah Jowitt, June 1985, New York City.

[23] Edwin Denby, "Edwin Denby Remembered" Part I, *Ballet Review*, Vol. 12, No. 1, Spring 1984, p. 5–7.

critic "brings to consciousness the means of performance," making a work "new" as part of the process of being known afresh.[24]

Denby's appetite for seeing, his creating a climate of acceptance for Balanchine, his susceptibility to dance values and poetic values side by side, his very sense of seeing being liberated through watching Balanchine, his sensual and analytical descriptiveness, his moral and at the same time intensely pleasurable view of dance and his risking of hypotheses in order to get closer to the cause and effect of dances — all these constitute Denby's legacy for the New York School of critics. It is a legacy that both draws them together and, in the way they act on that legacy, distinguishes them from each other.

From the early thirties to the time of his death, in 1983, Denby lived mostly in New York City. From 1936–1943 he wrote dance criticism for *Modern Music* magazine and from 1942–1945 he was the dance critic for the *New York Herald Tribune*, and a regular contributor to *Ballet* magazine and *Centre* magazine in London. Denby's dance writing was also published in *Dance Magazine, Dance News, The Nation, the Hudson Review, Saturday Review* and *Art News*. His collection of dance criticism called *Looking at the Dance* was published in 1949. In 1965 he published *Dancers, Buildings and People in the Streets*, a collection of dance essays originally prepared as reviews and lectures to dance students. Other works included fiction, poetry, libretti, and film performances. If there can be said to be a *School of Denby*, as Croce comments, "it was comprised of his fellow artist friends with whom... he had more in common than with the pack of inattentive children who were trying to be dance critics." The imposing list of Denby's circle included artists such as

> the poets Frank O'Hara, Kenneth Koch, James Schuyler, John Ashbery, Ron Padgett, Anne Waldman, Alice Notley, Ted Bettigan; the painters Willem and Elaine de Kooning, Franz Kline, Alex Katz, Red Grooms, Larry Rivers; the composers Virgil Thompson, Aaron Copland, Roger Sessions, John Cage; the photographer and filmmaker Rudolph Burkhardt; the choreographers Merce Cunningham, Paul Taylor and Jerome Robbins.[25]

"But far from writing for a coterie" asserts Croce, "Denby was working to broaden access to the subject on its deepest levels, both for the reader and for himself."[26] The widely varied dance culture available to Denby in New York in the Thirties and his willingness to look at and respond to all

---

[24] R. P. Blackmur, *The Lion and the Honeycomb*, New York: Harcourt Brace, 1955.

[25] Arlene Croce, "Edwin Denby", *Sight Lines*, New York: Alfred A. Knopf, 1987, p. 341.

[26] Ibid.

of it clearly helped to establish this critical precedent for the New York School. Musicals, "ethnic" dance, the early modern movement and the changing face of ballet from Russian dominated classical style to a new era of American themes, style and identity surely presented a critical challenge of the highest order.

The American ballet pioneering spirit, informed by the Diaghilev tradition and the Russian teachers who flocked to America at the end of the company's era in 1929, shaped itself into both an American classicism and a philosophy of experimentation. Like its original Diaghilevian ancestor, Paris, "the city of experiment and at the same time of ferment and discord,"[27] New York both inherited and invented *a tradition of the new*. By choice and by necessity Denby also viewed an extremely eclectic range of material that surely helped stretch his imaginative and poetic response to dance. His regular contributions to *Modern Music*, for example, well illustrate the range. Under sections called "Theater and Dance" and "With the Dancers" he covered spectacles at the World's Fair where he complained of their timidity, proposing his own, bigger marvels such as "Virgil Thompson lecturing on Wagner from a parachute, his voice all over the fair grounds" or Aaron Copland "improvising a cannon concert during a thunder storm;"[28] folkloric dance forms, character dancing, Broadway show dancing, circus pageantry, nightclub dancing like the "Negro dancing" at the Savoy, WPA works, the "moderns" such as Martha Graham, Doris Humphrey, Helen Tamiris, Hanya Holm, the Ballet Russe de Monte Carlo, and the emerging American ballet companies such as Ballet Caravan (1936) and later the New York City Ballet (1948). Broadly speaking Edwin Denby's criticism captured the essence of the emerging American neo-classical style of ballet. His was an inventive critical vocabulary, locating and articulating a dance impetus as yet unrecognized by the audience.

Denby's efforts in making the dance experience, particularly the Balanchine dance experience, accessible to American audiences created a receptivity, a climate of acceptance towards American dance culture and, ultimately, an influential style of *writing* and *thinking* about dance that serves as an enduring reference for the New York School of critics. It is this same self absorbed process of investigating dance so deeply that the New York critics share with Denby — an activity which is both intensively specialised and subjective and yet so broadly educating. "Edwin spoke and

---

[27] Marie Rambert, "What the Diaghileff Ballet Meant to Us", *Ballet Annual*, Tenth Issue, 1956, pp. 62–63.

[28] Edwin Denby, *Modern Music*, Vol. XV, No. 4, May/June 1938, p. 249.

wrote" said Arlene Croce, "as if everyone saw things the way he did. His genius made us believe it was true."[29]

Denby's essential contribution to the aesthetics of this school lay in the depths of his *subjectivity* and in his *process of seeing*. For these critics, it is Denby's eloquent subjective response to dance and his *pioneering in feeling* about dance (contained most significantly, perhaps, in his writings on Balanchine) that links their motivation.

Croce, who admits to having spent years "combing Denbyisms out of her prose" said that it was his feeling which *moved* her, "...... his willingness to let his love show." What *impressed* her were the things he showed her that could be done with language, like his description of Nijinsky's hands in *Jeux*, "as mysterious as breathing in sleep."[30] Jowitt recognizes Denby's way of seeing Balanchine as:

> *a way of seeing how dancers are expressing feelings.... Not so much about structure and steps as about men and women doing things in relation to music. He saw ballet as a world.... He wanted to convey to people the sensuous values in dance and he was saying to people that you have to allow for the sensuous value in dance.*[31]

Siegel, who dedicated her book, *The Shapes of Change* to Edwin Denby, states that he "was a model for us critics in so many ways, and he should continue to be a model... partly because of the seriousness and disinterested generosity of the way he examined things."[32] Denby's depth of feeling, transmitted through such accurately sensuous language is possible only to the extent that *one sees*... "In Denby I find two inspirations that have kept me going," says Siegel.

> *One is the way he sees time. He has more sensitivity to time than anyone — the rhythm, phrasing, insightful observations on how dancers use time. And his curiosity. He could look at a dance that he already knew as if it were new and he could look at a dance that was new and really see it.*[33]

Goldner has said that "the writing of Denby clinched it for us [critics]. Denby was the seer."[34] Clive Barnes, writing about Denby in *Ballet News* in 1983

---

[29] Arlene Croce, "Edwin Denby Remembered", *Ballet Review*, Summer, 1984, p. 30.

[30] Arlene Croce, *Sight Lines*, New York: Alfred A. Knopf, 1987, p. 335.

[31] Interview with Deborah Jowitt, June 1985, New York City.

[32] Marcia B. Siegel, *Ballet Review*, Fall 1984, p. 92.

[33] Interview with Marcia B. Siegel, June 1985, New York City.

[34] Interview with Nancy Goldner, New York City, June 1985.

made a particularly insightful comment regarding this influence on some of
the New York critics:

> *Two things marked Denby out as a critic. The first was the sheer quality of his writing. Denby*
> *has always been an exquisite stylist in a critical discipline that has produced comparatively*
> *little truly elegant writing. Then there was his attitude — he seemed to assume that the*
> *critic's role was that of a pair of articulate eyes. This latter assumption — as well as the*
> *example of his writing — has had a considerable influence on later American dance critics*
> *including some as otherwise diverse as Arlene Croce and Marcia Siegel. It cleaned up the*
> *writing and also, probably, cleaned up the vision.*[35]

## Denby's Legacy

Croce's own survey of Denby's critical method explained the process by
which Denby "cleaned up the writing." The first step in Denby's "method"
Croce calls a "description of how a classical ballet works in writing that is
entirely sensory."[36]

> *(Ballet) makes an image of behaviour, and many momentary ones; a sense of instinctive*
> *manners and cruel innocence; unconscious images suggested by devices of structure rather*
> *than by devices of gesture. So the individual keeps all her natural ambiguity as you see her*
> *decide, and see her swept on past the moment in the stream of dancing. And the force of the*
> *image comes not from her will but from the rhythm of the company's dancing and from the*
> *physical strength of the step.... For people who prefer to avoid human interest, I imagine the*
> *fantastic ingenuity of the arrangements, the costliest of hypertrophic pleasure-domes built up*
> *on nothing, the sweep and the lift of them is enough.*[37]

An image of behaviour, suggested by structure rather than by gesture, the
force of the image coming from the strength of the step. Again and again
Denby seems to uphold a sense of the *beautiful* in ballet through a formal
expressiveness. For him ballet is a vision of life, a world of physical clarity
and achievement and harmonious interaction. Croce refers to "seemliness" in
ballet, about the classical tradition being a "profound honoring of a certain
philosophy of life, a way of looking at the world." And in one of her
critiques on Balanchine's *Four Temperaments*, she says:

> *We can trust the ballet in performance because it is built of the things that dancers a̲ ̲ race*
> *know about. No small part of its moral beauty comes directly from the dancers, from their*
> *fastidious concentration, their ghetto pride....*[38]

---

[35] Clive Barnes, *Ballet News*, No. 8, February 1983, p. 46.

[36] Arlene Croce, "Edwin Denby", *Sight Lines*, New York: Alfred A. Knopf, 1987, p. 343.

[37] Edwin Denby, "The New York City Ballet," *Dancers, Buildings and People in the Streets*,
New York: Curtis Books, 1965, pp. 32–33.

[38] Arlene Croce, *Afterimages*, New York : Alfred A. Knopf, 1978, p. 190.

Returning to Denby's critical method, the next step is the process of reflecting on the *afterimage* of the dance, described by Denby as "the visual moment of climax that goes on gathering force in the mind."[39] It was Elaine de Kooning, wife of Denby's close friend and influence, the painter Willem de Kooning, who very early on used the expression "afterimage" when discussing Denby's perceptions. This is the period, explained Croce "that separates the processes of seeing and writing from "ballet in the theatre" to "ballet recollected in tranquillity."[40] Denby's description of it is that

> ...*There are flashes that come to you as if in slow motion like a landscape of lightening at night and then at the end the whole thing comes to you in a very big way inside yourself. And you put it all together intellectually. But the real emotion, the real thrill of it, is that extraordinary image that overwhelms you before you can understand....*[41]

In her first critical collection called *Afterimages* Croce defined her title as "the impression retained by the retina of the eye, or by any other organ of sense, of a vivid sensation after the external cause has been removed."[42] The image we are left with, she says, when the programme is over. "I never try to write immediately although sometimes I've had to," she says. The many repetitive viewings [of a dance] demand a synthesis. I seek to find the "residual impression."[43] For Denby, this afterimage, this image that overwhelms prior to understanding, was not always located in the visual or kinesthetic sense of a work. In classical ballet, for instance, he illustrates the notion of *afterimage* as a kind of expressive effect of a special ballet humanity — an abstract yet powerful aesthetic notion of morality.

> *Anyone who cannot bear to contemplate human behaviour except from a rationalistic point of view had better not try to "understand" the exhilarating excitement of ballet; its finest images of our fate are no easier to face than those of poetry itself, though they are no less beautiful.*[44]

The final step in Denby's critcal method is when he locates the causes of the dance's effects. An example of this is his writing in 1942 about Antony

---

[39] Laurel Quinlan, *A Way of Seeing: Edwin Denby's Ballet Criticism*, Masters Thesis, York University, Toronto, 1982, p. 18.

[40] Arlene Croce, "Edwin Denby," *Sight Lines*, New York: Alfred A. Knopf, 1987, p. 343.

[41] Edwin Denby, "A Conversation with Edwin Denby Part I" *Ballet Review*, Vol. 2, No. 5, 1969, p. 3.

[42] Arlene Croce, "Preface", *Afterimages*, New York: Alfred A. Knopf, 1978.

[43] Interview with Arlene Croce, June 1985, New York City.

[44] Edwin Denby, "Against Meaning in Ballet," *Looking at the Dance*, New York: Curtis Books, 1949, p. 44.

Tudor's ballet *Pillar of Fire*. Denby describes the emotional effect of the dance as being both real and poetic. He illustrates his point about locating the source of the dance's great effects through the following passage:

> *Again in* Pillar of Fire, *a chaste and frenzied young woman sees a vigorous young man. He looks at her suggestively. She leaps at him through the air in grand jeté. He catches her in mid-leap in a split and she hangs against his chest as if her leap continued forever, her legs completely rigid, her body completely still. How is it one notices the momentary pose so distinctly? It is partly because the stopped leap has a startling effect — like a fast tennis ball that goes dead. And the shock of the stop is heightened by the contrast to an onward full surge of the music. The timing, the placing of the pose, its contrast to the direction, the speed, the stopping and starting of the dance figures that went before; in brief, all the resources of what the cinema calls visual rhythm have been used to direct the eye to this special instance of bodily contact. The attention is focussed on the parts of the body, their relation to one another, the physical force involved in the leap and the lift, almost as if by a motion-picture close-up.*[45]

Several ingredients are contributing here to Denby's poetic analysis of *Pillar of Fire*. By the nature of his images, the "hanging leap" and the "fast tennis ball", and so on, one is immediately drawn into Denby's deeply subjective experience of the ballet. The imagery is inspired and active — it describes the essence of the dance's impact by constructing images which recreate the speed, the shape, the phrasing and the relationship between the music's rhythm and the movement. He also refers to a cinematic way of seeing to capture the power of the dance and analyze its effects.

Croce, writing in 1975 about Balanchine's *Four Temperaments* also employs a cinematic eye in locating the source of a dance's effects. In the following example her writing uncannily recalls Denby's writing in structure, type of imagery (subjective and poetic, yet at the same time analytical) and in the manner she draws you into her way of seeing the ballet as she has *felt*. Like Denby's, it is a kind of criticism that springs from a formal instinct yet exudes an infectious subjective passion, bringing to consciousness "the means of performance," to recall Blackmur's words from earlier in the chapter.

> *In the Sanguinic variation, for a virtuouso ballerina and her partner, the vista is wide, the ozone pure and stinging. The ballerina is an allegro technician; she is also a character. She enters and pauses. Her partner is expectant. But she pauses and turns her gaze back toward the wings. For a moment she seems to be wearing a demure black velvet neck ribbon, and then she is bounding like a hare in the chase, an extrovert after all. The Sanguinic variation takes us to the top of the world, and twice we ride around its crest, its polar summit (a circuit of lifts at half-height). In these two thrilling flights, the camera eye pivots on the pinpoint of a*

---

[45] Robert Cornfield and William Mackay, eds. *Edwin Denby, Dance Writings*, "Tudor and Pantomime" (July 11, 1943), New York: Alfred A. Knopf, 1986, p. 129.

**Plate 2** *Pillar of Fire*, choreography by Antony Tudor (1942), American Ballet Theatre. Dancers: Sallie Wilson, Marcos Paredes. Gift of Michael Maule, 1978. Courtesy of the Dance Collection, The New York Public Library at Lincoln Center.

*spiral, once to end the trajectory, once to start it. We see, as in some optical effect of old cinema, a scene spread from the centre of its compass, then respread in reverse.*[46]

Another vivid example of this investigation of *cause and effect* is Denby's writing in 1936 on the revival of Nijinsky's *"Afternoon of a Faun"* by the de Basil Ballet Russe, in New York, with Lichine in the title role.

*...it gathers momentum from the first gesture to the last like an ideal short story. ......The rhythm pattern in relation to the stage and to the music is so subtly graded that instead of monotony we get a steady increase in suspense, and increase on the eyes' perceptiveness and a feeling of heroic style at the climax.*[47]

Again, we see in Denby an attention to physical detail, to description of tension, shape, and gesture in plastic terms, and to the relationship of rhythm to movement. Forty-three years after Denby's piece, Nancy Goldner wrote about another revival of the ballet (by the Joffrey Ballet, with Rudolf Nureyev in the role of the faun). The tone of the piece astonishingly echoes Denby's perception and style:

*Sexual union between faun and scarf is also a union between the choreography's granite mathematics and the music's diaphanous qualities...... Although much has been written about the counterpoint between Debussy and Nijinsky and the revolutionary concept of dancing against the grains of rhythm and general atmosphere, no words could prepare one for the feelings of muted tension rising out of the contrast. It is precisely because kinetic and musical impulses scrape against each other that* Faun *is haunted by impenetrable power.*[48]

One of Denby's cherished beliefs about dancing, says Croce, had to do with "the persistence of image as key to comprehension."[49] The central image for his critique of *Concerto Barocco*, pulled from the climax of the work is such an instance.

*The correspondence of eye and ear is at its most surprising in the poignant adage movement. At the climax, for instance, against a background of chorus that suggests the look of trees in the wind before a storm breaks, the ballerina, with limbs powerfully outspread, is lifted by her male partner, lifted repeatedly in narrowing arcs higher and higher. Then at the culminating phrase, from her greatest height he very slowly lowers her. You watch her body slowly descend, her foot and leg pointing stiffly downward, till her shoe reaches the floor and*

---

[46] Arlene Croce, "The Four Temperaments," *Afterimages*, New York : Alfred A. Knopf, 1978, p. 189.

[47] Edwin Denby, *Looking at the Dance*, New York: Curtis Books, 1968, p. 178. (originally in *Modern Music*, Nov-Dec, 1936)

[48] Nancy Goldner, *The Nation*, April 7, 1979, p. 880.

[49] Arlene Croce, "Edwin Denby," *Sight Lines*, New York: Alfred A. Knopf, 1987, p. 341.

*she rests her full weight at last on this single sharp point and pauses. It has the effect at that moment of a deliberate and powerful plunge into a wound, and the emotion of it answers strangely to the musical stress....*[50]

Throughout his critique Denby repeatedly focusses on rhythm, flow, steps, body shapes and choreographic structure. The central image of his critique, the series of lifts and descent, described as "a deliberate and powerful plunge into a wound," is for Denby where the expressive effect of the whole dance is located. His imaginative description carefully balances human emotion with the value of movement. The net effect of the almost constant movement, the complex phrasing, the gathering momentum, the delicate distortions and inventiveness in the classical vocabulary, pouring out of the dancers in *Concerto Barocco* creates a stirring, sensuously revelatory experience.

As with Denby, the *image as key to comprehension* operates for the New York School as a critical method. All three 'stages' in Denby's method — the sensory writing about the way a classical ballet works, the framing of an afterimage and the locating of sources for a dance's effects — all engage *the image* as an investigative agent for demonstrating the meaning of a dance: its physical properties and internal dynamic relationships, the "nuts and bolts" of the choreography, the emotional-kinetic sense of the work. Constructing and 'reading' images — from poetic metaphors to concrete physical actions — is both the key to comprehension and the root of subjective response.

Goldner has described this critical process for herself as one of working and re-working images that seem to speak to the dance and of "writing them into focus." One of my favourite examples of this concerns a Béjart ballet that she described as being "Béjart frenetic, and bustling, but which achieved overall, the effect of tedium." Goldner traced her sensation of tedium back into the work to locate its source and found that it was Béjart's approach to the music that was the "culprit." She proceeded to analyze phrases of steps and discovered a "downbeat quality in the opening attack of the movement phrases," "drooping arabesques" and the like which produced this mysterious "tedium."[51] Such a "method" requires a remarkable kinetic memory which she has consistently demonstrated through her studies of steps in the ballets of Balanchine, Fokine and Petipa. The disclosures Goldner makes in her detective work on Bejart in this example are graphically reinforced by her fellow critics. Siegel refers to

---

[50] Edwin Denby, *Looking at the Dance*, New York: Curtis Books, 1968, pps. 108–9.

[51] Nancy Goldner, *Dance Criticism Seminar*, The University of Waterloo, Ontario, Canada, January 1979.

his choreography as being "stupefyingly anti-dance."[52] Croce compares him to the movie directors, Russell and Fellini, for being "a purveyor of sensation... ballet is just one of the glutting effects he uses."[53] Likewise, Kenneth MacMillan is exposed for examining "the subjects that dance cannot touch on, such as war, disease, poverty and death (as a fact, not as a symbol)."[54] Unlike Bejart, however, who elicits a consistent concensus of disfavour among these critics, MacMillan poses more provocative problems. "He pushes so insistently against the nature of his art and what it is equipped to express," says Croce, that "now and then he achieves breakthroughs and returns a kind of strength to it which has been long absent."[55] Clearly, an alertness to occasions of reform or innovation is ever operative here. In general, the critics are disturbed by those choreographers they view as unable to make dancing *move* physically or emotionally, the problem being that of concepts versus percepts in dance. They are disturbed by ecclecticism masquerading as invention. They are disturbed by choreography that exploits rather than enhances dancers. Values and biasses are confirmed and defined throughout the body of their writings.

In opening their eyes to images in dance, these critics also opened up their hearts. Croce once said that she found that Denby's perceptions "were closest to the emotions she felt while watching the ballet."[56] Goldner described Denby's process as "seeing what was in the *mind* (italics mine) of that dance...... not so much a recreation (of the dance)...... as an act of imagination, an act of good will toward what the best kind of dancing can be... he opens up a vision of dance."[57] Out of their articulate imagery "ideals" for a dance are envisaged by these critics.[58] We have seen that Denby's subjective way of looking at dance has been both formal and intensely emotive. It enables him to see on the one hand, the "plastic beauty" of Nijinksy's *Afternoon of a Faun*, the cinematic effects of Tudor's psychological ballet, *Pillar of Fire* and, on the other hand, the love story or

---

[52] Marcia B. Siegel, *At the Vanishing Point*, New York: Saturday Review Press, 1972, p. 129.

[53] Arlene Croce, *Going to the Dance*, New York: Alfred A. Knopf, 1982, p. 167.

[54] Ibid, p. 392.

[55] Ibid, p. 98.

[56] Arlene Croce, "Dance Books in My Life", *Dance Magazine*, March 1969, p. 39.

[57] Interview with Nancy Goldner, New York City, June 1985.

[58] George Beiswanger, "Doing and Viewing Dances: A Perspective for the Practice of Criticism", *Dance Perspectives*, No. 55, Autumn 1973, p. 8.

moral in Balanchine's neo-classical spectacles. These sensibilities are at work simultaneously in his criticism and illustrated in its best form in something like his piece on Balanchine's *Concerto Barocco* quoted earlier. This ability to see the sensuous in the formal means of dance and the formal means at work in a highly emotive and humanly expressive context is the poet and analyst at work — and in both sensibilities there is operating a *kinesthetic sympathy* which gives description of the dances viewed a life of their own. The New York School critics share this sense of *telling the story of a dance through active description*. We read dance criticism that not only conveys the look of movement and analyses the source of effects but conveys the *felt experience* of the dance. The following passage, by Deborah Jowitt, demonstrates this "gathering momentum" of ideas and images that vividly brings her dance subject to life, within the framework of active critical scrutiny. On Eliot Feld's *Mazurka*, she writes:

> *The form of the mazurkas defines the dancing. Perhaps that's why the ballet makes you sense motions and emotions pressing and shifting to fulfil themselves within severe limits. Almost every dance takes off with three repetitions of its opening phrase. Steps and gestures proper to the mazurka recur everywhere — folded arms, stamps, small side-travelling hops with one foot lightly beating the other. Bold, weighty moves often give way to a sputter of small, rapid, almost irritable ones.*
>
> *All the dances are passionate, but whether brooding, or exultant, or flashing, the dancers never stop to indulge in anything; the momentum of the mazurka pulls them along. "Mazurka" isn't ingratiating. It's too fast and too difficult for that. All that is strange and harsh and devious in those lovely sombre melodies has gotten hold of Feld. The dances are full of unrest; the dancers reverse directions seemingly in mid-air; while the impetus is carrying them one way, they somehow muster their weight to pursue a new path...... There are passages in "Mazurka" as beautiful and astonishing as anything I've ever seen. And in some ways, the speed of the ballet does make the complexity more dazzling.[59]*

Clearly what delights these critics is choreography that invents new relationships between action and emotion; choreography that demands "risking hypotheses" about the "nature" of dance and choreography that can also achieve a re-ordering of the senses.

### Dancers

Yeats' question "How can we know the dancer from the dance?" comes at least close to being answered in the writings of Denby and later in the writings of the New York School critics. The detailed *dancer portrait* emerges

---

[59] Deborah Jowitt, *Dance Beat*, New York: Marcel Dekker, 1977, p. 14.

**Plate 3** *Concerto Barocco*, choreography by George Balanchine (1941). The New York City Ballet. Dancers: Conrad Ludlow, Patricia McBride. © The George Balanchine Trust. Courtesy of the Dance Collection, The New York Public Library at Lincoln Center.

as a major force in these writings. In these portraits the meaning of the dancer as distinct from the meaning of the dance unfolds through description and analysis. This approach refers both to the dancer's uniqueness in his or her approach to the activity of dancing and to the value that that dancer draws out of the choreography. We get an insight into how a dance "lives" in the body of a particular dancer and how the two mutually direct each other. Denby's dance portraits established a precedent, it appears, for the later New York critics.  Denby's description of Markova, for example, achieves the kind of physical detail that seems to go beyond the kind of observation possible in review writing. His way of seeing Markova is *intimate*. He describes how she steps into her passages, how she relates to music, how the music sounds in the grip of her dancing, etc. The details of her musculature and shaping seem extremely probing — a zoom lens that can record the stretch of her instep and the power of her thigh. Croce, also, achieves this quality in her descriptions of dancers. Her scrutiny of Suzanne Farrell seems almost too intimate to be possible for the naked eye. Another aspect of these portraits is their *cause and effect* structuring. They pinpoint the nature of the illusion the dancers create and the elements at play in those great moments of dancing that have the most expressive impact on them. This kind of attention to how individual dancers achieve their own identity in dance makes the whole topic of role interpretation open up enormously. Not only the depth of detail but the effort invested into recognizing distinctions between one dancer and another creates a literature for dance that parallels and often surpasses notable theater criticism. The comparative ways in which dancers treat choreographic "texts" through approaches to music, physical structure, virtues and flaws in technique, their visible attitude to the choreography being danced, is the material for these critical portraits.

Look at the following examples of such writing by Denby, Croce and Goldner, for example, to see their similarities in purpose and style. Denby on Markova:

> *For the full effect of being stilled and immobile, she often brings forward her low shoulders into a droop, a gesture like a folding in of petals, like a return into herself.... Her softening forward droop in the shoulders also alters the look of the next, new start since the dancer takes an up-beat of straightening her shoulders, and so seems to lift and unfold into the new phrase. Such nuances of color or breathing or dynamics give to the old-fashioned style its fullness; but they easily become fullsome. One can watch Markova, however, use them to carve more clearly the contour of a phrase, to make it more visible and more poignant.*[60]

---

[60] Edwin Denby "Impressions of Markova at the Met," *Looking at the Dance*, New York: Curtis Books, 1949, pp. 55–58.

Denby's observations on Markova at the Met, above, and Goldner's comments on Gelsey Kirkland that follow both share an unmistakable interweave of tender reverence with a pristine analytical edge — a kind of scrutiny and reverie at the same time. Twenty years after Denby's above review, Nancy Goldner writing in *The Nation* about a performance of Robbins' *Goldberg Variations* says:

> *Gelsey Kirkland does one solo that is actually about rubato. Each balance in arabesque is held a fraction longer than the beat allows, and she makes up for time lost in the little glissades that take her from one balance to the next. Interestingly, the dance reaches its climax when rubato yields to the straight beat of the music, as Kirkland makes big jumps toward the back of the stage. The restored steady rhythm is deliciously luxurious, like the calm after a storm. The dancers also swallow space.*[61]

In another set of startlingly similar descriptions of dancers, Goldner describes Baryshnikov dancing in 1976 and Denby describes Youskevitch dancing in 1934. One might be hard pressed to distinguish between them.

Denby:

*At the moment, Youskevitch is at the peak of his classic style. His style is calm, rich and elastic. It is completely correct. You see easily what the action is, how the trunk takes the main direction of the dance and how the limbs vary the force and the drive by calculated counter movements. The changing shape of the dancing body is vigorously defined. The weight of the body and the abundant strength of it are equally clear and the two aspects blend gracefully in the architectural play of classic sequences. The distribution of energy is intelligent and complex. In his leaps, for instance, the noble arm positions, the tilt of the head sideways or forward, make you watch with interest a whole man who leaps; you don't watch, as with most dancers, only the lively legs of one. And while most dancers leap for the sake of the bound upward only, Youskevitch (like Markova) leaps for the entire trajectory, and for a mysterious repose he keeps as he hangs in the air.*[62]

Goldner:

*Well, yes, Mikhail Baryshnikov takes off in a very interesting way. For a big jump he takes a few running steps, but they're unusually skimming and light. They seem to give him speed rather than a boost, and maybe that's why the extraordinary height of his jump is initially shocking. With such a preparation, you would expect him to float forward rather than bound high. By the second or third jump, you notice that Baryshnikov gives a little clue as to where he's going. Just before leaving the ground, his eyes focus on a spot high in the air, buttonholing it in a glance. He kicks his front leg up toward that spot, and the rest of his body follows. I love to watch him "decide" how high and where he's going to jump and I think that being able to share with him the moment of decision makes his jumps thrillingly visceral.*[63]

---

[61] Nancy Goldner, "Goldberg Variations", *The Nation*, July 5, 1971.

[62] Edwin Denby, *Looking at the Dance*, New York: Curtis Books, 1949, pp. 128–9.

[63] Nancy Goldner, *The Village Voice*, July 12, 1976, p. 124.

Both critics analyse the impact and effect of the dancer's leap — mechanically as well as stylistically; both critics exude a passion and love in their act of observing a dancer they clearly admire; both passages are active in their observation, as if step-by-step they are apprehending every detail of motion and impact. Goldner's analysis of Baryshnikov's "initially shocking" jump, created by the speed of his preparation immediately brings to mind Denby's observations on Markova's calculatedly "drooped" shoulders creating a heightened sense of phrasing in her dancing, and Youskevitch being described above as "a whole man who leaps." But for all the detective-like investigation into how the dancers achieve their performance effects neither critic implies that there is any myth or mystery put to rest or a formula identified. Rather, the more they see the more they seem to be preserving the freshness of discovery and, in the process, they empower the dancers even more. Nancy Goldner describes this very experience in a review of a Merce Cunningham's work, specifically, a solo section performed by Cunningham himself:

> What fascinates me about it is that it is as energetic and sharp as the preceding group dance — and as tingly and staccato too. He shows us that an arm can shoot out of its socket, with as much surprise and off-angled precision as a leg; that port de bras and slight hunches in the lower back can have as much brio as a full battement. Of course, it's this kind of discovery that Cunningham is always interested in. He's able to make it out of dispassionate investigation of the body, but its theatrical effectiveness bespeaks passionate concentration. He's what you call a great dancer. Through sheer brain power, I think, he can enrapture the audience in the thing, anything, he's doing. How many times has it been said that he dances with the quivering sensibilities of an animal? That he turns his audience into equally sensitive animals is as extraordinary. We sniff him out, goose-pimpled with the excitement of discovery.[64]

Denby, in his own early encounters with Cunningham's performances in 1945, recorded in an article called *The Modern Dance: Two Kinds* observed "he is a virtuoso, relaxed, lyrical, elastic like a playing animal". Denby also illustrated a precision of seeing when he analyzed that Cunningham had "an instinct for a form that makes its point by repetition, each repetition being a little different, and the phrasing of each difference, exceptionally limpid."[65] This notification of Cunningham's phrase structuring at that very early stage, foresaw what was to become his signature quality as a choreographer. Denby also empowered Cunningham with an "American Classicist" identity which was investigated and classified and protected with a curator's care by

---

[64] Nancy Goldner, "Merce Cunningham's Event No. 206", *The Bennington Review*, September 1978.

[65] Edwin Denby, Edwin Denby, *Looking at the Dance*, New York: Curtis Books, 1949, p. 282.

the New York School of Critics twenty years later. "Mr. Cunningham reminds you that there are pure dance values in pure modern technique," says Denby in his 1945 review, and these dance values, particularly Cunningham's "elastic rhythm," he values as being "peculiarly American" and "delicately supported by the elastic phrases of John Cage's music."[66] The collaborations between Cunningham and Cage, as well as those between Graham and Horst, and Balanchine and Stravinsky, were appraised by Denby and later by the New York School for their roles in shaping the particularly American value (and virtue) of *pioneering classicism*. This core aesthetic orientation was promoted and defined also in the works of choreographers such as Taylor, Tharp and Morris. The celebration of these values, as clarified in the works of their much admired choreographers, is encountered throughout their writings. The source for these values most evidently springs from the work of George Balanchine.

## Balanchine

Denby described his first experience of seeing Balanchine's company as "finding a friend." One of the most energetic examples of this "friendship" can be found in Denby's review of the "Stravinsky-Balanchine *Apollon*" by the "Metropolitan" (Ballet) in 1938. In a second viewing of Balanchine's *"Apollon"* he draws us into the very activity of his seeing and shares with us, almost in a re-creative account, his discoveries about Balanchine's choreography that so thrill him. He asks his readers about half a dozen questions: "Did you see the way Balanchine shows you how strangely tall a dancer is?" ......"did you see how touching it can be to hold a ballerina's extended foot?" ...Did you notice the counter-movement, the keenness of suspense within the clean onward line of Callope's variation?" ......"And did you notice how much meaning — not literary meaning but plastic meaning he gets out of any two or more dancers who do anything together?"....[67] For each question, really asking the reader to see what he sees, Denby illustrates the motive of the question and its answer in physical facts and poetic imagery. He describes a moment of extreme balance as "touching and impersonal as a mathematician's faith in extreme human reasoning" and the effect of the dance as "a kind of play that exists in terms of dancing."[68]

---

[66] Ibid, p. 283.

[67] Edwin Denby, *Modern Music*, Vol. XV, No. 3, March/April, 1938, pp. 184–85.

[68] Ibid.

Balanchine is perceived by the New York critics to be both the most enduring and current of choreographers. In sometimes overt and sometimes unconscious ways these critics, like Denby, see Balanchine as a way to the future, as a choreographer who could reorient the convention of classical ballet.

For Nancy Goldner the personal bias about watching Balanchine ballets transcends matters of taste into a more objectified "natural consciousness" when she says: "His ballets have convinced New York that it needs ballet...... Balanchine's ballets are as necessary a part of the city as subways and do unique honor to the city, as does its skyline."[69] This New Yorker's "pride" regarding the Balanchine repertory is an expression of what Marcia Siegel refers to when she speaks of dance as "cultural artifact": Balanchine's dance is performed by a company of dancers whose performance temperament, attitude and style symbolizes and shapes an American dance identity. The foundation of this identity is the complex environment of New York out of which Balanchine has forged a distinctly American-style classicism.

All these years later Balanchine's ballets are still a challenge for ballet audiences and critics to "read." And although the New York school of dance critics are not necessarily united by a "Balanchine aesthetic," they are concerned to identify and analyze what constitutes American style in theatre dance and also to clarify distinctions between European and American sensibilities. Balanchine is an American institution, a school of thought, an aesthetic viewpoint which is a product of the unique environment in which it developed. The critics of the New York school have largely followed Denby's lead on appreciating Balanchine. Their investigation has been an elaboration of Denby's instincts about the meaning of Balanchine's ballets. Siegel, writing about Balanchine's *Four Temperaments* for example, says:

> But with Four Temperaments *"he also liberated the dancer's body, and this proved decisive in establishing him as a choreographer of and for Americans. After years of cultivating American ballet dancers, demonstrating that this training could be accomplished far away from the European academies, he was now able to take chances with the dancer's line, succession, attack, phrasing, weight and balance, yet not have them be mistaken for anything but ballet dancers.*[70]

[69] Nancy Goldner, *The Stravinsky Book of the New York City Ballet*, New York: Eakins Press, 1974, p. 66.

[70] Marcia B. Siegel, "Balanchine's Four Temperaments," *The Shapes of Change*, Boston: Houghton Mifflin, 1979, p. 211.

**Plate 4** *Four Temperaments*, choreography by George Balanchine (1946), New York City Ballet. Dancers: Miranda Weese, Damian Woetzel. © The George Balanchine Trust. Photograph by COSTAS.

Later, in the same book, in the section called "Balanchine's America," Siegel comments on the ballet *Agon* that:

> *The dancers, stripped to their most minimal practice clothes, come before us in a mode for moving…. Perhaps it isn't too much to suggest a relationship between these confident, unadorned bodies of Balanchine's and the sense Americans have of being at ease in space. We don't need to be surrounded by artificial vistas, decorative landscaping, or reassuring architecture because space to us is a limitless challenge, a field for conquest.*[71]

Whereas Denby was tapping at the tip of the iceberg — discovering a new way of looking at ballet through Balanchine and formulating a vocabulary about New York City Ballet style, Siegel is here using Denby's terms of reference to further construct an identity for American dance. Of all the New York school she is the most concerned with this theme, as her book *The Shapes of Change* illustrates throughout.

Arlene Croce, writing about *The Four Temperaments* in 1975 is infused with Denby's particular brand of passion about Balanchine's classicism:

> *What a monumental decade it was! Balanchine was by then established in America, but not solidly established; from* Concerto Barocco *and* Ballet Imperial *on through* The Four Temperaments *to* Theme and Variations *and* Symphony in C *he is on the attack. His objective: to make plain to American audiences the dynamics of classical style.*[72]

"Since Balanchine's death and Edwin Denby's suicide," says Siegel "ballet is finished as far as I am concerned."[73] "Can there be anything more difficult for a choreographer," asks Croce, "than making classical ballet in the Age of Balanchine?"[74] Such all-consuming loyalty to the canon of one choreographer comes perilously close to insular, in-house bias or even fanaticism rather than open-visioned, renewed critical response. Having revelled in the seeming limitlessness of Balanchine's vocabulary, the critics of the New York School seem nostalgically intractable concerning his *living* legacy. Their doubts about the capacity of succeeding choreographers to sustain the innovative imperative of true American (Balanchine) classicism seems at odds with their often optimistic spirit. On the other hand, it confirms their view of the profound, almost sacred, nature of this notion of *the new* as the

---

[71] Marcia B. Siegel, "Balanchine's America," *The Shapes of Change*, Boston: Houghton Mifflin, 1979, p. 228.

[72] Arlene Croce, "The Four Temperaments," *Afterimages*, New York: Alfred A. Knopf, 1978, p. 186.

[73] Marcia B. Siegel, Discussion, New York City, September 1994.

[74] Arlene Croce, "Postmodern Ballets," *Sight Lines*, New York: Alfred A. Knopf, 1987, p. 320.

most challenging and demanding aspects of Balanchine's artistic heritage. "Making something new out of something old" is one definition that Nancy Goldner offers of classicism. All four critics persuade us of the consistently and insistently "new" ethos of Balanchine's choreography. Therefore, the question they seem to be posing is provocative rather than pessimistic. It is: How can a choreographer "in the Age of Balanchine" create something new from something that is *always new*? Croce elaborates:

> *The curse of Balanchine… how the great choreographer created 20th century ballet and put it off limits at the same time…… He incorporated into the mainstream everything there was to incorporate — jazz, Bauhaus, twelve-tone music, American pop, yes, even the modern dance — and left the academy at a peak of virtuosity, with nothing further to express. Balanchine's progeny re-work his accomplishments; they can honor his precedents, but they can add nothing to what he has said.*[75]

## Formalism

From the time Beaujoyeulx described ballet in *Ballet Comique de la Reine* as "no more than the geometrical groupings of people dancing together, accompanied by the varied harmony of several instruments"[76] the pendulum was swinging back from Aristotle's representational treatise on dance in *Poetics*. It has continued to swing back and forth in dance history in a struggle to reconcile technique and expression as meaningful either via elements external to itself or inherently expressive as an autonomous art form. While Aristotle "assigns to dance an aim outside of itself…."[77] Valery asserts that "a formula for pure dance should include nothing to suggest that it has an end."[78] Mallarmé claimed of ballet that the dance steps "…expressed that which would be inexpressible in any other language."[79] Levinson pondered on behalf of critics why "no one has ever tried to portray the intrinsic beauty of a dance step, its innate quality, its aesthetic reason for

---

[75] Ibid, p. 319.

[76] *Dance as a Theatre Art: Source Readings in Dance History*, ed. Selma Jeanne Cohen, New York: Dodd, Mead & Co., 1974, p. 113.

[77] Andre Levinson, "The Idea of the Dance from Aristotle to Mallarmé," *Theatre Arts Monthly*, Vol. 40, 1927, p. 572 (volumes collected).

[78] Paul Valéry, *Aesthetics*, trans. Ralph Mannheim, Vol. 13 of Collected Works, New York: Pantheon Books, 1964.

[79] Stephen Mallarmé, "Ballets," *Mallarmé*, trans. Bradford Cook, John Hopkins Press, Baltimore, 1956.

being...."[80] In Beaumont's view ballet is "a composite art, in which music, painting and sculpture are as essential as dancing itself."[81] Beaumont's contemporary, the critic Rayner Heppenstall, on the other hand, responds with a sweepingly formalist assertion that

> *Ballet, itself, without representational interest of any kind, is one epitome of the total history of the West. The pure devoted practice of it, therefore, not attempting to deviate from, but only to fulfill, to enrich tradition, is enough. Style for style's sake in the Dance is not the same ideal at all as Art for Art's Sake elsewhere. Style in the Dance is all-comprehensive. It contains the whole riches of a whole experiential order.*[82]

Likewise, Clement Greenberg's formalist manifesto establishes the view that what had to be made explicit "was that which was unique and irreducible not only in art in general but also in each particular art... It quickly emerged that the unique and proper area of competence of each art coincided with all that was unique to the nature of its medium... Thereby each art would be rendered 'pure'."[83] The impact of this argument, recently assessed by Roger Copeland as a "purist philosophy" amounting to "a sort of loyalty oath... to the underlying nature of an artist's medium"[84] appears in numerous guises throughout the writings of the New York school. Goldner states outright that her way of looking is "formalist" and that

> *the structural relationships are the things that draw you in. It works the same in each medium. For example, in a painting: look at the lighting, the drapery, etc. [......] The source of the meaning is what I am looking for through this structure.*[85]

"I do notice structure first," says Deborah Jowitt and she continues:

> *It thrills me, if it is there, because it gives the work coherence. What impresses me is the way structure works with feeling. My focus on structure is not deliberate. It is more a predilection of mind and the fact that certain works demand that way of seeing.*[86]

---

[80] Andre Levinson, "The Spirit of the Dance," *Dance as a Theatre Art: Source Readings in Dance History*, ed. Selma Jeanne Cohen, New York: Dodd, Mead & Co., 1974.

[81] Cyril Beaumont, *Dancers and Critics*, ed. Cyril Swinson, London: Adam & Charles Black, 1950, pp. 10–12.

[82] Rayner Heppenstall, *Apology for Dancing*, London, 1936, p. 145.

[83] Clement Greenberg (1965), "Modernist Painting," *The New Art*, ed. Gregory Battock, New York: E. P. Dutton & Co., 1993, p. 68.

[84] Roger Copeland, "Backlash Against Balanchine," *Choreography and Dance*, Issue Editor, Eleni Bookis Hofmeister, Harwood Academic Publishers, Vol. 3 Part 3, 1993, p. 5.

[85] Interview with Nancy Goldner, June 1985, New York City.

[86] Interview with Deborah Jowitt, June 1985, New York City.

Marcia Siegel says that while she does not think of herself as a formalist she is "interested in, fascinated with structures because they connect with the verbal, intellectual part of myself."[87] Writing about Balanchine's *The Prodigal Son*, Goldner clearly frames this way of seeing when she observes, for example:

> *In Balanchine the source of movement stems from music rather than dramatic situation. This rule is actually an aesthetic, and it even holds for something as overtly dramatic as* The Prodigal Son. *The magnificence of the crawl home lies less in the fact that it is a crawl, or that it is a sustained crawl, or that it is the touchstone of the plot, than that it is commanded to happen by Prokofiev. The Prodigal Son inches his way into his father's arms not mile by mile but note by note. The pathos and grandeur of this episode derive from the way emotional experience is funnelled through an external, rigorously formal medium. All of Balanchine's ballets sting us by their distillation of emotion into metrical units.*[88]

Balanchine's own declaration that "the ballet will speak for itself and about itself"[89] was rigorously mediated by Lincoln Kirstein in his critic-publicist role for Balanchine saying "Balanchine has refined his repertory by clarifying his composition to what it can express in no other medium."[90] Croce writes about Balanchine's use of academic technique in the ballet, *Apollo* as an assertion of "cardinal priorities of substance over decoration, invention over representation."[91] Denby, in acknowledging the choreographer Antony Tudor as a "choreographer of genius" found him nonetheless flawed because his ballets were "not primarily dance conceptions."[92] And Massine, described by Denby as an "inexhaustible" "pictorial arranger" nonetheless leaves "a void in the imagination" because his dances "arrest the drama of dancing which the imagination craves to continue, stimulated by all the kinetic senses of the body."[93] This specifically kinetic interactiveness is something that Croce suggests is, paradoxically, essential to dance yet exclusive in nature.

> *The appeal (of dance) is so directly physical... that it doesn't occur to us to notice its limitations as such, though once we notice them they are startling. Six motions...... are all a body can manage at once (torso, limbs, head)...... But as we know who love it, dancing is the*

---

[87] Interview with Marcia Siegel, June 1985, New York City.

[88] Nancy Goldner, *The Nation*, July 2, 1972.

[89] Roger Copeland, "Backlash Against Balanchine," *Choreography and Dance*, Issue Editor, Eleni Bookis Hofmeister, Harwood Academic Publishers, Vol. 3 Part 3, 1993, p. 7.

[90] Lincoln Kirstein, "The Position of Balanchine" (1955), *Salmagundi*, No. 33–34, S/S 1976, p. 213.

[91] Arlene Croce, "News from the Muses," *Going to the Dance*, New York, Alfred A. Knopf., 1982, p. 107.

[92] Edwin Denby, *Looking at the Dance*, New York: Curtis Books, 1968, p. 23.

[93] Ibid, p. 181.

**Plate 5** *Prodigal Son*, choreography by George Balanchine (1929, revived 1950 by NYCB). Dancers: Baryshnikov, O'Brien. © The George Balanchine Trust. Photograph by COSTAS.

*language of things uncommunicable apart from... its own way of doing, and not everybody loves that.*[94]

Directing an audience's attention to the sensuous (and pleasurable) aspects of pure dance was something Denby saw as a kind of mission.

> *the value of watching ballet is unlike trying to make sense and order from the "disjointed fragments of impressions" one sees in everyday life. The ballet performance is arranged so that it is convenient to look at, and easy to pay continuous attention to [......] The excitement in it seems to have points of contact with the excitement of one's own personal life.*[95]

This "arrangement" of form in ballet is what Roger Fry articulates on the subject of painting as an organizational means of appreciation in his *Essay in Aesthetics*.

> *The greatest occupation of the graphic arts is to give us first of all order and variety in the sensuous plane, and then so to arrange the sensuous presentment of objects that the emotional elements are elicited with an order and appropriateness altogether beyond what Nature herself provides... The formal ingredients which they isolate and describe and the relationships which can be pointed out directly are important not in and of themselves: their importance lies in the way they focus our attention on the work [......]*[96]

These formal ingredients, essential canon for Fry and Greenberg, constitute equally for Croce the "bedrock definition"[97] for dance. It is exemplified as much in the academic technique of Balanchine as in the anti-academic investigations of Nijinsky, for instance, in a ballet such as *Faune*, specifically because "its first concerns were with balance, gravity, rhythm, proportion...."[98] Most essentially, claims Croce, "Nijinsky showed that the aim of dance techniques was essentially clarification."[99] Further, Croce concludes that because of the power of demonstration in these elements in Nijinsky's choreography "theatrical dancing, which was growing pretty,

---

[94] Arlene Croce, "Sylvia, Susan and God," *Ballet Review*, Vol. 1 No. 1, 1965.

[95] Edwin Denby, *Looking at the Dance*, New York: Curtis Books, 1968.

[96] Roger Fry, "Essay in Aesthetics", extracted from Laurel Quinlan, "A Way of Seeing: Edwin Denby's Ballet Criticism", *Masters Thesis*, York University, Toronto, 1982, p. 50.

[97] Arlene Croce, "News from the Muses", *Going to the Dance*, New York, Alfred A. Knopf., 1982, p. 108.

[98] Ibid.

[99] Ibid.

grew beautiful once more."[100] Similarly, when Jill Johnston responded to Cunningham's work by saying "he has brought us back to the reality that dancing concerns dancing"[101] she is celebrating, as Sally Banes suggests, "the expressive intensity of abstraction." For Johnston this is "more human and exacting than the sledgehammer technique of a doubled-over grief or a chest expanded joy."[102]

Objectified expression, integrated invention, diversifying through clarifying, purity of means — all these guises or variations on the central notion of formalism — have entered these critics' dialogue with their dance subjects. Choreographers like Graham, Humphrey and Taylor did not necessarily purge their dance of "all extraneous to the underlying nature of their medium"[103] but they did exercise a purity of means regarding structural and gestural devices — so much so it seemed to Denby, reviewing Graham's *Chronicle* for the first time in 1937, that

> *she allows her dance to unfold only on a dictatorially determined level. But a dance unfolds of its own accord on a great many contradictory levels. And I miss the humanity of these contradictions. To speak more in terms of dance, it seems as though Miss Graham were too neat.... Even her so-called angularity springs partly from a fear that the eye will be confused unless every muscle is given a definite job. The eye would be confused. But our bodily sense would not. Our bodily sense needs the rebound from a gesture, the variation of hard and soft muscle, of exact and general......*[104]

The "dance revolution pioneered by the early 'moderns' who established new representational connections between movement and lived experience,"[105] according to Copeland, was a different interpretation of medium-oriented formalism. The New York school critics could write about both Graham's *Primitive Mysteries* and Balanchine's *Swan Lake* for their clarity about dancing and consequently for their powers of expression. It is vital therefore to understand that the humanity of the *expressive effect* of dance is an integral part of the formalist view. By his own admission, in his essay called *Complaints of an Art Critic* Clement Greenberg asserts that a

---

[100] Ibid.

[101] Sally Banes, "Jill Johnston: Signalling Through the Flames," *New Performance*, Vol. 2, No. 1, 1980, p. 12.

[102] Ibid.

[103] Roger Copeland, "Backlash Against Balanchine," *Choreography and Dance*, Issue Editor, Eleni Bookis Hofmeister, Harwood Academic Publishers, Vol. 3 Part 3, 1993, p. 3.

[104] Edwin Denby, *Looking At The Dance*, New York: Curtis Books, 1949, pps. 252–3.

[105] Roger Copeland, op. cit., p. 4.

work of art has content because of its *effect*.[106] Greenberg, in defending himself against accusations that formalism "concentrates upon the effect of works of art,"[107] asserts that content, form and effect cannot be prised apart. Analysis of the consequences of formalist aesthetics in dance is in-the-making, as the post — "dance boom" debate continues. Anna Kisselgoff has argued that "the formalist view made dance more accessible to a public who, relaxed in their search for the "message" of dance, accepted its physicality. In so doing they may have lost the ability to recognize the place of expressionistic and romantic dance.[108] But Goldner has maintained throughout her career that "only the expressive power of dance is important."[109] On the other hand, as Copeland impresses upon us, the formalist framework has the capacity to extend the fullness of the moment and enhance one's powers of perception in other contexts.[110] While in a work like Balanchine's *Agon*, for example, he says

> *the meaning of the work is concentrated into the sensuous surface of the dancers' bodies, it is entirely there, that the dancers don't represent anything that lies beyond the confines of their own bodies — that doesn't mean that the perceiver who experiences this intensified sense of thereness will not ever again return his or her gaze to the "outside world"... he or she may well see that world more freshly and more fully.[111]*

## Critical Repertory

> *From this time on familiarity began and I like familiarity. It does not in me breed contempt it just breeds familiarity. And the more familiar a thing is the more there is to be familiar with. And so my familiarity began and kept on being. (Gertrude Stein)[112]*

Whether watching modern, classical or any other type of dance, the viewer always experiences dance within the integrated context of space, time and energy; in the context of immediacy; within the sensory and emotional context of one human body perceiving another human body; and within the

---

[106] Clement Greenberg, "Complaints of an Art Critic," *Modernism, Criticism, Realism (Alternative Contexts for Art)*, ed. Charles Harrison and Fred Urton, London: Harper and Row, 1984, pp. 3–9.

[107] Ibid.

[108] Anna Kisselgoff, "The Search for New Definitions," *New York Times*, Sunday, March 13, 1983.

[109] Interview with Nancy Goldner, June 1985, New York City.

[110] Roger Copeland, op. cit., pps. 7–8.

[111] Ibid.

[112] Jill Johnston, "Fresh Winds," *The Village Voice*, March 15, 1962, p. 13.

illusory and dynamic context of performance. Since a dance unfolds before the viewer's eyes and cannot be experienced in totality in one complete moment, familiarity with the dance work is essential for rigorous criticism. Familiarity develops memory and anticipation and frees the viewer to focus more closely on specific elements of the particular dance experience. As will be seen in later chapters this familiarity, an agent for "critical repertory," is a very important advantage and strength in the development of the New York School of Dance Criticism.

We have seen that Edwin Denby left a legacy of critical sensibilities — romantic subjectivity, kinetic imagery, analytical and sensuous description and an appetite for seeing that strongly influenced and inspired these four women critics. They came to their task of dance criticism with this and many other influences and professional experience to shape their own critical syllabus and styles. But the climate of critical dialogue which is a significant factor in the crystallizing of many of their ideas and which helps view them as a school, is something that developed from their own momentum as critics rather than something which they inherited as part of a dance criticism scene in New York.

This dialogue among the New York School of critics has been brought about largely by two factors. The first is that these four critics have consciously aimed for and developed a highly articulate set of ideas on dance criticism and have set about teaching criticism to students and addressing the topic with fellow critics in areas such as the Dance Critics Association Conferences and other symposia and institutes. The second factor is the phenomenon of critical repertory possible to these critics in New York dance viewing over this period. Having access to retrospectives of choreographers' works, enormous numbers of performances, alternative castings and productions, and more journalistic freedom to investigate this dance in terms of space and in terms of format, the New York School critics have industriously chronicled both the conditions and the evolution of their critical processes within this framework and formalized a working aesthetic (however unconsciously) between the covers of their collections or when studied in collected form. Denby lacked this critical repertory and, though he was in dialogue with fellow artists, he was largely observing and commenting on dance in relative isolation compared to Jowitt, Siegel, Croce and Goldner. As Arlene Croce points out in her essay on Edwin Denby, "Nothing is harder to spot than the unconscious patterns that connect the work of contemporaries."[113] These connections comprise the network of this critical repertory and, in discussing, for instance, Denby's ability to see a connection between aspects of Massine's choreography and Graham's choreography without being able to comment on it, Croce states:

---

[113] Arlene Croce, "Edwin Denby," *Sight Lines*, New York : Alfred A. Knopf., 1987, p. 340.

*Yet Denby's eye saw something — probably the only thing — in Graham's work that was like Massine's. That he didn't make a critical point of the similarity is immaterial. He may not have had the chance. Companies didn't perform, and critics didn't write often enough in those days for such tight connections to be made.*[114]

The four critics under examination have been very largely responsible for taking full advantage of their dance environment. They have seen and commented on the connections among choreographers and have detailed the family tree of dance not only in their time, but as critics with keen historical consciences, in the preceding generations of dance that formed the roots of the tree. In evolving a critical repertory, these critics have created a dance cultural literature rather than a body of review writing. The review of the single performance format has been gradually replaced by a far more enduring and protective literature about performed dance of an era.

At the start of their careers as dance critics in New York, the dance criticism scene was markedly sparser than it is now. Jill Johnston was writing criticism for *The Village Voice* and at the *New York Times* John Martin was chief dance critic. With assistance from Selma Jeanne Cohen and Jaqueline Maskey the dance critics that followed at the *New York Times* were Alan Hughes, Clive Barnes, Don McDonagh and Anna Kisselgoff. Mary Watson, the original dance critic for *The New York Herald Tribune*, was succeeded by Walter Terry and then Edwin Denby. Terry reclaimed his post from Edwin Denby in 1945 after he completed his military service during World War II. Denby never wrote for a newpaper again, concentrating instead on his poetry and contributing only the sporadic dance essay. Other dance writing was mainly in the hands of Louis Horst in *The Dance Observer*, Selma Jeanne Cohen as editor of *Dance Perspectives* and Doris Herring, as editor of *Dance Magazine*. Another publication, *Dance News*, had a succession of three editors — Anatole Chujoy, P. W. Manchester and Helen Atlas, with major contributions from Nancy Goldner and Walter Sorrell. Marcia Siegel started *Dance Scope* in 1964 but moved on to a much broader criticism career soon after.

This, largely, was the criticism scene that Croce, Goldner, Jowitt and Siegel inherited. And it was in this environment of dance criticism that these four women made their collective stamp. Today's New York School of critics, like Denby in his day, are "willing to risk hypotheses" about what they view again and again and in the process they have made the passionately subjective response ring true in their grasp of the issues and essence of American dance.

---

[114] Ibid.

# 3

## WOMEN AT WORK

### Description

Description can be seen as the first, natural step in responding critically to dance and little discussion can develop without some attention to this task. As T. S. Eliot once commented, the critic must have "a highly developed sense of fact."[1] Description can achieve vivid visual and kinesthetic imagery and help recreate the immediacy of the dance experience. The phenomenological attitude of "being present to the phenomenon" and "elucidating structures apparent in the phenomenon,"[2] describes in part the way in which description operates in the criticism of the New York School. What distinguishes these critics is their ability to reconcile technique and expression within the descriptive framework of their criticism,[3] revealing the expressive value of dance through its formal structures.

The objectives of description in dance criticism appear to be: firstly, the re-creation of the action, the physical facts, in order to establish a framework for interpretation and evaluation; secondly, the creation, through imagery, of the immediacy or kinesthetic experience of dance; thirdly, a means of illuminating the critic's aesthetic values by the nature of the description itself (setting forth the imaginary presence of the dance); fourthly, a tool for historic preservation of dance.

In this last context, the livelier and more accurate descriptive criticism is, the greater value it possesses for the historian and also for "discovering the fundamental and continuing values of the art not from

---

[1] T. S. Eliot, *Aesthetics and History*, Purdue University: Open Court, 1962.

[2] Maxine Sheets, *The Phenomenology of Dance*, University of Wisconsin Press, 1963.

[3] George Jackson commented that "The factualness of criticism seems discredited now in New York. The post-dance boom critics claim at most to be writing about their memory of facts, about images. Is what you see determined by what you know? With even Siegel now disavowing plain description, have we entered the post-descriptive era of dance criticism?" (Washington, D.C. January 10, 1990).

past works but in contemporary works themselves."[4] I find myself drawn to dance criticism as a way into dance history. For example, the liveliness and detail of an account by a critic writing in the *Morning Chronicle* in 1839 on Romantic ballerina, Fanny Elssler's "fall from grace" and an account written in 1968 by Arlene Croce about New York City Ballet ballerina, Suzanne Farrell reveal astonishing similiarities in concern and style of scrutiny of their dancer subjects. The first example is from John Chapman's marvellous research in *British Ballet Criticism in London (1785–1850)*. The second is from Croce's *Afterimages* in a piece called "Dancers and Dance Critics." I quote these passages in considerable length to reveal the full extent of their compatibility and to demonstrate how such writing can be both provocative and practical as a preservational tool for historian and audience alike.
On Elssler:

> *Would that she applied her rare talents to their legitimate uses, instead of striving to accomplish feats destitute of intelligence, and movements calculated to disguise rather than illustrate the loveliness of her form. The style in which FANNY danced in London last year approached nearer to our standard of excellence than that of any other female dancer we ever saw, excepting TAGLIONI; the appropriate action of her limbs, always in harmony with each other, her expression when in repose, the blending of vigour and agility with dignity and grace — those various modes, in short, of exhibiting a finely moulded human form in motion, which both gratify the imagination of the beholder, and produce that delicious torment of admiration and envy which the realisation of the 'ideal' in any lofty branch of art, inspires in its votary.*

> *We deplore Mademoiselle FANNY's manner of dancing the more, because this new style is infinitely beneath her powers. To behold her symmetrical person, elevated on the extreme digitals, or tottering across the stage as though she wore gyves on her ancles, with rapid beetle-like steps, body erect and stiff — or else, executing that most senseless of all 'tours de force', the whirligig spinning round! How can we applaud such a misdirection of her faculties? Let FANNY ELSSLER but cast aside that fatal error of our day- the rage for performing what is new in preference to what is perennially enchanting — and delight us once again by her unrivalled elasticity and poetical movements; let her but throw herself into natural postures — into simple saltatory action and undulation, and we predict a tribute of the most heartfelt applause for her.*[5]

## On Farrell:

> *In her earlier seasons as a featured soloist, starting about 1962, Miss Farrell was an altogether different dancer — sensitive, light, fluid and simple without, as yet, much projective force.*

---

[4] Thomas Barnes Herthal, *John Martin, Dance Critic: A Study of His Critical Method in the Dance as Theatre Art*, PhD Thesis, Cornell University, 1966.

[5] John Chapman, "British Ballet Criticism in London 1785–1850" in *New Directions in Dance*, ed. Diana Theodores Taplin, Oxford: Pergamon Press, 1979.

*This force began to appear in* Meditation, *with its new, for Balanchine, use of emotionally expressive gestures and poses that seemed more in the vein of* Bolshoi moderne *than the NYCB repertory at that time. The Farrell of that period was not only a beautiful dancer in the variety of styles that Balanchine had established in the ballerina roles of the repertory, she was obviously the dancer whom Balanchine had chosen to lead him into fresh areas of composition and to set a further style of her own. She was one of the few dancers I have ever seen who could make any movement, no matter how unorthodox, look classical, at any speed. Expression seemed to pour from her. She was incapable of ugliness or insecurity. Today, in the dances of the third act of* Don Quixote, *she can still persuade me that she is among the greatest dancers on earth — in the great sighing lifts in which she holds the shape of her pose in its continuing arc, in her entrance a moment later with the torso twisted to be back as she breaks into fleet, low jumps, both feet lifted and held above the ground like an illusion in stop-time photography. These moments, for me, sum up Farrell's greatness, a greatness which the critics still write about, and the public pays to see, as if it were present in everything she does.*

*The break came in the* Rondo all Zingarese *movement of the Brahms-Schoenberg* Quartet, *which Balanchine set for Farrell and D'Amboise as a rowdy escapade with the kind of amorous, tongue-in-cheek byplay that might have been staged for a floor show in a Hungarian restaurant. In addition to flashing through the movements, which were a sophisticated version of the backbends and heel-and-toe work common to that style, Farrell apparently decided, or was encouraged, to play for powerful climaxes and sexiness on a big scale. This wasn't inappropriate, but soon it began to seem as if this role had become the expressive norm for her entire repertory. One now saw, in almost every part, the same worked-up shape to every phrase, everything delivered with utmost impact, no subtlety, no coherence. One saw a formerly fluid line distorted for maximum dynamic thrust in every direction, continual flaunting and flailing through the spine and neck, limp wrists, dismissive hands. Worse than this, there were movements that were repeated from ballet to ballet whether they belonged there or not: simple arabesques were converted in extreme arabesques penchées (in, for example, the second movement of* Concerto Barocco, *where the distortion was blatant), and I was astounded to see her kick her hand (in a grand battement) even as Terpsichore in* Apollo.

*All this is not only vulgar, it is immodest. It exhales self-importance. Paradoxically, it contracts the expressive range of her performance.*[6]

Both critics clearly hanker for their dancer's return to purer, simpler, more seemly and accurate modes of expressiveness. Elssler's critic is witness to the turning point of virtuoso display in female dancing of the time and fears the erosion of "poetic" clarity in the face of technique trends of the time. Farrell's critic is witness to the super-technical status of dance in her time, promoted to some extent by Farrell herself, and requires of this dancer that she be conscious of her role as guardian of that style. Again, accuracy and clarity are sought in the cause of preservation. Audiences have the advantage of film

---

[6] Arlene Croce, "Dancers and Dance Critics" in *Afterimages*, New York: Alfred A. Knopf, 1978, pps. 336–7.

**Plate 6** *Don Quixote*, choreography by George Balanchine (1965), The New York City Ballet. Dancer: Suzanne Farrell. Courtesy of The Dance Collection, The New York Public Library at Lincoln Center.

**Plate 7** *Don Quixote*, choreography by George Balanchine, The New York City Ballet. Dancer: Suzanne Farrell. Courtesy of The Dance Collection, The New York Public Library at Lincoln Center.

and video to inform them of past dance generations but dance literature such as the descriptive accounts above enlivens and sustains this impact of the visual record of dance or creates a visual record where none exists. Certainly it extends the parameters of descriptive documentation.

The subject of description as a keystone in dance criticism incites increasingly divided views. Denby, in his highly influential essay on criticism in *Looking at the Dance* proposed that clear and credible image-making essentially creates the setting of acceptance for interpretation and evaluation.

> *Dance criticism would be clearer if it found a way to describe relationships in theatre effect; and to describe just what the dancers' bodies do, the trunk, legs, arms, head, hands and feet in relationship to one another. The expression of a reviewer's personal reaction, no matter how violent or singular, becomes no immodesty when he manages to make distinct to the reader the visible objective action on stage he is reacting to.[7]*

The critic George Beiswanger argues that the task of dance critics is to "translate a kinetic into a verbal actuality" and that "setting forth an image of its presence becomes the substance of the critic's judgment of the dance."[8] Another view, voiced by *Washington Post* critic, Alan Kriegsman is that description tends to overshadow other approaches and needs to be reshaped or checked. With the advancement of technology which can preserve the faithful experience of dance the ideas of a "report proximation" of the performance is less necessary.[9]

The more current argument, that descriptive criticism is minimalist, impressionist or anti-theoretical, may arise from both a "backlash" against the formalist pure-dance orientation of the last two decades and from under-developed criticism which describes for the sake of description itself and fails to deliver the analysis upon which it is contingent.

Curtis Carter asserts that by the mid-seventies descriptive criticism had made it "unfashionable" to consider ideas, meanings, myths and feelings and that criticism based solely on the description of movement reflected only the kinesthetic experience of movement — the dancers' point of view.[10] The problematic and unsatisfactory divide between dance criticism that seeks to

---

[7] Edwin Denby, *Looking at the Dance*, New York: Dance Horizons Press, 1968, p. 338.

[8] George Beiswanger, "Rakes Progress or Dances and the Critic" in *Dance Scope*, Vol. 10, No. 2., S/S 1976, pp. 29–34.

[9] Alan Kriegsman, Panel Discussion at Conference entitled "Illuminating Dance: Philosophical Enquiry and Aesthetic Criticism" Temple University, Philadelphia, May 5, 1979.

[10] Curtis Carter, "Some Notes on Aesthetics and Dance Criticism" *Dance Scope*, Vol. 10, No. 2, S/S 1976, p. 36.

discuss ideas and criticism that describes movement is grounded, Carter believes, "in a misguided separation of sensibility from intelligence."[11]

Roger Copeland adds a new twist to the age-old body/mind split that has infiltrated the history of doing and viewing dance. "Dance is heralded as the most participatory of the arts" he says, "even if that participation remains virtual rather than actual." Dance is thereby "entrusted with preserving the participation mystique," in anthropological terms, a feature of primitivism.[12] The "virtual" participation in dance attributed to the kinesthetic experience of dance — viewing is analogous here to the "primitive" aspect of the act of describing as a form of critical writing.

In the Spring issue of *DCA News*, 1989, Marcia Siegel took the position that there is no such thing as "simply describing dance." She argued that "our account of a performance is profoundly affected by subjective considerations as well as practical ones" and that sensuality in description is vital because "dance's fascination is based largely on its sensual and expressive qualities."[13]

For the New York School of Critics description is a product of seeing. Description activates memory and language. Description is an organizing agent. "Describing is a way to find out what I might know"[14] says Marcia Siegel. Nancy Goldner believes that

> description works only when the reader is told why it is important to know about that which you are describing. You have to first intuit the whole work and make that judgment about what is important right away. Then description is necessary...... I go back to the works again and again to find out more.[15]

And Arlene Croce claims that her critical consciousness

> comes from the frustrations of reading about dance without being able to see it. Dance literature is so largely eyeless, but not Denby's. I prefer Denby's way of describing. I want from criticism not choreographic notation but impressionistic description — poetic metaphor.[16]

---

[11] Curtis Carter, "Intelligence and Sensibility in the Dance" in *Arts in Society*, Vol. 13, No. 2, S/F 1976, p. 62.

[12] Roger Copeland, "Dance Criticism and the Descriptive Bias" in *Dance Theatre Journal*, Vol. 10, No. 3, S/S 1993, p. 29.

[13] Marcia B. Siegel, "Dance Criticism" in *DCA News*, Spring, 1987, p. 3.

[14] Interview with Marcia B. Siegel, June 1985, New York City.

[15] Interview with Nancy Goldner, June 1985, New York City.

[16] Interview with Arlene Croce, June 7, 1985, New York City.

Deborah Jowitt values description and sees it as being "more important in dance than in the other arts," adding, "I never thought I was just describing."[17]

The highly descriptive nature of these critics' writings points to a remarkable kinetic memory about dance. They demonstrate the power of interpretation liberated by the accuracy of the dance image. The term *description* or *descriptive writing* is, in itself, problematic. It suggests a reactive, imitative and essentially passive process (recording what one sees) rather than the *activity of seeing* in all its facets. For this reason I propose to replace the term descriptive writing with the term *perceptual writing* which I believe more accurately defines the mode of writing particular to the New York School. Perception takes in the whole apparatus of vision, of the imagination, sensation and cause and the "intuitive recognition of a moral or aesthetic quality."[18] "Receptivity to visual experience" as Siegel puts it, or active seeing, is central to these critics' processes. Active seeing, so impressed upon Siegel by Denby has remained a lively issue for her throughout her career. For years Siegel and Jowitt went so far as to "train" with leading vision therapy specialist Dr. Richard Kavner in New York.[19]

At its very heart, the writing of the New York School, re-creative, sensual and analytical, "examines ideas generated from the systematic reflection of the sensory experience of dance."[20] Ironically this point, quoted from Roger Copeland's essay *Dance Criticism and the Descriptive Bias* was made in arguing that the "descriptive" writing of critics like Croce and Jowitt precluded any such generation of ideas. The pure dance values of the formalist vanguard of choreographers who predominated in the New York dance scene, the argument goes, inspired a predominantly anti-interpretive, theory-impoverished critical literature, vividly reflected in the descriptive genre of many of the New York critics. Other writers have examined the post-dance boom in New York, assessing the issues of decentralization, the rise of regionalism in American dance culture, the emergent popularity of European-inspired expressionist theatricalities, the representations of performance artists, world dance, physical theatre and the hybrid forms spanning all three. With these forms setting the aesthetic agendas in the

---

[17] Interview with Deborah Jowitt, June 1985, New York City.

[18] *The Shorter Oxford English Dictionary*, Third Edition, ed. C. J. Onions, Oxford: Clarendon Press, 1973, p. 1551.

[19] Interview with Marcia B. Siegel, June 1985, New York City.

[20] Roger Copeland, "Dance Criticism and the Descriptive Bias" in *Dance Theatre Journal*, Vol. 10, No. 3, S/S 1993.

1990s some have argued that the value and contribution of the New York critics discussed here were particular only to a formalist milieu, now eroded. Their body of work is therefore relegated to an irrelevant status. Neither of these arguments stand up to much scrutiny. The New York School of criticism, represented in the work of these four women, has been central to issue-based, aesthetics-based, values-based dance discourse.[21] Croce has consistently voiced that the "seriousness of dance and its literacy needs to be emphasized."[22] But by that she does *not* mean the "reduction of the dance experience to ideas and constructs with little or no sensuous response."[23] To do so, in her view, would constitute "the wrong sort of intellectual interest in dance."[24]

Their particular mode of perceptual writing straddles the acts of "revealing sensuous surfaces"[25] and maintaining a consciousness of heritage.[26] It is about seeing clearly and constructing an active language of dynamic scrutiny. The "accurate, sharp, loving description of the appearance of a work"[27] avowed by Susan Sontag, for instance, is informed in their criticism by a reckoning with, a reference to and a reverence for heritage. Inherent in their writing is an alertness to *the new* rooted in an awareness of the past. In a "golden age" of choreography witnessed by a group of such conscientious and innovative critics the seeds for a golden age of dance criticism were surely planted.

Through description these critics excavate the physical facts of the dance for investigation. Their active description recalls the vivid rhythms, physical discovery and visual attitude of dances and dancers. Their poetic description conjures up the enduring imaginative value of the dances they view. Their analytical description investigates how a dance achieves its impact. By describing *what* they see they reveal *how* they see. Amongst these critics description becomes a way of *telling the story* of the dance. Again, Deborah Jowitt's review of Martha Graham's *Primitive Mysteries*,

---

[21] Janet Adshead Landsdale, "Dance and Critical Debate" *Dance Theatre Journal*, Vol. 11, No. 1, Winter, 1993–4, p. 24.

[22] Interview with Arlene Croce, June, 1985, New York City.

[23] Ibid.

[24] Ibid.

[25] Susan Sontag, *Against Interpretation and other essays*, London: Andre Deutsch Ltd., 1987, p. 13.

[26] T. S. Eliot, "Tradition and the Individual Talent" in *Modern Criticism Theory and Practice*, eds. Walter Sutton and Richard Foster, New York: Odyssey Press, 1963, p. 141.

[27] Susan Sontag, *Against Interpretation and other essays*, London: Andre Deutsch Ltd., 1987, p. 13.

quoted in Chapter 2, is an example of such "story telling."[28] Such writing meets dance on its own terms and finds the motivation for language within the movement. Croce, too, whose writing is more inclined towards complex *enchainments* of references and issues also features this "story telling" mode. Capturing the sassy, colloquial, irreverent style of Tharp in a 1971 performance of *Eight Jelly Rolls*, a dance at the other end of the temperament spectrum from *Primitive Mysteries*, she observes:

> *The piece has a slow, easy start. Rose-Marie Wright, the group's long tall Sally, does a lazy, slew-footed shuffle, the arms lifting and falling in an imitation of shadow boxing…. Right in the middle of this, at an entrance for two gravel-throated trombones, two other dancers make an upstage cross in a state of high spastic agitation, like a Marionette act being pulled slowly across the scenery… Rudner falls down dead once, twice…. It's Twyla's turn and she's loaded; sick, filthy, drunk. She's flat on her nose and can't get up. She's up and off balance, legs spiralling, knees sinking, keeling and careening the length of the stage…. Avant garde, with its connotations of elitism, is…. a miserably ineloquent term of description for Tharp's special atmosphere of novelty. I should prefer to call this atmosphere baroque, bearing in mind that the original meaning of "baroque" was "bizarre." Her love of paradox, of radical possibility and permutation… makes the bond of communication one of a mutual respect for form.[29]*

Siegel's *The Shapes of Change* is a landmark experiment in dance criticism written in description-analysis form, creating a "reading" of dances at a level of literacy never before known. *The Shapes of Change* is a whole book dedicated to describing in words the moment to moment progress through a dance, and it reads with astonishing interest. Can it be that the dances Siegel chooses to describe are such exciting pieces of craftsmanship that it is possible to "play them back in words" and still achieve a satisfying sensory experience? I think the answer lies as much in the descriptive powers of Siegel as in the dances themselves. Interestingly, although *The Shapes of Change* is based on long-term and repeated viewing of performances and videos which allows for the resulting in-depth analysis of the works selected, this documentary descriptiveness can also be found in the single review pieces of all four critics, to similar effect.

In her own intensive account of *Primitive Mysteries* Siegel exercises all three modes of descriptive or perceptual writing outlined earlier. Overall, one is impressed with her ability to be both guardian of a heritage and open to the ways in which the values of a preserved work *change*. We know that Siegel, by virtue of having selected the dance for inclusion in *The Shapes of Change* defines *Primitive Mysteries* as an American classic, a cultural artifact

---

[28] Deborah Jowitt, *The Village Voice*, May 30, 1977.

[29] Arlene Croce, *Afterimages*, New York: Alfred A. Knopf, 1978, pp. 393–5.

which is a "zeitgeist" of a period and place. Accordingly, she acts as preserver, analyst and catalyst for the dance in dialogue with her audience.

To give a sense of this description and to see how it reads as both active and emotionally descriptive, I quote the writing of Section I of the dance. After this follows about five pages of descriptive documentation of the dance in chronological order.

> *They begin strutting backward and forward around her to a marcato five-count melody that the piano and flute play in unison but in different registers. At each end of the groove that they're digging by backing up and treading forward, they lash their arms around their bodies, clasping them behind and pulling back on the forward step, and clasping them in front, pulling the upper body toward the ground, when striding back. Though it's a five-count phrase, the steps and turns are set up so that each woman remains in the same segment of the circle, making no headway in either direction.*
>
> *The phrase gains a beat and accelerates. As if the regularizing of the beat — from five to six — had fortified their intention, the dancers begin making a complete turn on their back-and-forth pathway. They emphasize the vertical, jumping into the air or bouncing down to the ground on each turn, at the same time as they pedal their hands up and down in front of their bodies. They seem to be pushing off from the earth, being sent heavenward by a great propelling force. The bodies have stopped wrenching forward and back, and have become straight and taut, like arrows shot into the sky.*
>
> *Suddenly, on a cadence in the music, they stop, turn to the center of the circle, where the Virgin has been sitting. She rises, keeping her arms in the same iconic position, and they fold their bodies from the waist and bow to the ground. After a pause, they march off the stage in formation.*[30]

The language is abrupt, lean and forceful, reflecting the choreography. Siegel keeps the sense of *the story* of the dance alive through an active and emotional coloration. The dancers "dig grooves" by "backing up and treading forward" rather than simply move back and forth; they "emphasize the vertical" when they jump; their bodies stop "wrenching forward" and become "taut like arrows." Siegel's way of seeing is dynamically, almost *fiercely* attentive. It is in itself a critical commentary on the central value of this dance that is vital to its preservation and yet has already changed irrecoverably over generations. The mysterious, amazonian female strength inherent in the original choreography is somehow summoned from this revival and freeze-framed in Siegel's writing, clinging to its intended performance ideals through her words.

Nancy Goldner's 1977 review in *The Nation*, written the same year as Siegel's above work is based on a later revival of the dance rather than the 1964 revival on which Siegel bases her piece. (Siegel's is also based largely on

---

[30] Marcia B. Siegel, *The Shapes of Change*, Boston: Houghton Mifflin, 1979, p. 106.

viewing the film of the 1964 revival). Nonetheless, striking similarities in their accounts of *Primitive Mysteries* are evident. These similarities are all the more interesting in that the two reviews were designed with different purposes, for very different publications. Goldner's detailed description reads like a condensed version of Siegel's in-depth study. The fact that *The Nation* published such a descriptive account of the work as a "review" says a lot for Goldner's ability to convince the editor and readers of the significance of the work and to make the work so readable through that kind of approach. Again, like Siegel's piece, Goldner's review of *Primitive Mysteries* is very sensitive to movement quality and to images which speak for the overall effect of the dance. Also like Siegel, Goldner analyses the source of the dance's effects and works towards defining the dance in the context of Graham's significance as a choreographer. The "rigor and intensity" that Siegel notes about the work is referred to by Goldner as being "shocking for its rawness." Both critics are riveted with the way in which the dance achieves such expressive impact through such spartan, formal means. Both critics go on to define what those means are and how they are unique in the Modern Dance Movement.

Structurally, too, Goldner's piece on *Primitive Mysteries* is very like Siegel's. The first paragraph assesses the whole dance as a ritual empowered by symbolic and concrete expression. There follow several paragraphs of moment to moment description, also emotionally coloured and intensely visceral. The last of these paragraphs reads:

> *Now the central figure is accompanied by one woman. She stands behind the woman in white, a shadow and an extension. The group jumps in quick little fountains of energy. The central figure rests on the ground while her shadow, looming above, crowns her with splayed fingers. The group falls to the ground. The two women in the center fall to the ground. Then they all rise and recess in the same formation in which they had entered at the beginning of the dance, except that now two women occupy the center of the square. The Virgin is dead; long live the Virgin.*[31]

Notice again how *narrative* this description is. It never appears as merely an account of the action but as a *story of movement*. The last section of the review is an analysis of the dance both in terms of how it achieves its effects and where its significance lies in American choreographic history.

> *What is absolutely certain is that the architectural grandeur of* Primitive Mysteries *rises out of a choreographer at the peak of her incisiveness. Just as the dance is about a group of women who know exactly what they must do, so is this dance made by a woman who knows. Its austerity and purposefulness are not to be confused with Bauhaus grimness, however. Rolling*

---

[31] Nancy Goldner, *The Nation* (volumes collected) June 4, 1977, p. 697.

**Plate 8** *Primitive Mysteries*, choreography by Martha Graham (1935). Photograph © 1980 by Barbara Morgan.

*up behind every jagged line is a curved line. The square becomes a circle. For every heel locked into the ground there is a subsequent spring onto the ball of the foot. The celebrants' clenched arms find release in the Virgin's full-faced open-bodied stances, assumed once she has the group's permission to be its symbol. That first circular run, its momentum nipped in the bud, is unleashed the second time around. The tensely asymmetrical groups of the crucifix yield to symmetry in the hosanna.*

*Yet despite the care with which Graham weighs dissonance against harmony,* Primitive Mysteries *is shocking for its rawness. As much as it is about the rites of passage so is it about elbows and knuckles.*[32]

Locked heels become "sprung feet," runs become "unleashed," "behind every jagged line is a curved line." These descriptions, so terse, again, reflect the very starkness of the landscape of the dance. These critics are able to delve into the essence of the dance and return with a language of response that is in dialogue with it. Images are active or delicate or economical or grittily visual; they appropriately activate in the reader the kinetic and sensual experience of the dance. They "take on" in words the language of the choreographer's movement. The dance is "about the rites of passage" and it is "about elbows and knuckles." The *story of the dance* is utterly believable in those terms.

We are brought time and time again to the fact that all experience of the dances viewed come from and return to the dances themselves. Description, organised around the three components: active re-creation of the dance; sensual or poetic imagery that qualifies the essence of the movement; and analysis that links effects to actual dance moments and assesses in larger terms the dance's value and significance, is motivated and informed by the dance's terms. We are made party to the critic's discovery of this.

What is so fascinating in these descriptions is the sense that there is a "preserving eye" at work selecting what is essential, finding the vocabulary to bring the image into action, telling us how these characteristics act as the matrix of the dance observed and how they can help us to appreciate the works more fully. Goldner describing Cunningham's movement traits in *Signals* is yet another example:

*The tendus that don't quite hit their destination, the passés that scamper about the knee, the off-kilter tilts to the side, the attitude with the arms in the "wrong" position, at chest level rather than held above the head — it's precisely this kind of play with basic vocabulary that's allowed Cunningham to revitalise classic dance. But the way the steps unfold — as a quick*

---

[32] Ibid.

**Plate 9** *Primitive Mysteries*, choreography by Martha Graham (1965 revival). Dancer: Yuriko. Courtesy of the Dance Collection, The New York Public Library at Lincoln Center. Photograph © 1980 by Barbara Morgan.

*succession of flash cards instead of daisy chains — gives his dance new, pristine momentum. It explains why a style so elaborate in content can be so tonally austere at times.*[33]

And Jowitt, as a final example, describes the movement traits of Paul Taylor:

*Today,* Aureole *can almost be viewed as a primer of Taylor dancing; in it you can see the chains of ground-skimming leaps; the parallel feet (as opposed to the turned-out ones of ballet); the archaic Graham poses with jutting hips which give the dancers the look of frolicking satyrs; the flyaway hands, twin-armed gestures; the fluent knot. And above all the buoyancy. Taylor is a big man, but his style had a light, smooth, spongy quality, which all of his dancers acquire. However difficult the steps, however perverse the choreographic non sequiturs, the easy, almost tactful way the dancers exert their strength minimises all effort and imparts a fluidity to whatever they do. So by taking his idiosyncratic movement style and treating it as if it were neutral, by performing it dispassionately, by patterning it with grace and ingenuity, Taylor has arrived at his extremely odd brand of classicism. The dances that he's made since 1966 might also be considered as classical art in that they're neatly balanced, formal equations in which his inescapable quirks of thought are framed or resolved in images that have theatrical vividness and comprehensibility.*[34]

The physical facts of the dance yield expressive effects. The dance is *felt* as much as understood. Consistently these critics identify the telling characteristics of a dance and comment on the way in which these characteristics create the stylistic outcome (the choreographer's point of view) and the expressive and kinesthetic resonance.

Description operates as a provocative and meticulous methodology. Description penetrates the dances. Time and again, whether in confronting new choreography, identifying and defining a choreographer's characteristics, assessing the place of a dance in choreographic history, investigating the sources of a dance's effects, distinguishing between performers, and observing the changing values of dances, the critics of the New York School anchor their experience of dance in those three essential components of description to construct the framework of their investigations: the recreative, the sensual and the analytical.

Sometimes the descriptive language of these critics imbues work with a romanticism bordering on the mythological. In Denby's day, dancers sometimes complained that some of the things he described could not possibly have happened. Certainly these critics have at times been aggressively imaginative seers. Croce, for instance, tends to make

---

[33] Nancy Goldner, "Cunningham Diary" in *The Bennington Review*, September 1978.

[34] Deborah Jowitt, "Rebel Turned Classicist" in *Dance Beat*, New York: Marcel Dekker, Inc., 1977 p. 108–9.

**Plate 10** *Signals*, choreography by Merce Cunningham (1970). Dancers: Douglas Dunn, Valda Setterfield, Ulysses Dove. Photograph © James Klosty. Courtesy of Cunningham Dance Foundation, Inc.

**Plate 11** *Aureole*, choreography by Paul Taylor (1962). Courtesy of the Dance Collection, The New York Public Library at Lincoln Center.

sweepingly heroic statements about the definitiveness of a particular production of a dance or over-scrutinizes a dancer's performing characteristics. Sometimes the connections the critics make between dances are too insistently forced. Sometimes the dances they review "do more" on the page than they ever did on the stage. Ironically, this problem of making a medium do more than it can do or needs to do is a problem these critics often refer to in reviewing choreographers who, in their opinion, attempt to "do more" to classical ballet but only succeed in deforming the medium.

## Style as Meaning

There are two phrases that one encounters in the writings of the New York School with regularity and reliability. They are "the curtain rises" and "the dance is about." Both phrases are introductions to detailed description. The phrase "the curtain rises" literally sets the scene for the re-creation of the physical facts of the dance. Thus Goldner writes about Balanchine's ballet *Violin Concerto*:

> *The curtain rises and the music begins. Mazzo and group stand alertly in stage center, but do not move a muscle, while Stravinsky is off and running. You sit poised, then anxious: when will they begin to dance to music that begs for dancing?*[35]

What follows immediately and runs to about one thousand words, is a vivid description of the movement throughout the dance in the chronological order of the choreography. In a critique on Balanchine's *Symphony in Three Movements* Goldner again starts the actual description by announcing:

> *The curtain rises on a long diagonal of girls in white leotards.... Stravinsky's chords blare out and the girls swing their arms violently in big circles... It seems a demonic invocation to which Helgi Tomasson responds.... by leaping from the wings onto the stage.*[36]

Again there follows an account of the action before she probes the ballet analytically. In a collection of critiques of Balanchine's ballets from the Stravinsky Festival she proceeds in the same fashion. But it is by no means only Balanchine's ballets that promote this approach. *Four Last Songs* by Leonide Massine, for instance, is handled in a like fashion when she writes

---

[35] Nancy Goldner, "Stravinsky Violin Concerto" in *Repertory in Review*, ed. Nancy Reynolds, New York: Dial Press, 1977, p. 290.

[36] Nancy Goldner, *The Nation*, February 26, 1973.

"When the curtain rises seven dancers are exercising at a silver coloured barre at the back of the stage...."[37] The use of the phrase "when the curtain rises" is a stylistic device that organizes and alerts the reader to the task of focussing on the subject of movement as if he or she were present at the event itself. In dances in which movement is clearly its own subject as in the ballets of Balanchine, this device serves as a reminder for the reader. It reminds us that it is the choreographer's intention that the dance be recognized and perceived in those terms — the terms of movement. Jowitt, also using the phrase, writes of Balanchine's *Vienna Waltzes*: "The curtain goes up and we see a couple arm in arm, wandering through a glade..."[38] She proceeds with atmospheric and active description. But the use of the phrase "the curtain rises" or its equivalent is also a reminder to the critics themselves to be alert to the movement properties of any kind of dance they view. Jowitt's use of this device in an account of Eiko and Koma's dance *Grain* operates in such a way. Writing about a work that is not a theatre of steps but a theatre of images, she begins her description "When the audience enters the deep, narrow performance space, Eiko and Koma are sprawled far apart, face down, naked, on a white platform less than a foot high that almost fills the room."[39]

From this introduction Jowitt proceeds to look at how the images in the work are essentially motivated by and effective through the manner of Eiko and Koma's movement. Even Arlene Croce, who of the four critics relies the least on re-creative description, engages in this structural device. In a critique on Paul Taylor's *Runes* she begins "The curtain rises on a dark stage, its horizon lit by a full moon."[40] There follows an involved description of the movement passages and the structure of the choreography. Again, it seems that the phrase is a kind of technical "cue" for the critics to attend to the task of setting the scene, establishing the physical facts of the dance before weaving in other forms of commentary. Croce even uses this device as a way to set-up the emotional re-creation of the dance's effects. In a lovely example she writes of Balanchine's *Liebeslieder Walzer* "I have never been able to experience the rise of the second curtain, on those girls now suddenly frozen on toepoint, without a tightening of the heart."[41] Following

---

[37] Nancy Goldner, *The Nation*, November 11, 1978.

[38] Deborah Jowitt, *The Dance in Mind*, Boston: David Godine, 1985, p. 19.

[39] Ibid, pps. 185–6.

[40] Arlene Croce, "Runes" in *Going to the Dance*, New York: Alfred A. Knopf, 1982, p. 367.

[41] Arlene Croce, *Afterimages*, New York: Alfred A. Knopf, 1978, pp. 409–10.

that phrase Croce describes the sensations of the dance's images not so much in movement terms but in emotionally coloured atmospheric terms.

The phrase "the dance is about" has a narrative style of delivery about it. The critics are saying, in essence, "this is a story about a dance and it goes like this." What we see, they tell us, is a dance about a dance and to get to the expressive core, the heart of the story, you must believe what you see. There is a filling in of the stage canvas that includes detailed features of movements, the order of events, the look and effect of the movements, the relationships between movement and music, between one work and another, the performing attitude of the dancers, and the nature of the dance's challenge to our perception and aesthetic sensibilities. The term "the dance is about" frames the issue of style -as- meaning. This is what these critics mean when they describe the story of the dance. With eye-catching consistency the phrase introduces the reader to works which instigated a new order of sensibilities. Goldner wrote of Tharp's *As Time Goes By*, for example, that "it is about the elements intrinsic to dance composition."[42] Jowitt, writing about the same ballet said "If the dances look improvised at times, it's because the movement — which is what Tharp's dances are all about — looks so complex, so spontaneous, that you can hardly believe that someone taught it to someone else."[43] Later in the same critique Jowitt stated "Although Tharp's dances are mostly about dancing they are also intermittently about how dances get made."[44] Siegel, writing in 1973 about Tharp's *Deuce Coupe* said "This dance is about the flow and immediacy of crowds as much as it's about individuals doing their thing in crowds."[45] Writing about *As Time Goes By* she described it as being "about that different look and about how that kind of dancing goes with Haydn's music."[46] There is something quite playfully formalist about these statements, much like Cunningham's retort "it's about forty-five minutes long" when once asked what one of his dances was "about." In their descriptions of Cunningham's dances the same device is used repeatedly. Siegel describes *Summerspace* as being "about irregularity and unpredictability." *Winterbranch* is described as being "about resistance — about falling so slowly the dancers might be tempting gravity...." Goldner describes *Signals* as being "about something

---

[42] Nancy Goldner, *The Nation*, December 1973, p. 604.

[43] Deborah Jowitt, *The New York Times*, February 1973, p. 159 (collected).

[44] Ibid, p. 160.

[45] Marcia B. Siegel, *At the Vanishing Point*, New York: Saturday Review Press, 1972, p. 207.

[46] Marcia B. Siegel, *The Shapes of Change*, Boston: Houghton Mifflin, 1979, p. 353.

...... as a kind of metaphor of the dancers' discipline and as a study in contrast between measured movement and release, between the dancer practising and performing."[47]

Again, as with the phrase "the curtain rises" the phrase "the dance is about" operates as a release mechanism for delving into choreography that most challenges and inspires these critics. These choreographers are the "classicists" who reflect a purity of means in their dance-making. The New York School critics experience their works as meaningful within the steps and structures. As Croce said of Tharp's *The Fugue*: "The dance's only subject is itself."[48]

In an essay called *More Geese Than Swans* which is particularly revealing for its seizing of style-as-meaning, Marcia Siegel fantasizes about a new *Swan Lake* whereby all the pantomime would be discarded and a dramatically believable story ballet out of the *material of movement* would arise in its place. Siegel uses Balanchine's version of *Swan Lake* as a potential model because he "lets his dancers make use of the expressive possibilities within the ballet technique... This is the magic that *Swan Lake* should have. It is created by the infusion of expressive qualities into the movement itself. It speaks to our deepest kinesthetic sense."[49]

Croce wrote at great length about Balanchine's *Swan Lake* being the definitive version for precisely the same reason that Siegel states. For these critics the expressive content and emotional meaning of dance comes from the impetus to move. And Balanchine's choreography, in spawning a whole lineage of American classicism, both inspired and responded to that criterion.

Through their characteristic examination of style-as-meaning, their "telling of dance stories," these critics pioneered the creation of a text for dance and set about guiding us through a reading of dances in ways literary, philosophical, imagistic and narrative. Denby's ideal for dance criticism "to quote passages as illustration" becomes a reality through their work.

## Classicism

> *Classicism, like everything else, evolves (Diaghilev)*

Rarely in the writings of our pas de quatre of critics does one encounter a specific definition of classicism even though this concept is proposed as a characteristic of the school. Croce quotes Cunningham to get to the matter:

---

[47] Nancy Goldner, *The Nation*, December 7, 1970.

[48] Arlene Croce, *Afterimages*, New York: Alfred A. Knopf, 1978, p. 391.

[49] Marcia B. Siegel, *At the Vanishing Point*, New York: Saturday Review Press, 1972, pp. 54–7.

*That a dance be, as he once wrote, 'Unprompted' by references other than to its own life is the first requirement of Classicism. The other two requirements — academic legibility and virtuosity — are also part of his canon.[50]*

This reference to Cunningham offers at least a partial definition of classicism. Certainly the three "requirements" that Croce raised were recognized by her fellow critics as being present in the works of their "essential" choreographers. Recognizing the frequent reference to the notion of classicism in her own writing and that of her colleagues, Nancy Goldner recently attempted to define the term as

*...meaning revealed through structure, through dance language, through a certain purity of form.... The use of the body itself is very schooled, clear, based on a codified vocabulary — one that is investigated over and over. Classicism is a language that has a clarity, a certain sense of measuredness... anytime you can intuit that a choreographer is trying to make something new from something old.[51]*

Recalling Siegel's comment about "the plenitude" of ideas that Balanchine discovers in the arabesque, one understands through the writings of these critics that the invention of style is in itself an act of classicism, arrived at through a "pure" manipulation of means. The form is the route to expression and meaning. "The only subject of classical dancing is classical style" said Croce. Speaking about Balanchine, she observed that "The formal values are not Balanchine's invention but the emphasis on them is. He extracts the essence of a form and gives it expansion."[52] Copeland, in describing Balanchine as a "modern neo-classicist" expands on the definition:

*His relationship to the past, specifically the classical vocabulary codified by Petipa, recalls the relationship of Picasso to the work of Goya and Velasquez, of Stravinsky to Tchaikovsky, Joyce to Homer and Elliott to Shakespeare. These artists affirm their continuity... with classical predecessors. They proceed on the assumption that the principle dilemma facing artists in the 20th century is not the burden of tradition, but the lack of an organic connection to the past.[53]*

"Just as Vladimir Nabokov is not really an American writer," says Goldner, "Balanchine has not created an American style of ballet, as is often said, unless that statement means that his style flowered in America. Balanchine

---

[50] Arlene Croce, *Going to the Dance*, New York: Alfred A. Knopf, 1982, p. 10.

[51] Interview with Nancy Goldner, September 1994, New York City.

[52] Arlene Croce, *Going to the Dance*, New York: Alfred A. Knopf, 1982, p. 328.

[53] Roger Copeland, "Backlash Against Balanchine" in *Balanchine: New Approaches*, Volume 3, Part 3, 1993, p. 9 of *Choreography and Dance*, ed. Eleni Brooks Hofmeister, Switzerland: Harwood Academic Publishers.

has created the Balanchinian style, whose godfather is the Russian choreographer, Petipa."[54]

Again, referring to Balanchine these critics saw in Tharp's expansiveness a Balanchine lineage. Siegel, described Tharp's ballet, *Push Comes to Shove* in Balanchinian terms, saying "It seems to me just as classical and just as daring for its time as *Concerto Barocco*. Croce wrote of the same ballet by Tharp that:

> *When you've seen Van Hamel deliver a high developpé kick from under the hat, you've seen the beginning of the synthesis that is Tharp's answer to the proposition "American Ballet Theatre." The synthesis involves an amalgamation of high and popular art which no other choreographer except Balanchine has achieved in this country.*[55]

Writing about Tharp's ballet *As Time Goes By* Goldner also compared her classicism to Balanchine's by saying: "For the more I see her manipulation the more convinced I become that she is redefining balletic concepts as Balanchine did.... *As Time Goes By* would seem to offer classical dance's unlimited possibilities."[56]

"Integrated innovation," choreography that is both inventive and restorative, clearly emerges throughout their writings as being another property of classicism. Choreographers such as Balanchine, Taylor and Tharp had landmark impacts on these critics because over and over again their choreography re-conditioned their critical sightlines with its astonishing individuality and its vigorous assertion of the immortality of classical ancestors. Jowitt referred to Taylor's choreography as "an unconservative but comprehensible form of classicism — ballet in a foreign language."[57] Croce asserted that Tharp was "moving toward a new quality of plain speech in classical choreography... on the verge of creating a new style, a new humanity, for classical ballet dancers."[58] Similarly, Croce writing in 1975 about Tharp's *Eight Jelly Rolls* and other of Tharp's "jazz" ballets observed that

> *in working to jazz musicians of other eras, in treating them with the same respect she gives to the constructions of Bach or Mozart and with the same omnivorous idiomatic sweep, Tharp*

---

[54] Nancy Goldner, "Who Cares?" in *The Nation*, March 2, 1970, p. 252.

[55] Arlene Croce, *Afterimages*, New York: Alfred A. Knopf, 1978, p. 197.

[56] Nancy Goldner, *The Nation*, December 1973, p. 604.

[57] Deborah Jowitt, "Under the Arch, Over the Trellis" in *The Village Voice*, April 29–May 5, 1981.

[58] Arlene Croce, op. cit., p. 24.

*is doing more than salvaging a lost art — she's reconditioning it and restructuring it as a modern art.*[59]

These critics' need to excavate, to turn over the pages of dance history and other art histories, to assess connections and identify influences  is activated most intensely at these times. The more innovative the choreography, the greater the need to find out, to clarify, and to celebrate.

Croce's first encounter with the work of Twyla Tharp in 1969 is an exhilarating example of a critic rising to the occasion of *the new* and finding a language to articulate the nature of the challenge. It is no surprise that, again, Croce refers to Balanchine and Cunningham as a means of "placing" Tharp's impact in a context for historical, cultural consideration.

> *Twyla Tharp is the first of the new generation of avant-garde choreographers to develop a choreographic style ordered entirely by considerations of time and space… Watching a piece like* Group Activities, *one has the feeling of having emerged on the other side of some barrier to perception… In* Group Activities, *you grasp immediately its difficulty and then its beauty of precision… The animation is so intense, the stop and go action of the piece so unpredictable, that one hangs on in quasi-dramatic suspense. The unforeseen logic of these calculations has a peculiar relation to the imagery of abstract ballet… they look brilliantly irrational to the eye. I know only two other choreographers who give the same effect, and they're Mr. B and Merce.*[60]

And in a piece on Tharp's ballet, *Deuce Coupe* Siegel observed that it "demands that the audience overhaul its habitual way of looking at ballet."[61] Confronting Tharp's work, *As Time Goes By* for the first time, Croce appraised the power of the work as being "like Nijinska's" in that it "exacts a primitive force of expression for its subject which is classical ballet…."[62] In her review of Paul Taylor's *Le Sacre du Printemps* (The Rehearsal) Croce cross-references a complex tapestry of themes, images, musical manipulations and expressive motivations, with Nijinsky's ballet *Le Sacre du Printemps* and illustrates that Taylor's ballet takes its place as the definitive treatment of this work. Goldner cross-referenced Taylor's work in a different way when she observed in a review in 1976 that

> *This quality of nonserious seriousness is hard to get at with Taylor. Merce Cunningham delivers it through whimsical non sequiturs; Twyla Tharp through irony; Frederick Ashton through a not so simple simplicity. Taylor's sleight of hand has neither the stimulating*

---

[59] Ibid, pp. 132–33.

[60] Ibid, pp. 342–3.

[61] Marcia B. Siegel, *Watching the Dance Go By*, Boston: Houghton Mifflin Company, 1977, p. 59.

[62] Arlene Croce, *Afterimages*, New York: Alfred A. Knopf, 1978, p. 24.

*tensions of the other choreographers nor their flaws — Cunningham's feyness, Tharp's fear to*
*face her audience squarely, Ashton's banality. Taylor's manifests itself in content.[63]*

Paul Taylor's distinct place in these critics' regard is in being a "one choreographer genre." The critics see Taylor as a dance artist who has uniquely managed to span the ballet-modern bridge, remain stylistically outside all the "hybrids" yet equally at home in modern or classical repertories. Taylor is perceived as someone who has established an exacting position between the two idioms and at the same time defies imitation. Altogether, the critics consider Taylor to be perhaps the most formal of modern dance choreographers because of his balletically presentational style and his purity of composition. The term "classicist" is applied to him as it is to Balanchine, Tharp, Ashton and Cunningham. He is considered to possess a boldly appropriate sixth sense about movement-music relationships. Stylistically, all four critics respond vividly to the bizarrely beautiful shape, line, and phrasing that contribute to the look of Taylor's dance. Their descriptions of the look of his movement focus unanimously on elements like speed vs. weight, and other oppositional tensions like fluidity vs. strength, masculine muscularity vs. softness of texture in the movement, archaic-like, twisted, two-dimensional stances the bodies often assume, subject matter and Taylor's penchant for the "geniality of the grotesque."

Again, in all their reviews, the critics demonstrate a deep familiarity with the Taylor repertoire, with the ways in which the works change and the way in which the company changes. They all assess the place Taylor occupies in the modern dance history-in-the-making and place him in a choreo-historic context, pinpointing the elements of his style, his innovations, and so on. They also, each of them, find vivid and active images that describe the look of Taylor's choreography, its effects and how it affects them as spectators.

In the following review of Taylor, Nancy Goldner gets to the "nuts and bolts" of his style. In the first few paragraphs she analyses Taylor's appeal, identifying the way in which music functions in his dances, how jumps are at the foundation of his technique, what the "anatomical layout" of Taylor dancers is and so on. Then, with equal directness and economy, Goldner assesses the Taylor dance "attitude" against those of Cunningham, Tharp and Ashton and places Taylor in a relevant historical context. Throughout her review Goldner refers to a cross-section of works in the Taylor repertoire to give the reader a firmer understanding of where any

---

[63] Nancy Goldner, *The Nation*, June 25, 1976, pp. 795–97 (volumes collected).

one work stands in the development of this choreographer's total output. She returns again and again to the issue of style and how to clarify and define it in "Taylor" terms. This is the "critical repertory" of the New York School in operation. A section of her review reads like this:

> *What the public forgets or perhaps, despite Taylor, has never learned, is that modern dance can be utterly genial and as vividly seductive as ballet… One obvious distinction between him and others is that he uses music as a meter for dancing. Not only are his dances usually rhythmic but the impetus to dance is readily understood; the music helps us empathize with the dancers' "need" to move. And the Taylor dancers move a lot. Jumps are as essential to Taylor as they are to Bournonville. Considering Taylor's passion for massive movement and modern dance's eschewal of fancy footwork, his choreography is remarkably allegro. The dancers move fast in defiance of the choreography's clunkiness and wayward propulsion and this endows the dancing with aspects of virtuosity. The visual interest of Taylor's work is more elusive, but I think it has something to do with the principle of opposition, transposed from painted to live bodies. The pelvis lunges one way; the torso and shoulders corkscrew back. Equilibrium is sustained through perpetual motion. The dancers extricate themselves from one extreme position by plugging or dipping into another, "other added" one. As long as they keep moving they're all right. This law of physics Taylor turns into a law of entertainment.*[64]

Goldner's "law of physics" echos Paul Valéry's analysis of balletic illusion saying,

> …… *From this arises this amazing impression that in the Universe of Dancing rest has no place; immobility; something forced and unnatural, a passing and almost violent state while leaps, counted steps, pointés, entrechats, and giddy rotation are natural manners of being and doing.*[65]

For Valéry, dancing was not only an intrinsically beautiful activity but one characterized by a particular notion of instability and stability and it was the instability of dance that was so immensely thrilling and unnatural. Valéry, along with Mallarmé, those French impressionists regarded as "essential reading" by Croce also assert their influence on *her* writing on Taylor when she refers to the "unstoppable energy of what Taylor has set in motion"[66] in a review of *Runes*. At other points in the review of *Runes* her writing, in reference to Mallarmé and Valéry, becomes increasingly esoteric —

---

[64] Ibid.

[65] Paul Valéry, "The Philosophy of Dance," in *Aesthetics*, trans. Ralph Manheim (Vol. 13 of Collected Works), New York: Pantheon Books, 1964, pp. 197–211.

[66] Arlene Croce, *Afterimages*, New York: Alfred A. Knopf, 1978, p. 201.

referring to Carolyn Brown as "not the agent of transformation — she is transformation itself" and at another point locating the essence of the work's powers with the term "the transubstantiation of dance energy."[67] To Mallarmé, ballet was the visualization of a metaphysical world, and poetry was its ideal language. He described dance as "the whirl of fleeting impetus"[68] and "perpetual illusion which suggests but never states."[69] He saw the dancer as transcending human nature and moving into the idea, the "element she incarnates."[70] His critical conception of the dancer in physical terms was a necessary but inferior agent to some higher form. The language that Paul Valéry shaped for the expression of both philosophical thoughts on dance and the description of dance was, like Mallarme's, richly poetic and vital. The godfather for their poetic pursuit of the dance was Théophile Gautier who was deeply susceptible to the feminine charms of the dancers whom he indulged in his writings and who showed how "a poetic vision can suggest the almost indefinable essence of a dancer's art."[71] Gautier applauded the achievements of the Romantic ballerinas in emphasizing dance values above all others and, as Alastair Macaulay suggests, in the supernatural realm of pure dancing, a "classical afterlife," dance values could be liberated from dramatic context.[72]

The art of idealization, and the envisioning of ideals for dance, from the French Romantics to Denby, was inherited by the New York School. They were highly susceptible to the ideal of classicism as much for its ruled and ordered expressiveness as for its spirituality, morality and romance.

In her book, *The Stravinsky Festival of the New York City Ballet*, Goldner comments, "The only constant has been Balanchine's belief that courtly dancing is a fine and proper thing to do, and many times his ballets have transformed dancers, theaters and audiences into their better selves."[73]

---

[67] Ibid, p. 200.

[68] Dierdre Pridden, *The Art of the Dance in French Literature*, London: Adam & Charles Black, 1952, p. 66.

[69] Ibid

[70] Ibid, p. 65.

[71] Ivor Guest, "Ballet Criticism and the Historian's View" in *Ballet Annual*, Volume 16, 1963, p. 63.

[72] Alastair Macaulay, "Notes on Dance Classicism" *Dance Theatre Journal*, Volume 5, No. 2, Summer, 1987, p. 7.

[73] Nancy Goldner, *The Stravinsky Book of the New York City Ballet*, New York: Eakins Press, 1974, p. 66.

In a review of Balanchine's *Duo Concertante* she proposes that Balanchine is ultimately a *love* choreographer. For the fullest appreciation of Balanchine's art, plotless, dissonant and lean as it is often described, one must see that it is charged with the human condition. One must also see that because its roots are so clearly in the social order of classical conventions (Petipa's ballet) it refers over and over again to the ideals of love: "In his most noble ballets he elevates the dancer into an image of love, a Muse-ballerina who inspires but is unreachable. And so this ending is an apotheosis of Balanchine's art."[74]

Croce swoons over the "formal values of dancing" in Cunningham's work, saying one can be "moved to ecstasy in the course of an evening."[75] And Goldner, writing on Cunningham (in a piece that sounds like Croce writing about Balanchine) says,

> In many instances the.... delicate pillars of support he offers are more often than not decorative; its the idea of support, rather than the physical need of it, that seems paramount. That's why, I think, Cunningham's duets have such powerful strains of love in them.... When Cunningham partners ...... he becomes the woman's guardian angel, touching her... not only to balance her, but as though to command her to our attention.[76]

This romantic response to the technical and metaphorical workings of the pas de deux is something that all four critics produce unabashedly. Not literal romance, but, rather, the essence of romance that is the product of classicism's stylistic purity. Two major perceptions emerge. The first is that *classical behaviour* is manifested through a particular vocabulary and that vocabulary embodies a response to the human condition: "instinctive behaviour in complex situations." Cunningham's work, for instance, instigates some distinct critical responses to this notion. "Its from a standpoint as much moral as anything else," says Macaulay,

> that Cunningham chooses to dance independently of music. Dance for him is a system or systems of behaviour: part of the system is his instinctive or deliberate choice to carry on acting without tagging along to soundtracks. (And it was from no less committed and profound moral standpoint that Balanchine chose to choreograph to music....)[77]

Roger Copeland places Cunningham's work within a moral dimension insofar as there is a "profound connection between what we choose to look

---

[74] Nancy Goldner, *The Nation*, July 10, 1972.

[75] Arlene Croce, *Afterimages*, New York: Alfred A. Knopf, 1978, p. 51.

[76] Nancy Goldner, *The Bennington Review*, September 1978, p. 81.

[77] Alastair Macaulay, "Notes On Dance Classicism" *Dance Theatre Journal*, Volume 5, No. 2, Summer, 1987, p. 37.

at and how we live our lives."[78] Where everything seems to clamor for our attention in modern city life, "Cunningham's work does serve as an end beyond itself; that of perceptual training."[79] As Peter Brook puts it, Cunningham's work is "a continual preparation for the shock of freedom."

Resolutions to formal problems, a code of manners, clarity, logic and the constant discovery of existence through the state of motion — the "shifting equilibrium" — all constitute the behavioural repertory that informs classicism through the language of ballet technique. The second perception that emerges is that the "afterimage" leaves its imprint not only through particular passages of steps, gestures and timings, but also as a humanly expressive drama arousing our emotions in a particular way. It suggests a mood, a point of view, a way of experiencing life within a given ballet 'environment'.

The ideas of love and morality in choreography are appreciated as a timeless condition as well as a style of investigation. Ashton and Balanchine, for example, might exquisitely express or describe conventions of behaviour between men and women through a rigorous pursuit of classical technique but the key to their place as aesthetically celebrated classicists lies in their *manipulation* of the classical technique in expressing this. Ashton's work expands the criteria for classicism to include the concept of *restraint* in structure and by means of a code of etiquette in his choreography. Like Balanchine's ballets, Ashton's ballets are experienced by these critics as being "about love" and love as being the *product* of this restraint and etiquette. Through the means of academically legible style and virtuoso technique these ballets uphold a timeless courtly relationship between men and women.

Motion and musicality are other components in an equation that is at the root of (e)motion, from plotless to narrative ballets alike. Deborah Jowitt located the essential values in an Ashton ballet,

> A Month in the Country...... *shows Ashton in terrific form doing what he does better than almost anyone else: working with literary plot and characterization in dance. He can make you accept movement as a metaphor for conversation without confusing you or making the dancing look inhibited and ridiculous. And he's a master of the business of creating solos and duets that fulfil the function of arias in opera, without stalling the momentum of the drama. Perhaps this is because these "arias" tell you something new and vital about the characters instead of frilling what you already know.*[80]

---

[78] Roger Copeland, "The Politics of Perception" *Contact Quarterly*, Winter, 1981, p. 23.

[79] Ibid.

[80] Deborah Jowitt, *The Village Voice*, May 11, 1982.

Responding to the same ballet, Croce delves into one of her passions, the analysis of a dancer's performance and the chronicling of her or his performing style. She focusses for instance, on Lynn Seymour's dancing as Natalia Petrovna in *A Month in the Country* and signals a breakdown between style and attitude in Seymour's performance. Jowitt plunges into movement description as a means of appreciating Ashton's drama of suggestive steps. She describes Vera's feet "shivering" in the air, the folk quality of Beliaev's dance with the maid, the bourrées and wanderings of the lovesick Natalia. In discussing Ashton's *Enigma Variations* Goldner investigates the source of the dance's effects and impact by saying "But now I have given away a secret of the ballet's power. Although it matters how people dance, it matters more what those people do in the presence of which other people...." In another piece she ponders,

> Can a dance give life to people's inner lives? Ultimately, perhaps not, but Graham, Tudor and Ashton himself in Enigma Variations *have given us some very beautiful and convincing moments in their struggle with the challenge....*[81]

All three critics respond to Ashton's pure dance moments that reveal dramatic depths. For instance, both Jowitt and Croce discuss the variations that introduce the characters in *A Month in the Country* as the essence of the work. All note the movement motifs, particularly that of Natalia Petrovna. Goldner says:

> Toward the end of this one-act ballet, when Natalia Petrovna and Beliaev finally declare themselves lovers in a pas de deux, the young tutor wafts the elderly woman forward in a lazy zig-zag path while her arms twine about her in the air. She could be nestling in silk or idly fingering chains or pearls, but in fact it's the luxuriousness of love she is touching. That moment is the one moment of truth in a Month in the Country, *true to the emotion, true to the heat of summer, true to Chopin, and true to the economic status of the household....*[82]

Croce observes,

> Certainly the most wonderful section of the ballet is the suite that introduces five of the six main characters.... But perhaps the essence of the matter is that Ashton's skill as a dramatist is invested mainly in his dances. Such characteristic passages as the meandering bourrées for Seymour at the end of her pas de deux with Dowell (and the recurrence of this passage in her final solo) or the muted military flavour of the tutor's steps when he dances alone — steps that seem to be tokens of his manliness — give us more "story" than any official scenario could.[83]

---

[81] Nancy Goldner, "Real Life is Unrealistic" in *Saturday Review*, July–August, 1983.

[82] Nancy Goldner, *The Nation*, May 22, 1976, p. 639.

[83] Arlene Croce, *Afterimages*, New York: Alfred A. Knopf, 1978, p. 220.

Writing about their favourite choreographers such as Balanchine, Cunningham, Taylor, Tharp, Feld and Ashton, the critics' definition of classicism expands with the challenges of the choreography they encounter. Their criticism, like the innovations of vocabulary they respond to in choreography, seems imbued with a sense of abundance and discovery. Collectively, then, classicism is defined as being "about" objectivity, "about" dance being its own subject, "about" revelations of meaning through structure, "about" the romance of choreographic restraint, "about" academic legibility and virtuosity, "about" the investigation of vocabulary to produce "something new from something old" and "about" the renewal of a heritage rather than an erosion of one from making ballet technique "do more" for the sake of novelty. While these perceptions evolve as a kind of acquired taste — often courageous, insightful and uncharted — they almost always result in an anchoring of references to those choreographers who form their essential aesthetic "canon." But the purity of means they sought so unrelentingly was at times "seduced" by their responsiveness to innovation. Like the American culture itself, the values of this critical school tread this perilous line between the puritanical and the decadent. "The American reformative conscience in action" as Croce said of Graham's early work, and the most elaborate of their descriptive scrutinies were most often inspired by the same choreographic sources. The work of these choreographers was preciously protected by them through careful clarification, distinguishing between the differences and grasping the connections. On the one hand the "less-is-more" aesthetic, instigated by Balanchine's richly "lean" choreography constantly led these critics to voice a reverence for the power and integrity of classicism while on the other hand they sought to push their writing, make it do more and more, to penetrate the sensations of dance.

In *Denby Remembered Part II* the painter Alex Katz describes an incident in which Edwin Denby took him to see a dance concert by Paul Taylor. "Gee," he said to Denby at the interval, "the technique is brilliant and it's intellectually brilliant, but there's no feeling there." Denby replied to Katz, "What else do you want?" Denby's response, a metaphor for classical style being its own subject (and therefore being enough), was the view argued by the New York School of critics in various guises throughout the body of their critical literature.

### The Critics as Women

All four critics examine dance aesthetically, poetically and politically, from the highly conscious position of themselves as women writers. Their critical point of view about dance often reveals a sympathy with the woman-ascreator, strong feelings about how women are portrayed in dance and how choreographers express man-woman relationships. These relationships reveal the humanity of the choreographer and in addressing this issue there is often a highly charged moral tone in their writing, operating as a kind of guardianship of taste. In discussing the theatre of Martha Graham, for example, Arlene Croce distinguished between the difference in treatment of women in the hands of a pioneering modern dance choreographer versus the classical ballet, where men dominate as choreographers.

> *But the tragic heroine is also a triumphant heroine. Implicit in the rigor of her self-discipline is the certainty of her reward — self discovery. No Graham heroine dies unilluminated. The difference between her and the fated heroines of nineteenth century ballet — a Giselle or an Odette — is that the Graham heroine possesses, herself, the key to her mystery. She does not entrust it to the hero; she herself must unlock the inner door.*[84]

Marcia Siegel, in one of her major essays about gender in dance called *Siegfried's Revenge* approached the issue in this way:

> *In dance as well as life, it hasn't worked out yet. I think the early modern dancers were searching for it. Doris Humphrey more than anyone could use men for their tenderness and women for their strength, without making them seem neurotic... Today a lot of dance isn't concerned with discovering new forms and new roles at all, but with telling a story or exhibiting a technique... The men are virile and the girls are feminine in the old familiar ways. We hardly notice how this reinforces sexism because it's so attractive and entertaining...... Today's leading men seemingly don't need any dimension or character, nor do the women who oppress them... there isn't simple warfare between men and women. The message goes beyond sexual partisanship.... Their sex determines their role in society and their role in the dance. The man is always either a stud or a sensitive ambiguity. The woman is always a calculating bitch or a clinging vine.*[85]

There is a striking unity of expression regarding "anti-female" traits in choreography — that which "humiliates" the dancers or sexually abuses women. Compare some of their writings on Béjart and MacMillan in this regard. On MacMillan's *Isadora*, *Manon* and *Gloria* Croce had this to say:

> *There are so many floor-slamming, whizbang adagios, with so many acrobatic crotch held lifts, that they cancel each other out; the heaving and flailing limbs, the convolutions that turn Merle Park's body into silly putty cease to have impact. The only one of these panting pas de*

---

[84] Arlene Croce, "The Blue Glass Goblet and After" in *Afterimages*, New York: Alfred A. Knopf, 1978, p. 50.

[85] Marcia B. Siegel, "Siegfried's Revenge" in *Watching the Dance Go By*, Boston: Houghton Mifflin Company, 1977, p. 105–111.

*deux that carries any expressive charge after the first big one (with Craig) is the one with Essenin, in which Isadora really is pulped, and her desperation and exhaustion ought to be moving. But by the time Essenin appears, in Act II, the audience is punch-drunk. And we're also confused: is MacMillan showing us a series of sadomasochistic relationships or is the violence inherent in his idea of heterosexual passion? The only other key MacMillan composes in — rapture — is the same as violence, but with heads thrown back in ecstasy. Thus it is that Isadora, radiant, ravenous, succumbs to Craig, and thus it was for most of the way in Manon ...... sex is the ruling metaphor; it's what lends urgency and fluency to his dance language ...... in Gloria MacMillan's acrobatic—expressionistic dance language is similarly ambivalent. In its continual self-investigation, its kneading and twisting and joining of body shapes and body parts, it reaches a kind of creative delirium — a mystique of physique, .... and he doesn't stop until he's got an image of the woman pronged between the two men. It's like that so much of the time in Gloria .... If death is present at all, it's in the orgasmic extinction of a metaphor.*[86]

And in a piece called "Knocking About the Jungle" Deborah Jowitt described exactly what she saw in Kenneth MacMillan's *The Wild Boy* with rather alarming results:

*The Wild Boy is a joyride for sadists, disguised as a moral tale about corruption and the loss of innocence. Here's how it goes: In a vine-draped jungle we see a slinky woman (Lise Houlton) preening.... On come two violent, ragged men (Kevin McKenzie and Brian Adams). They share her. That is, one holds her foot and the other her armpits while they twist her around lasciviously.... MacMillan's sense of theatre seems to have left him at the scent of this ballet. While he can express the men's boisterous camaraderie through adroit close canon, the sex duet starts at fever pitch and stays there. I think that audiences can and should be shocked by violence sometimes; but I don't like being stroked by it.*[87]

If the violent sexual behaviour of men toward women is what the critics find distasteful in MacMillan, it is the anti-female attitude described through unisexuality and homosexuality in Béjart's work that offends equally. "Béjart's soft, sensuous movement and heavy-handed kitch may be the new turn-on", said Siegel, "but they mask a virulent anti-feminism and a re-routed sexuality that seem to be his real message."[88] Goldner unequivocally stated in a discussion with me in September, 1994 her moral indignation over choreographers like Bejart who "deformed classicism, who claimed to build something new from something old (a lie), who beautified men and uglified women, who deformed second position, who practiced Eastern philosophy pretensions and whose Bach constructions were childish when New York audiences were, after all, seeing Balanchine's *Concerto Barocco*.

---

[86] Arlene Croce, *Going to the Dance*, New York: Alfred A. Knopf, 1982, pp. 392–6.

[87] Deborah Jowitt, *The Dance in Mind*, Boston: David Godine, 1985, pp. 222–3.

[88] Marcia B. Siegel, *At the Vanishing Point*, New York: Saturday Review Press, 1972, p. 133.

In the moral tone that infiltrated such writing, "villains and heroes"[89] were constructed and various critical issues emerged from this moral order. One was the issue of the choreographic "hybrid" riddled with an "impoverished dance vocabulary" rather than sustained by an innovatively pure one. Look at the difference in their tone when describing Tharp as a ground-breaking choreographer in contrast to their response to European neo-expressionist choreographers as sensationalist borrowers. The classicisms of Balanchine, Ashton, Taylor, Cunningham and Tharp were embraced for possessing the greater aesthetic value than the mannerisms, symbolisms and ritualisms of choreographers like Béjart, MacMillan, Van Dantzig, Van Manen and others. Their identification of American dance as distinct from European theatricalities was charged with nothing less than patriotic territorialism. Siegel, who of all the critics being discussed has been perhaps the most concerned to define American dance style and record its heritage, had this to say about the Royal Ballet's performance in the Metropolitan Opera House in 1969:

> If Ashton's Jazz Calendar *is jazz, we might as well call Paul Whiteman a soul brother. And if you are as steeped in the classical tradition as the Royal Ballet, I can see how you would think that Roland Petit's twitchy, ugly, going-nowhere movement for* **Pelleas and Melisande** *is modern. We in America know better, to the everlasting credit of our own choreographers....*[90]

But, again, nowhere is this moral tone more aroused than it is on the subject of the treatment of women. Deborah Jowitt, writing about the "Béjart phenomenon" pointed to what she considered to be Béjart's offensive treatment of women as getting in the way of the subject of dance:

> A charge of prudishness or snobbery is often levelled at those who don't adore Béjart. My distaste may stem from something even more fundamental and inescapable. I'm a woman, and Béjart's choreography is savagely anti-female. Not only are the women in his company almost invisible but they're usually either being mauled or being bitch goddesses.... I'm not even sure why Béjart needs women in his company. One of the features of his style is that his men often perform movements related to those considered feminine in traditional dancing.[91]

What a contrast was offered up by Croce in her discussion of her very much American "hero" Balanchine, in his treatment of women:

> If George Balanchine were a novelist or a playwright or a movie director instead of a choreographer, his studies of women would be among the most discussed and most

---

[89] George Jackson used this term in discussing the material for this book with me in correspondence, January 10, 1990.

[90] Marcia B. Siegel, *At the Vanishing Point*, New York: Saturday Review Press, 1972, p. 49.

[91] Deborah Jowitt, *The Dance in Mind*, Boston: David Godine, 1985, pp. 215–17.

*influential artistic achievements of our time...... It is part of Balanchine's genius to make the extraordinary seem natural; how many contemporary male artists, in ballet or out of it, can compete with him in depicting contemporary women? ...... his women do not always live for love, and their destinies are seldom defined by the men they lean on. Sexual complicity in conflict with individual freedom is a central theme of the Balanchine pas de deux, and more often than not it is dramatized from the woman's point of view...... We can make comedy or tragedy, and sometimes a blend of both, out of the conflict between a woman's free will and her need for a man; he can carry you step by step into dramas in which sexual relationships are not defined by sex or erotic tension alone, and in this he is unique among choreographers....[92]*

Morality, romance, codes of behaviour, restraint, purity and innovation were the central concepts in the major choreographic influences they guarded, documented and claimed for an American dance identity.

### Possessing, Preserving and Purifying

As early as 1967 Croce was expressing a wariness of a 'misguided' movement in dance which she and the other critics of the New York School saw largely as a misunderstanding and misapplication of the territory they claimed as American *pure dance*, or what Croce called *'dance totalism.'* In her passionate essay called *Ballets Without Choreography* she said:

*...perhaps it's necessary to look narrowly, even suspiciously, at choreography as the big ballet companies produce it. A lot of it is vile, and most of it is vile on principle.... The ideal is absolute expression, dancing for its own sake — might what be called dance totalism; and it has become a major international trend.... I have no argument against it.* La Bayadere, Les Sylphides, Primitive Mysteries, Serenade, Concerto Barocco, Agon, Moves *— they are all examples of dance totalism in successive epochs.... If I refrain from labelling dance totalism the new orthodoxy, it is only because the formulas have kept its production looking disparate and old-fashioned; never was there so ill-managed a renaissance. Means have been imitated, but meaning has been confounded.... The totalist formulas are applied across the board... And the more sterile the means of expression, the more compulsive the effort becomes to create excitement through kinetic emphasis... In its struggle to avoid literalism, the younger generation of ballet choreographers has plunged into the opposite kind of doctrinal snare to totalism. Anything less than total dance metaphor seems proscribed...[93]*

Goldner, too, had similar thoughts on the topic which she described as the "Americanization of European choreography" which, in her opinion, was inaccurate and inappropriate. Writing in *The Nation* on May 8, 1972, she said: "When Americans decided to purify dance of literal meaning, they

---

[92] Arlene Croce, *Afterimages*, New York: Alfred A. Knopf, 1978, pp. 125–7.

[93] Arlene Croce "Ballets Without Choreography" in *Afterimages*, New York: Alfred A. Knopf, 1978, pp. 319–350.

did not mean for it to be meaningless."[94] And another direct hit by Siegel the following year when discussing the Royal Ballet season at the Met, to honour Ashton's retirement went:

> *One new work was premiered in New York, Rudi Van Dantzig's* The Ropes of Time *a "modern ballet" created for Rudolf Nureyev. I suppose in places where dancing hasn't advanced very far beyond the nineteenth century they think this piece is sensational — the British critic John Percival gave a reverent analysis of this in* Dance Magazine *— but many New York ballet-goers were appalled. I can remember when we used to speculate what would happen if a modern dance choreographer had all the manpower and scenic resources of a big ballet company to work with. Van Dantzig is not a modern dance choreographer, since he only borrows Martha Grahamisms and glues them to the balletic body. But his attempt to amalgamate the two styles results in pomposity beyond all tolerating....*[95]

And Jowitt in a later essay comments:

> *A while back people started talking about an eventual marriage of ballet and modern dance... I forget just why it is supposed to be a good idea. It never happened. ...Ballet makers like George Balanchine or Frederick Ashton or Jerome Robbins have kept right on making ballet — concentrating or pushing deeper into the possibilities inherent in the classical vocabulary... But a cross-pollination did occur, and it produced a hybrid style that is... showy... and intricately convoluted.... Deep weighted pliés, rippling arms and contracting and expanding torsos, frequent falls to the floor, these are just some of the modern dance "discoveries" so suitable for dealing with 20th century angst — which have been helpful in beefing up the repertories of ballet companies here and abroad.*[96]

Croce wrote similarly on the"collapse of purity" in film trends in 1959.

> *The confusions of the international hybrid and the inadequacies of wide screen technique are compounded by the labors of the assiduous adaptation industry which has sprung up, in recent years, not only in Hollywood, but on Broadway and in the mills of television. The process of book-into-play-into-film (not necessarily fixed in that order) has brought about a mutual destruction of forms from which all our dramatic arts suffer.*[97]

There is an insistence on distinguishing between invention and trend, between eclecticism and erosion. Erosion of style and of definition very much concerns these critics who are all viewing dance in historical, social, aesthetic contexts. They are unwilling to view dance as only a "performing instant."

---

[94] Nancy Goldner, *The Nation*, May 8, 1972.

[95] Marcia B. Siegel, *At the Vanishing Point*, New York: Saturday Review Press, 1972, p. 52.

[96] Deborah Jowitt, "The Hybrid: Very Showy, Will Root in Any Soil" in *Dance Beat*, New York: Marcel Dekker, Inc., 1977, pp. 64–5.

[97] Arlene Croce, "Hollywood the Monolith" in *Commonweal*, January 29, 1951, p. 432.

Hence, "anti-female" choreography is seen not only as a politically hostile trend, but it also bespeaks of "impoverished" vocabulary and of a rejection of, rather than of a revolution within, enduring dance values expressed through male-female relationships. The "erosion," the impoverishment, also effects audiences' perceptions and their ability to distinguish between pure dance meaning and hybrid meaninglessness.

Siegel clearly questioned the desirability of dance as a mass-popular art form. Her plea for dance practitioners and audiences to know who the "Bachs and Beethovens of dance are" was about wanting to protect performers by respecting the historical and contextual situation of their work and illustrating "dance in its time" for viewers. In 1972 she expressed her misgivings about the City Center American Dance marathon at the ANTA theater that featured 18 dance companies in six weeks and in 1973 about the Jacob's Pillow Festival that announced twenty-four names, from Margot Fonteyn to Alvin Ailey, during its nine-week season as "the perfect image of how utilitarian and undifferentiated dance had become in the minds of its entrepreneurs...."[98]

And in another review she surmised that

> *this sudden jump into prominence has hurt modern dance...... The producers have chosen to underplay the form's strongest assets — its individuality and seriousness — and have encouraged audiences to look at it superficially...... Merce Cunningham, Joe Athlete, T.V. Susie, it's all the same — or so the promoters would have us believe. Cunningham's was the last of the several "resident" companies...... the crowds that filled the Academy were completely bewildered and turned off.... They didn't understand enough about the dancing to be angry with it.[99]*

Perhaps the New York School of critics are sometimes guilty of being too "in house" and too territorial and even too precious about the purity and sanctity of American dance and of their best loved choreographers. I would argue, however, that it is merely a side-effect of their collective campaign for rigorous, active viewing of dance, for the defining of styles and for the opening up of the frontiers of deeply literate and passionate criticism. Do these critics mistakenly assume they have a much wider audience available to them than they really do? Over and over there is evidence in their writings that the notion of mass-popularity does no service to dance and that they are writing for quality of thought in their audiences rather than mass consumerism.

---

[98] Marcia B. Siegel, *Watching the Dance Go By*, Boston: Houghton Mifflin Company, 1977, pp. 157–8.

[99] Ibid.

Siegel comments about audiences not understanding Cunningham, about promoters not understanding the values of dance to promote, about the seriousness of modern dance compared to television shows or athletic heroes in the popular imagination. These comments reflect the views of a dance boom critic in New York who believes that dance is the most important activity in the world and who appears vulnerable to a population who do not share that view let alone distinguish between the aesthetic challenges of different choreographers.

Croce's manifesto on "dance totalism," the trend in choreography to create movement at the expense of meaning, suggested that it may have been sparked off by the mishandling of Balanchine as a role model by a younger generation of choreographers.

> *If more bad ballets are being produced each season than there used to be, possibly it's not because there are too many bad choreographers but because too many choreographers are making the same kind of bad ballet... The ideal is absolute expression, dancing for its own sake — what might be called dance totalism; and it has become a major international trend. Dance totalism is everywhere taken to be the sign of an art in its purest state.... My quarrel with the form is with its fetishistic reductions, with the fallacies and confusions that surround its present-day practice, with audiences and critics so seized by visions of "autonomous" movement that they cannot tell purity of expression from poverty of means... All dance ballets were good because they trained audiences to see meaning in movement. But today it is possible to speak of overtrained audiences who presuppose meaning where there is only movement... And the more sterile the means of expression, the more compulsive the effort becomes to create excitement through kinetic emphasis... Choreographers, both American and European, of non-ballets have inherited an audience that knows dancing isn't susceptible to verbal formulations; knows, in short, that dancing is movement. Only, these same people who respect movement couldn't be less concerned with whether the movement is expressive or not. Having stopped looking for literal sense in what they see, they're stopped looking for any other kind of sense and stopped trying to distinguish real invention from pointless ingenuity....[100]*

All four critics are concerned to preserve, clarify, define and distinguish between movement qualities and movement styles. This characteristic link which I call the *preservation mode* operates in different degrees of intensity and in relation to different issues amongst them. All four see their task as critics as being informed by the responsibilities of historian. This firm insistence upon dance being understood in the context of its developing history applies to choreographers, dances and audiences. They plead for distinguishing viewing from audiences; they demand stylistic clarity of dances; they applaud or discredit choreographers depending on their

---

[100] Arlene Croce, "Ballets Without Choreography" in *Afterimages*, New York: Alfred A. Knopf, 1978, pp. 319–325.

means of innovation or disregard for traditions. Marcia Siegel reminds us that without careful attention to language that clarifies dance style there is no permanence to dance, no sense in which it can signify as "cultural artifact." "Perhaps if dance were not such a passing phenomenon," she says

> *if we had more dance repertory, films, scores, or other methods of preservation, we might not place such a high judgmental value on its immediate relevance. Perhaps we might be able to say that there is such a thing as a good dance or a bad dance, apart from fashion or contemporary thought. But even now, we should be able to tell with some accuracy whether a piece is authentic for its time, and that quality might give it staying power over the many reconsidered versions of old dances that we see.*[101]

In another essay she writes: I think the fact that dance has no institutionalized history imposes extra responsibilities on its critics. We are its reporters and sometimes its interpreters, but we are also its memory, its conscience....[102] Croce treats the topic differently. "Preservation" she says

> *has become a cry, a right, a guarantee...... If dance does develop a visible past, like other visual arts, it will take a great step forward in legitimization, perhaps the greatest since the Royal Academy of Dance, founded under Louis XIV, codified and named the various positions and movements.*[103]

All four critics are in sympathy with Croce's appeal against what she describes as "the eyeless critic" who does not distinguish between dancers and their individual qualities. The reason for seeing *how the dancer dances* is not merely a concern to evaluate the thrill or disappointment of performance but, in the context of preservation and clarification, it is a concern for how dancers themselves project and protect the distinctions between styles of one choreographer and another. "The life of a repertory company" says Croce, "lies in its performers."[104] But there seems to be an unresolvable problem regarding the issue of preservation. While performers keep the works alive, the question of a dance's endurance is also ever-present. As Croce says when writing about Graham's *Primitive Mysteries*: "In the sixties, we could be impressed by the power of structure alone; perhaps that isn't enough now. Perhaps there is a statute of limitations on how long a work can be depended

---

[101] Marcia B. Siegel, *At the Vanishing Point*, New York: Saturday Review Press, 1972, p. 230.

[102] Ibid.

[103] Arlene Croce, *Going to the Dance*, New York: Alfred A. Knopf, 1982, p. 101.

[104] Ibid, p. 37.

upon to force itself through the bodies of those who dance it."[105] And Jowitt, writing about the same work, concludes after a 1977 performance: "These women now, taken as a whole have about half the strength and fervency of the 1964 cast. Barely enough candle-power to light up the dance, let alone sear your eyeballs for good."[106] Goldner responds to this problem much more dismissively by saying that to compare original and revival productions is an exercise in "nostalgia." Despite these differences *the dance work* is perceived as being a whole history of performances and not just the single performance event.

Siegel has talked about wanting to establish American dance as a *"cultural artifact"* to situate dances in American culture, to see them as representative of the zeitgeist of their periods, like paintings or movies — only there are no records of the dances in the same sense."[107] With both critical and political territorialism, pure dance was claimed as American, misconstrued pure dance alien (foreign) and alienating, resulting in not just the offensive dance totalism but worse, the cheap, titillating hybrid that blurred the boundaries between invention and trend, eclecticism and erosion. Within this school of criticism notions of morality permeate all facets of responding to dance. The identification of the Americaness of dance and the preservation of that identity is informed by a sense of cultural morality; the investigation of classicism is informed by a behavioural morality; and choreography is understood, not only as a dynamic structure of incidents in time and space, but as a philosophy of men and women being in the world and informed by a gender morality.

---

[105] Ibid.

[106] Deborah Jowitt, *The Village Voice*, May 30, 1977.

[107] Interview with Marcia B. Siegel, New York City, June 1985.

# 4

# THE MARCIA B. SIEGEL FILE

Marcia Siegel was born in 1932 and grew up in Long Island, New York, leading a "small-town American life during the 30's and 40's."[1] Her father was a journalist and film publicist and writing was always her ambition. She attended Connecticut College as a French major and graduated in 1954. From there, she went to live in North Andover, Massachusetts, working as a reporter for a daily newspaper — an experience she loved. The travelling, spontaneous newspaper reporter instincts were later a characteristic feature in her developing career as a dance critic.

Siegel did not get involved in dance writing until she was in her thirties, nor was theatre-dance a part of her cultural experience until then. Rather, her "style, taste and culture came from music, literature, popular dance, jazz and World War II." In 1962 she worked as a press officer and publicist for the *American Dance Festival* at Connecticut College. The next year she moved to New York City, started writing about dance (where she made "stick figures in the margins of her notes"), and trained at the Laban Institute for Movement, learning Laban's system of *Effort-Shape Analysis* and how to look at movement as "an immediate phenomenon." She received her certificate in *Movement Analysis* in 1971.

Dance criticism as a career did not begin until after five years of writing about dance. In 1963 the Dance Guild approached her to establish and edit *Dance Scope*. Their objective: the publication of a known writer and the promotion of serious dance writing. (the notion of serious writing on dance has been an ambition noted by all four critics) As Siegel described it, "We wanted to address what was wrong in dance criticism."[2] Siegel maintained her position with *Dance Scope* until 1966. From there followed, starting in 1967, a free-lance dance critic's beat in the *Kenyon Review, Kinesis, Ballet Review, Dance Magazine, Arts in Society* and *The New York Times Book Review*; with many other publication outlets accumulating over the decade,

---

[1] All quotes on this page refer to an interview with Marcia Siegel in New York City in June, 1985.

[2] Interview with Marcia Siegel, in New York City, September, 1994.

including *Eddy, New York Magazine, The Wall Street Journal, The Los Angeles Times, The Boston Herald Traveller, The Boston Globe, New York Times Arts and Leisure*, and *New York Dance*.

For years while reviewing dance, Siegel studied with an optometrist named Dr. Richard Kavner in a system of vision training called "Orthoptics." Kavner's understanding of "vision as a kind of movement" and "vision therapy as an experience in perception" with the aim of "seeing everything," was a very powerful aid in Siegel's looking at dance in all its complexity.

> *Through his training I learned about seeing and about how vision is variable. It has given me a whole range of perception and I consider the vision training to be as important as the movement in making apparent the bodily and intellectual connections with dance in my responses. For example, seeing the soloist moving against a larger group rather than making a choice between one or the other, as we usually do.... Seeing better is more than improving the field of vision, the content or quality of the image. It's getting rid of habits that limit your range of flexibility, your receptivity to visual experience, and ultimately, to all experience.*[3]

In 1971 Siegel became dance critic and contributing editor for *The Hudson Review*, a position she still maintains in addition to her other activities. An alternative paper in New York, called *The Soho Weekly News* was formed by a rock promoter in 1973 and a year later he hired Siegel as a regular contributing dance critic at $10.00 a review. Her first piece for that paper was about the debut of Gelsey Kirkland and Mikhail Baryshnikov dancing together in Winnipeg, Canada. The next piece she wrote was a quantum leap to Douglas Dunn's "Exhibit 101." Following that, she covered a series of

> *Dadaistic theatre pieces, happenings... clever improvisational ensembles like* Grand Union, *structured activities in untheatrical places like Trisha Brown's environment and equipment pieces, and planned events so bizarre they were guaranteed to destroy our inkblot reactions...*[4]

However lively the scene, Siegel was unable to make a living at the *Soho Weekly News* and she took a job at *New York Magazine* in 1978. She only lasted one year in the job, however, before returning to the *Soho Weekly News* saying "I preferred being an underpaid downtown dance critic to being an overpaid media fixture." Over the years at the *Soho Weekly News* Siegel chronicled her work by saying "I began to realize my pieces were hardly ever about trying to describe completely new phenomenon anymore, but about placing things in relation to their precedents." These reviews, then, formed the basis for

---

[3] Interview, June 1985, New York City.

[4] Marcia Siegel, "The Death of Some Alternatives," *Ballet Review* Fall, 1982, pp. 76–81.

an emerging but-as-yet-undefined critical direction — the consciousness of historian and cultural analyst. All four of Siegel's editors during her years at the *Soho Weekly News* were dance writers themselves: Rob Baker, Robert Pierce, Sally Banes and Lois Draegin. "They printed some good stuff" says Siegel, but she summed up the scope and vision of the paper by saying that "the paper was never angry enough for me, or argumentatively sharp enough."[5]

By the time the *Soho Weekly News* folded in 1982 Siegel had established herself as a regular contributor to many other publications. In addition to those mentioned earlier, she wrote regular reviews throughout the 70s' and 80s' for *Ballet International* and the *Village Voice*; critical essays for *American Poetry Review* and *Harper's*; and feature articles, interviews and book reviews for *Time Out, The Dial, The Washington Post, TDR* and *American Theatre*. Her early years of reviewing formed the material for her first major dance book, a collection of reviews called *At The Vanishing Point* published in 1972. This book, the first among the four critics under examination, was a *prime mover* in the development of the discipline of dance criticism. I can still recall the buzz of excitement the book produced among my generation of aspiring dance writers and dance enthusiasts. In collected form the reviews indirectly chronicled and directly illuminated an era of dance that was in an exciting phase of acceleration and also transition. It read like popular, lively literature and for me it was a turning point in dance criticism history. Siegel's tone in the book reflected her own excitement with comments like "Dance has never been in such a high and I for one am ready to come down." "Flowers.... is the ninth new ballet I had seen in five days." During this phase of her writing Siegel's critical standpoint separated the roles of historian and critic. Here she was occupied with the task of the vitality and thoroughness of personal response, and in the fullness of the reviewing format as a vehicle for cultural commentary and interpretation as much as for percolating description. At the end of her "Introduction" to *At The Vanishing Point* she advised her readers that "These articles are in part a record of myself as well as of the progress of dance... This book is not balanced or objective. It doesn't pretend to be history."[6] What precedes this statement, however, is a cultural and political appraisal of historic events

---

[5] This and the two previous quotes, ibid.

[6] Marcia Siegel, "Introduction," *At The Vanishing Point*, New York: Saturday Review Press, 1972, p. 6.

in dance such as the Hunter College Dance Series and the American Dance Theatre at Lincoln Centre during the 1964–65 season which

> ...*presented modern dance for the first time to a wide public and for multiple performances. Almost immediately, it seemed modern dance was on Broadway, at City Centre, and — under the enlightened direction of a former dancer, Harvey Lichenstein — in the splendid opera house at the Brooklyn Academy.*[7]

The result of this launching of "seasons" for modern dance performance was, according to Siegel, that "the one-night stand in New York just about disappeared..." And, turning her attention next to the rise of dance's popularity, she analysed:

> *The period covered in this book, from about 1967 to 1971, has seen continuing growth and adjustment... the most important factor in dance at the turn of the decade was its popularization ...Why did Americans suddenly turn to dance after all but ignoring it for more than three incredibly fruitful decades?... Precisely because it doesn't lend itself to any form of reproduction, dance was the only one of the arts that had not been cut up into handy packages and distributed to a mass market. Dance was the last precision-tooled American product that wasn't ready for recycling... The rise in dance is also closely related to the dissolving of Puritanism in our society. Gradually... we've increased our respect for the nonverbal.... Dance.... never loses it's connection with gut reality...*[8]

With the publication of *Watching the Dance Go By* in 1977, her second collection of reviews, Siegel was not only observing a period of dance in transition but was herself, undergoing ever-gradually, a transition and series of changes in her role as critic:

> *I think the fact that dance has no institutionalized history imposes extra responsibilities on its critics... what they tell us is our only systematic account of an ongoing history... I believe that the better I can do my job... the more I can help dance to have a history. Each separate dance experience carries its own unique and momentary life, but to consider only that singular evening's lifetime... is to deny evolution, to deny civilization....*[9]

As if in response to the cultural and commercial changes that liberated the modern dance in New York from "the one night stand," Siegel liberates herself from any sense of confinement implied in the single review format. Like Graham scanning the landscape and foreseeing the work cut out for

---

[7] Ibid, p. 3.

[8] Ibid, p. 5.

[9] Marcia Siegel, "Introduction," *Watching The Dance Go By*, Boston: Houghton Mifflin, 1977, p. xvi.

her in *Frontier*, Siegel, in her "Introduction" to *Watching The Dance Go By*, claims a new critical voice for herself in order to re-assess and respond to the job of dance criticism. As if to fortify herself in this pioneering endeavor she names Nancy Goldner, Arlene Croce and Deborah Jowitt as her colleagues *in seeing*.[10] and celebrates the "resonating power of dance itself." The Introductory essay from this collection chronicles several major issues in dance which include: the impact of government subsidy on the quality of choreography; notions of artistic freedom; negotiating between audience and critic in the arena of sexual morality depicted in dance; and the erosion of style. What emerges in the course of Siegel's discussion of these issues is a mini manifesto of her critical position. She believes in the innovative efficacy of her most celebrated choreographers: "No George Balanchine or Martha Graham or Merce Cunningham or Twyla Tharp could have survived in an antielitist America."[11] She upholds the "American" climate of artistic freedom — unsubsidized and independent — that gave rise to these creative forces: "Our initial toleration of the artist-outlaw, miserly and indifferent though we may have been, is what permitted our dance to reach its present state of excellence." She frames European opera house ballet as a reference point for a kind of cultural oppression: "Without that freedom, we probably would have been stuck from the beginning with empty, slick imitations of traditional European opera house ballet." She reprehends choreographic readings of sexuality that promote violence: "There's no use pretending dance doesn't turn people on; it always has. What's new is the extremity of violence, aggression, and ugliness cast as sexual encounter that audiences will accept." She asserts that art and therefore criticism engages with morality: "One of the hardest problems in criticism is finding how to tell what we see, without glossing over the moral implications... Why must we expose the maggots under the gold lamé'?" Finally, in advocating *seeing clearly* as the critic's primary task, she pushes open the borders of this definition to include interpreting, refining, and distinguishing. These labors can only be realized when the past is as visible to the critic as the present: "...we're more in need of critics who can make fine distinctions... Probably the most important phenomenon of the past five years is the blurring of dance's former lines of demarcation...

---

[10] In naming these critics Siegel was discussing the ways in which they see differently and how that reflects the resonance of dance. She was also describing seeing as a selective, individual and concrete process.

[11] This and the next five quotes that follow from Marcia Siegel, "Introduction," *Watching The Dance Go By*, Boston: Houghton Mifflin, 1977, p. xiii.

when a dance style begins to change... history starts to slip away from us." Near the end of this essay she steps back momentarily as if to appraise the impact of her new voice. "So this is my history as well as a fragment of dance's." However tentative that "fragment" might be, Siegel here is committed to the durability of dance via the critical act of seeing clearly as *history-in-the-making*: The history of incidents in a single dance, the personal history of the critic's perceptions and the history that forms itself around the written critical text.

Two years later, with the publication of *The Shapes of Change* Siegel's shifting attitudes of experiences with dance dovetailed into a powerful critical consciousness and aim: to address dances, in the spirit of historian, culturalist and journalist, as the "cultural artifacts" of a nation. Deeply investigating the works of selected American choreographers who Siegel felt were definers of American style, the book was, like *At The Vanishing Point*, a "first" in dance literature pushing out the borders, objectives and methodologies of dance criticism. But the book, almost entirely based on description, was not the product that Siegel had originally aimed for — a critical history of American dance. Rather, it became for her "the book she needed to write before writing a critical history" because, she discovered, "no one could know these dances without them first being described."[12]

In *At the Vanishing Point* Siegel wrote in her "Introduction" on the state of the discipline:

> As a critic looking at all this, I don't know whether the concrete experience or the evanescent metaphor is harder to capture. We have no traditions, no techniques or guidelines that tell us how to be dance critics. But this pleases me, because I was never good at following rules, and I like it when I can devise my own ways of accounting for experience...[13]

Compare this to Denby's statement of the critic's dilemma written in 1947:

> Unlike criticism of other arts, that of dancing cannot casually refer the student to a rich variety of well-known great effects and it cannot quote passages of illustrations. This lack of precision of data and of method is not without advantages. It saves everyone a lot of pedantry and academicism, and it invites the lively critic to invent most of the language and logic of his subject.[14]

---

[12] Interview, June 1985, New York City.

[13] Marcia Siegel, "Introduction," *At The Vanishing Point*, New York: Saturday Review Press, 1972, p. 5.

[14] Edwin Denby, "Dance Criticism," *Dance Writings*, eds. Robert Cornfield and William Mackay, New York: Alfred A. Knopf, 1986, p. 538.

A quarter of a century after Denby's opportunist view of a discipline inventing itself despite or even liberated by its very lack of methodology, Siegel's comments suggest little change in the conditions of dance criticism. But what occurs over these years is in fact the shaping of an exploratory language of dance criticism: formulating questions; identifying themes; creating a style; expanding a vocabulary; coming into clearer focus on methods and resources. This evolution is apparent with the publication of Siegel's *At the Vanishing Point,* and in the criticism of Croce, Jowitt and Goldner that followed. In these writings dance criticism "comes of age." Further examining the critic's task Siegel says that:

> *Dance is constantly in process, and whatever we think is true about it may very well not apply a moment later... I know I'm trying to catch the wind, and I like the impermanence of knowing that almost before you've written the words they're being superseded...*[15]

On one level this statement appears almost careless, haphazard. And yet any examination of Siegel's writings in this collection and others reveals finely observant, forward looking, committed criticism. The statement points to, rather, the notion of active viewing, the "risking of hypotheses" as Denby put it, the continually renewed response. In her second collection, *Watching the Dance Go By,* Siegel creates, in this genesis of critical consciousness, a link between the first work, *At the Vanishing Point,* and the latest work (within the time frame examined) *The Shapes of Change.* As discussed earlier, she positions the dance critic as a correlate to dance history when, in her introductory essay she refers to helping "dance to have a history" and to the evolutionary function of dance performance, beyond the single performance event.

We can appreciate here that it is not enough to "keep up" with the process of dance. It is not enough to actively describe the fleeting image, and forge a vocabulary to reflect the *process of seeing anew,* although that in itself is surely a monumental task. Significant criticism considers dance in the context of repertory and in the context of dance history. The active response to dance must be both accurately and imaginatively descriptive and analytical. The sense of a critic as a conscience and historian for dance is expressed with increasing insistence in Siegel's work particularly. Earlier in *Watching The Dance Go By* she appeals for a conscientiousness regarding history, definition of style and preservation — a dance history that can be recalled. Overall, there is a sense of alarm expressed that

---

[15] Marcia Siegel, "Introduction," *At The Vanishing Point,* New York: Saturday Review Press, 1972, p. 6.

the consequence of the popularity of dance is, contradictorily, a kind of immaturity of both audience and performer. Audiences begin viewing all dance the same way and dancers, with increasing technical fluency, begin performing all dance in the same way, "mucking around with their posterity," as Siegel says, effecting an "erosion of style."[16]

Just as Siegel says she "wishes people would care more about what critics see than what they think," (Croce keeps her company by commenting in her essay "Dancers and Dance Critics," "The question we ask is not 'How good is he?' but 'What is he doing?') Siegel's introductory statements in *Watching the Dance Go By* show her at her most poignant and persuasive. The essay demonstrates her drive to create in dance criticism an awareness of dance heritage, of dance evolution and dance values. Here is a dance critic who is at every turn, attending to both the immediacy of the moment, that is, the kinesthetic impact of performed dance, and the impact of an era: politics; morals; audience attitudes; differences and changes in style and choreographic objectives; the influence of one generation of steps upon another. In one of the major essays of this collection, "Modern Dance Now," Siegel picks up the threads of her introductory essay. Writing several years later about the same issue, she is still charged with urgency:

> *Not enough attention has been paid to the qualities and performing attitudes that made Limón's work look the way it did, or Graham's or Sokolow's. Companies that do a lot of repertory…. have acquired an all-purpose, technically stunning and stylistically bland way of doing everything. Their reconstructions overdramatise the drama and leave the movement unfulfilled. The creators did it the other way around. Converting the classic modern dance repertory into stable, contemporary dance is not only unacceptable, it's a rip-off.*[17]

Here Siegel has a tone similar to Croce's: defiant, biting, probing and scrutinizing. But, while Croce is a setter of taste, Siegel is a guardian of style and while Croce is a guardian of ballet, particularly Balanchine's ballet, Siegel is a guardian of the modern dance. Of the New York critics hers is the most persistent voice in identifying and preserving the American dance heritage and she sees that heritage largely through the modern dance.

> *I have been concerned to define an American sensibility, an American style. Some of the works lost from the 30's are, for me, particularly American culture… Specifically "American" works are for me, people like Dudley, Maslow, Bayles, and the political and protest dances of Sokolow and others, such as Hanya Holms's work… The early moderns like Humphrey and*

---

[16] Marcia Siegel, "Introduction," *Watching The Dance Go By*, Boston: Houghton Mifflin, 1977, p. xv.

[17] Ibid, p. 155.

*Graham are a great influence on me... Balanchine has undoubtedly had the greatest influence on American ballet sensibility. Robbins has had a great influence in his overt linking of ballet and commercial dance. But my sense of what is American style is not Balanchine. It is, perhaps, Twyla Tharp, the quintessential American stylist.*[18]

Siegel's fascination with the modern dance movement came largely from reading the criticism of John Martin, the prime-mover in building an audience for modern dance through his books and reviews in the *New York Times* from 1927–1962. From an essay in her first collection *At The Vanishing Point*, called "Modern Dance: The Process of Redefinition" — an eloquent and passionate plea from a voice that remains a unique force in American dance criticism is made:

*Modern dance, by its nature, must be constantly renewing itself. But we diminish the modern dance out of all conscience by assuming that the whole thing is only a phase. Why this failure to examine or even identify styles of modern dance, to preserve anything but its most anecdotal history, to capture it by whatever admittedly inadequate means are available? There must be a way to say modern dance is, now, at this moment, instead of always shoving it into the corner of not-quite-being. I'm not willing to consign forty years of creative achievement to oblivion without protest. Nor am I willing to see strongly personal styles get smoothed out and homogenised in the interest of more accessible theatre. Modern dance is the most eloquent and humanistic of theatre dance forms. In its several stubborn ways it speaks of and to the individual. For this reason most of all, we need to spare it from the increasingly mass-minded pressures of a depersonalised society.*[19]

For Siegel, the modern dance movement in America stands as one of the most eloquent and dynamic cultural sites. But it seems that the modern dance movement is threatened with extinction from three sources. The first being critics' unsympathetic grasp of the fact that modern dance *is* a tradition and not a phase. The second is the problem of undifferentiating audiences who are sold modern dance either in popular packaged terms which leaves them confused or hostile ("Merce Cunningham, Joe Athlete, T.V. Susie, it's all the same; or so the promoters would have us believe").[20] The third threat comes from the dancers themselves who, in the quest for technical versatility and marketability have often not grasped the distinctions between one style and another. With the erosion of style the signature feature and identifying characteristics that create a history and tradition for the modern dance are smoothed out or altered and both these

---

[18] Interview, June, 1985, New York City.

[19] Marcia Siegel, "Modern Dance; The Process of Redifinition," *At the Vanishing Point*, New York: Saturday Review Press, 1972, pp. 175–179.

[20] Marcia Siegel, *Watching The Dance Go By*, Boston: Houghton Mifflin, 1977, pp. 157–158.

factors lead to modern dance being reduced to a series of *phases* or a history of *becoming* rather than, as Siegel so urgently voices, maintaining a full-bodied history and tradition that can be understood *all the more accurately* in relation to the tradition of the new.

Siegel's sense of well balanced and reasoned indignation with what she feels is a "victim" status of modern dance is shared by the other three critics, most notably Arlene Croce. All have frequently written about undifferentiating audiences and the misguided popularization of dance among audiences. But whereas Croce's arguments are often aimed at the modern dance makers themselves, for misunderstanding the fundamental aesthetic principle of classical ballet in their search for the new, Siegel's comments are expressly aimed at preserving and dignifying the modern movement itself.

Focussing now on Siegel's active response to performed dance, her most outstanding trait is surely her eye for movement quality. "I had the news reporter's appetite for covering the irrecoverable; in dance, I found, you do it every time"[21] she commented in her autobiographical essay, "The Death of Some Alternatives." Being strongly influenced by her aforementioned study of Laban Movement Analysis, the system of analysis of shape, dynamism and the expressive properties of movement first codified by dance theoretician Rudolf Laban, Siegel says:

> During performances, I made stick figures in the margin of my notes... I kept on drawing. An event I remember vividly is an exhibition of Rudy Burckhardt's photos that I had just gotten a copy of... I looked at the photos and read Denby's poems about street life, about the way people behaved, his observances. It touched me. I did the same thing. I spent hours observing people on the streets and on subways (Denby is famous for his nocturnal prowls) and I sketched them and wrote about them.[22]

Besides the impact of Siegel's teaching activities in the field of dance criticism, one is always impressed by the ways in which Siegel can guide the reader through a dance by way of signs that start with the exact nature of the movements and lead to character, structure and themes. Although Siegel's writing style has undergone changes, perhaps even radical ones, from *At the Vanishing Point* to the present, the process of

---

[21] Marcia Siegel, "The Death of Some Alternatives," *Ballet Review*, Fall, 1982, pp. 76–81.

[22] Interview with Marcia Siegel, June 1985, New York City. During this interview, Siegel showed me her sketches and we talked about them. She has a remarkable collection. The striking thing about her sketches is the enormous feeling, mood and personality she manages to capture, mainly from the back of people or from extreme angles. We discussed how it might be her treatment of their weight or posture that pinpoints their individuality so immediately.

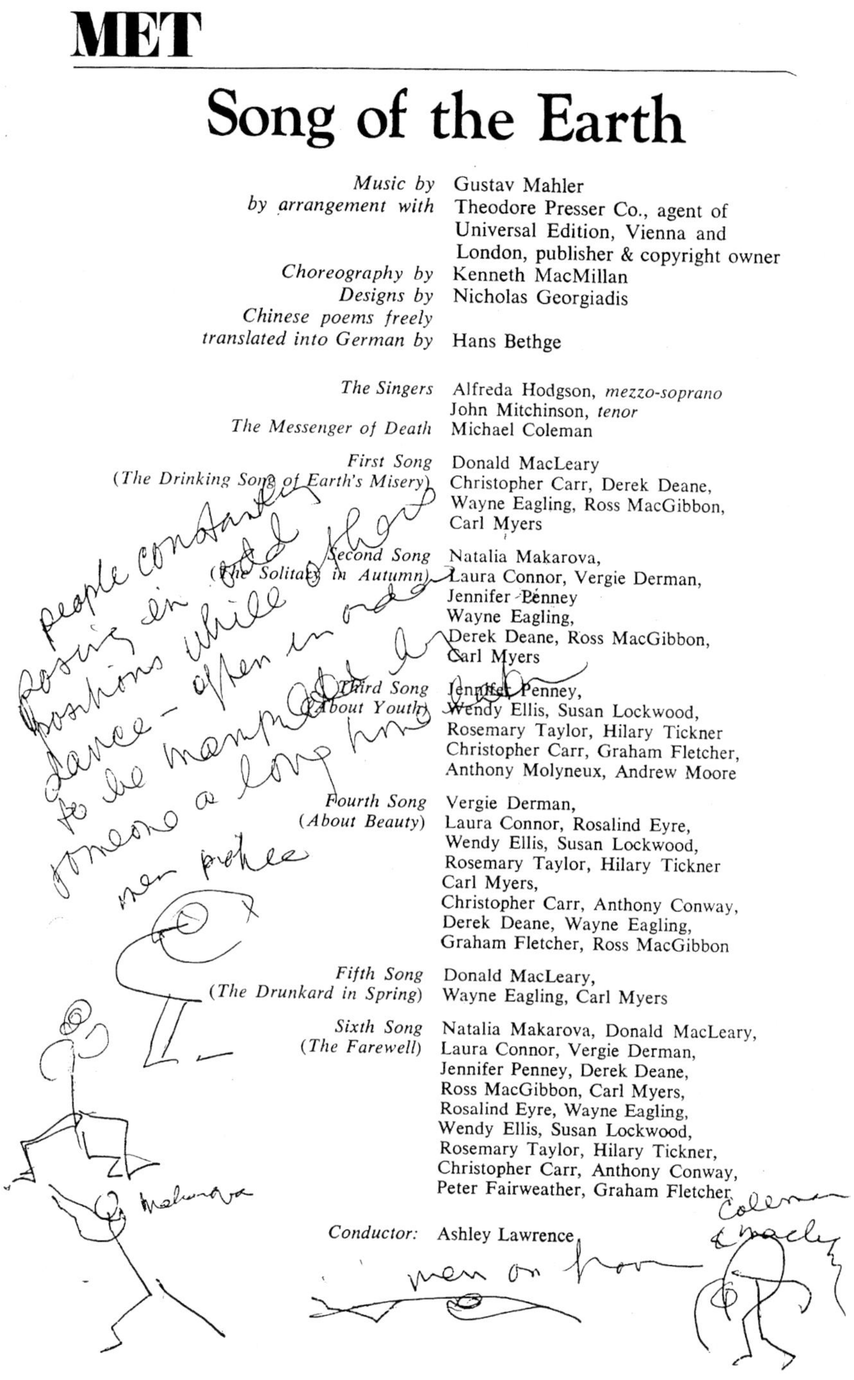

# Song of the Earth

| | |
|---|---|
| *Music by* | Gustav Mahler |
| *by arrangement with* | Theodore Presser Co., agent of Universal Edition, Vienna and London, publisher & copyright owner |
| *Choreography by* | Kenneth MacMillan |
| *Designs by* | Nicholas Georgiadis |
| *Chinese poems freely translated into German by* | Hans Bethge |
| *The Singers* | Alfreda Hodgson, *mezzo-soprano* John Mitchinson, *tenor* |
| *The Messenger of Death* | Michael Coleman |
| *First Song* (*The Drinking Song of Earth's Misery*) | Donald MacLeary Christopher Carr, Derek Deane, Wayne Eagling, Ross MacGibbon, Carl Myers |
| *Second Song* (*The Solitary in Autumn*) | Natalia Makarova, Laura Connor, Vergie Derman, Jennifer Penney Wayne Eagling, Derek Deane, Ross MacGibbon, Carl Myers |
| *Third Song* (*About Youth*) | Jennifer Penney, Wendy Ellis, Susan Lockwood, Rosemary Taylor, Hilary Tickner Christopher Carr, Graham Fletcher, Anthony Molyneux, Andrew Moore |
| *Fourth Song* (*About Beauty*) | Vergie Derman, Laura Connor, Rosalind Eyre, Wendy Ellis, Susan Lockwood, Rosemary Taylor, Hilary Tickner Carl Myers, Christopher Carr, Anthony Conway, Derek Deane, Wayne Eagling, Graham Fletcher, Ross MacGibbon |
| *Fifth Song* (*The Drunkard in Spring*) | Donald MacLeary, Wayne Eagling, Carl Myers |
| *Sixth Song* (*The Farewell*) | Natalia Makarova, Donald MacLeary, Laura Connor, Vergie Derman, Jennifer Penney, Derek Deane, Ross MacGibbon, Carl Myers, Rosalind Eyre, Wayne Eagling, Wendy Ellis, Susan Lockwood, Rosemary Taylor, Hilary Tickner, Christopher Carr, Anthony Conway, Peter Fairweather, Graham Fletcher |
| *Conductor:* | Ashley Lawrence |

**Plate 12**   Sketch by Marcia Siegel. American Ballet Theater, 13 May 1976.

**Plate 13**   Sketch by Marcia Siegel. Martha Graham's, *Herodiade*, 23 December 1975.

*Continued on page 29*

**Plate 14**   Sketch by Marcia Siegel. George Balanchine's, *Bugaku*, New York City Ballet, 3 December 1970.

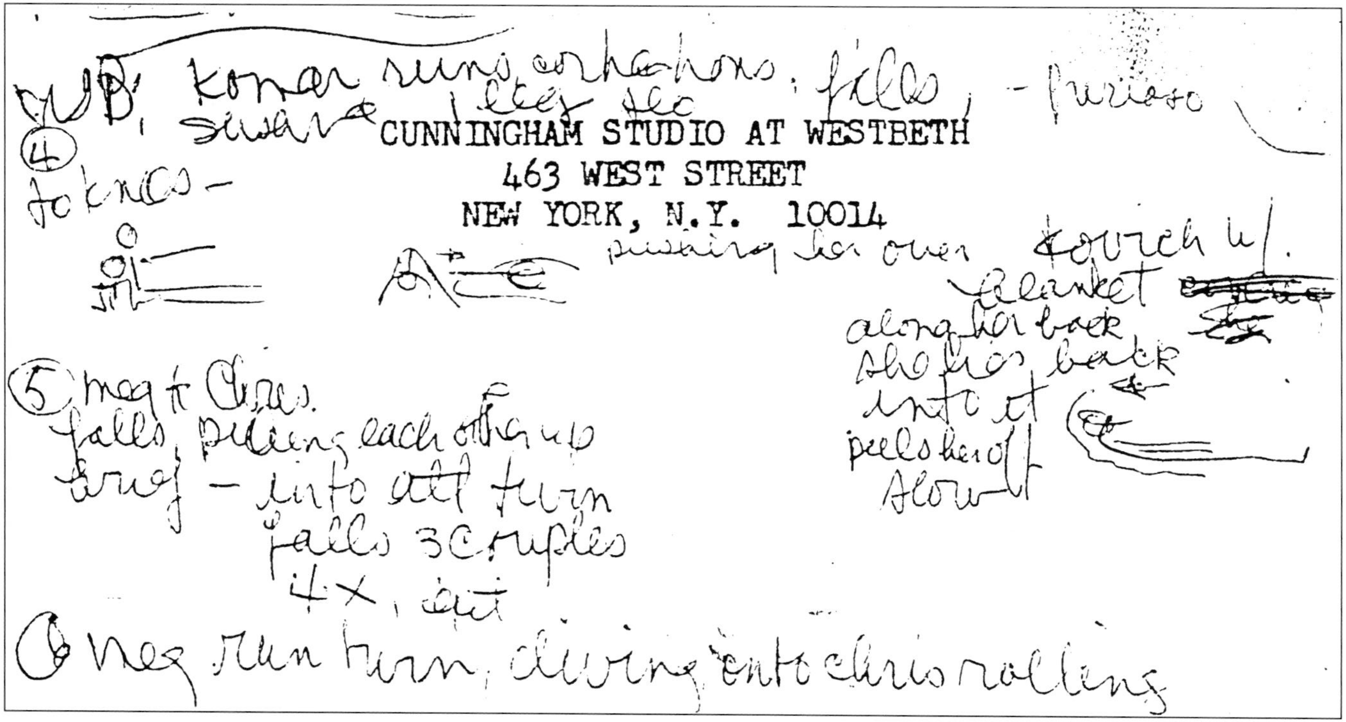

**Plate 15** Sketch by Marcia Siegel. Merce Cunningham, *Event #156*, 11 January 1976.

movement description and analysis is still an actively maintained discipline for her.

At its extreme end of the spectrum Siegel's writing has been compared, at times, to verbal notation, plotting out an almost frame-by-frame analysis of movement execution. But mostly, Siegel manages in journalistic reviews or in her lengthy and more comprehensive essays, to create a *drama of discovery* in the description itself. The following passage on Doris Humphrey's *Water Study*, quoted at length from *The Shapes Of Change* (based on a version reconstructed by Ernestine Stodelle for students at New York University in 1976) illustrates my point.

> *By 1935, the breath phrasing that formed the basis of* Water Study *had developed into an intricate language of rising, sweeping, soaring, suspending, pitching, sinking movement phrases initiated and carried on the dancer's inhalation and exhalation of breath. The lifting and expanding of the body into space was often prolonged, not by establishing a balance point as a ballet dancer would do, but by continuing the lift of breath and the progress into space to a point where it seemed the dancer might tip over. Then the plunge downward, in a continuation of the spatial design, usually a curve or spiral of some kind. At the bottom of the trajectory, instead of letting go his weight and giving in to the drag of inertia, the dancer remobilised his energy to initiate the phrase again. Basically I am describing a swing, the whole body active throughout the phrase, supporting and creating the shape. But how unusual it was in those days to imagine that the body's own momentum could be fashioned into dance patterns. It was much more common for the dancer to learn to hold back her weight, to resist her affinity for gravity. This acknowledgement of the body's relationship to the ground was one of the things that made the early modern dancers seems so much more human.*[23]

Doris Humphrey is a subject of continuing attention and inspiration for Siegel and she published a critical biography of the choreographer, *Days On Earth — The Dance of Doris Humphrey*, in 1987. The search for American dance roots, the evolution of a heritage is, as we see over and over again, the sine qua non to Siegel's criticism. In a work like *The Shapes of Change* where "determining what makes American dance American" is the aim of the criticism, this is thrown into sharp relief. So, close on the heels of a dancer's foot as she walks, an analytical description of her action also describes its significance in the context of American dance. Siegel's description of a swing in the above passage reads like a suspense moment from a novel. In intriguing and vivid increments, detail by detail, the dancer's execution of a swing comes into full focus and we marvel at the heroism of such a seemingly familiar act. The next passage which describes a section from Martha Graham's *Letter to the World* ties together both Siegel's forte for

---

[23] Marcia Siegel, *The Shapes of Change*, Boston: Houghton Mifflin, 1979, pp. 82–83.

**Plate 16** *Water Study*, choreography by Doris Humphrey (1928), Momenta Performing Arts Company. Photograph © Anne Bradley.

movement quality observation and the analytical drive to place those observations within an historical and aesthetic context. Here Siegel penetrates the *Graham walk* and comments on its significance both dramatically (assessing its choreographic importance) and stylistically (noting the erosion of its salient features amongst contemporary dancers. And, to complete the picture, she claims the style as peculiarly American. The passage compactly weaves together a statement on Siegel the critic as much as it critically assesses a moment of Graham's choreography.

> *The dance begins with a wonderful walking duet. Wearing long, full, Victorian-type dresses and holding their arms in squared-off, head-framing positions, the two women enter and stride through the space, acknowledging one another confidently. This walk of theirs has an amplitude and a weight that epitomises the whole modern dance period for me. Younger dancers don't really achieve it. The dancer steps with her whole foot, and the weight of the body transfers as the foot is placed down, not after it has set its position — in other words, the dancer makes an immediate, firm contact with the ground through her foot and leg as she is traveling forward. Today's ballet-trained modern dancers hold back their weight from the stepping leg, and they look careful, correct. But they don't have the quality of assurance, of oneness with the space into which they're going and the ground to which they entrust their progress. People don't walk like this naturally, but as Graham designed these women they couldn't be anything but American.[24]*

In *The Shapes of Change* Siegel develops her philosophy of dance criticism from its original "perishable activity" *(At The Vanishing Point)* to the task of preservation. She expresses the motivation behind this landmark book as being a "desperate and continuing sense that not enough was being done to impede the extinction of yesterday's dance." Discussing the book in an interview she added:

> *I began Shapes as a critical history of American Dance. But I could not talk about these dances as cultural artifacts because no one knew what they were unless they were described, brought to awareness. By cultural artifacts I mean that I wanted to situate the dances in American culture, to see them as representative of the Zeitgeist of their periods, like paintings or movies — only there are no records of the dances in the same sense. They don't leave objects behind for us to study or enjoy whenever we want to. So, I had to go back and explain the progression of the work.[25]*

I have described *The Shapes of Change* as a landmark in dance criticism in that it is thematically consistent in objective and in method. Accordingly, Siegel

---

[24] Ibid, p. 178.

[25] Interview with Marcia Siegel, New York City, June 1985. In correspondence through March 1991 she commented that Martha Graham has said, "I do not know whether my dance will live. This is not my concern…" She has allowed none of her dances to be notated so each reconstruction has required the intensive efforts of any dancer who can remember some part of the work…

organizes her book into chronological groupings of dances from which spring statements on American style, developments, links, and characteristics that make up American dance. From "Beginnings" to "Neo-Classicism II," Siegel salutes works from the American Dance repertory that are sometimes represented by different periods of certain choreographers' works: earlier and later works of Humphrey and Robbins; groups of works in the repertory of single choreographers such as Graham and Balanchine; and single efforts of different choreographers such as Tudor and Ailey that have an autonomous impact. This attention to identifying characteristics in dance repertory can also be seen in the writings of the other critics in this school, usually in the locating of movement traits within a given choreographer's style.

The method that Siegel uses in *The Shapes of Change* is analytical description. For each dance she selects, Siegel describes, almost moment to moment, what the action and the structure of the dance looks like. This results in our being able to literally "read" the dance. Each description is preceded by and also coloured by commentary that places the dance in its time, in the context of the choreographer's development, and in relation to other dance surrounding it. *The Shapes of Change* is both a dance archive and literary dance criticism. Let me illustrate what I mean by "literary" dance criticism with a passage from *The Shapes of Change* about the ballet choreographer, Antony Tudor.

> *Time and time again Tudor gave his character the refuge of tradition or asceticism — in* Lilac Garden, *in* Shadowplay, *in* Dark Elegies, *they draw back from experience and risk, into the safety of tribal codes.*

> *I think, in some way, Tudor's social concerns had an influence on the way he structured his ballets. He didn't make them character studies or encounters, the way Graham or Limón did, because they really were about whole societies in flux, the stabilising effect of the community against the forces that threaten to destroy it.* Pillar of Fire *is diffuse where Graham's theater dances are specific. People run in and out constantly, and scarcely ever do the main characters get to be alone long enough to think. Only Hagar has any dancing that might correspond to Graham's soliloquies, and her solos are more like hurried notations than monologues, for the demands of others constantly crowd in on her privacy. Everything you know about these characters you learn from their actions — how they behave, what choices they make — not from the way they describe themselves. Graham's dances are self-directed, Tudor's are other-directed. Groups of people pass in and out of Tudor's world because to him, individuals are part of their society and share its ills and benefits. To Graham, I think, the individual is at odds with society in some way; a psychic life takes place apart from the group and must come to terms with itself before it can be lived at peace. Tudor's individuals suppress their differences and learn how to fit into society. What he seems to be saying is that society is big enough to hold even the most divergent of them.*[26]

---

[26] Marcia Siegel, *The Shapes of Change*, Boston: Houghton Mifflin, 1979, pp. 162–163.

Siegel interprets dances through their characteristic movements, their overall physical attitude and their structure. From these facets of a dance she shapes a theme — political, social, moral, emotional. The impetus for her interpretation is always the movement itself — the dancing on its own terms. From the particular language of the dance emerges the implications of the choreographer's view of his subject. It is important to remember that it is the movement that directs one's way of perceiving the content. In other words, the movement makes the theme apparent, illuminates a particular view of the world — not the other way around. Encompassed within Siegel's interpretation of a dance is a choreo-historical principle at work. The discovery of one dance is accomplished within the context, the sphere, of other dances. Hence Siegel sifts out the essence of a Tudor philosophy (via movement) in contrast to a Graham philosophy in this instance. In approaching her subject in this way Siegel further clarifies and elaborates on the properties of each and also opens our imagination to the range of possibilities between. Again, we see operating here, the "critical repertory," a complex series of cross-referencings from one dance to another to elucidate ideas and meanings. This passage and many others quoted illustrate Siegel's capacity to take on the subject of dance writing as a novelist, through metaphor, narrative structures,themes, characters and actions. Ultimately, it is this creation of dance texts that has so profoundly changed my notion of dance criticism.

In her book review of *The Shapes of Change*, called "The Textures of American Dance" Selma Jeanne Cohen refers to Siegel's pieces as "brilliant explications of texts." She also supports the readability of the book by pointing out that "While verbal descriptions may lack the concrete immediacy of action, or even filmed, performance, words can move the mind in a way that visual images cannot." "The historian may well sigh," she adds, "if only the dancers of previous centuries had been seen with such eyes."[27]

Siegel, like her fellow critics in the New York school possesses a particularly responsive attitude to the tradition of the new — an alertness to dance innovation and an anticipation of developments or consequences of those innovations. Siegel is as much a co-creator of the dance evolution as she is a critic of it. Her means of preserving and interpreting the dance she views and even past dance that she can only guess at, always embraces new ways of looking at the dance in front of her and always to look at the new possibilities of future dance. Hand-in-hand is an aliveness to the *now* of

---

[27] Selma Jeanne Cohen, "The Textures of American Dance," *Dance Chronicle*, pp. 64–66, Vol. 11, No. 3, 1988.

dance, its links to the past, to the dance that surrounds it and to the properties of its individuality. This is a flexible but meticulous critic viewing and renewing the dance experience. Vivid evidence of it can be found, for example, in her encounter with Paul Taylor's *Orbs*:

> But in 1966 a single work brought together so many postmodern dance concerns that I now see it as a turning point, a symbol of a new era... Orbs shocked and dismayed me at the time... It was, as far as I could see, a ballet, despite its nonclassical movement and bare feet... I couldn't accept the idea that a modern dance choreographer... would relinquish the obligation to search for new movement or new forms... or that he would use "classical" music... to create a programmatic, illustrative dance. I couldn't explain the calculated, almost businesslike way Orbs looked... Orbs wasn't the first modern dance to do any of these things, but it was probably the first to acknowledge all of them as not merely by products or shortcomings of the creative process. Everything that the modern dance had been trying so desperately to avoid, Paul Taylor allowed to happen in Orbs. And the act was all the more telling because Paul Taylor was not some failed genius grasping at expedients...[28]

In another section of the same piece she addresses the phenomenon of Pop dance, saying:

> In one sense, modern dance now is just going through what happened to most of the other arts long ago. It is establishing a popular version of itself... If we stopped thinking of it as commercialized modern dance, or pretentious show dance, maybe we'd stop being disappointed in it.[29]

One wonders here if Siegel is speaking on behalf of audiences and critics at large or a select group of colleagues. But, in as much as her comments are addressed at her own critical faculties, the promptness of her response to an event-in-the-making is significant. Ten years later she commented on how to appreciate the significance of the historical Judson movement in contemporary terms by saying "to make a real revival of Judson today, you'd have to ask new questions, but work on them with a Judson frame of mind."[30]

Although her major thrust in critical literature is decidedly in the area of the modern dance, Siegel's vigorously attentive view to all dance subject matter and her characteristic analytical descriptiveness operates throughout. With such a diversity of publications generating the material

---

[28] Marcia Siegel, *Watching The Dance Go By*, Boston: Houghton Mifflin, 1977, pp. 152–3.

[29] Ibid, p. 153.

[30] Marcia Siegel, "The Death of Some Alternatives," *Ballet Review*, Fall, 1982, pp. 76–81.

of her dance criticism career it is almost impossible to pigeonhole her work. She has always had an eye for world dance (having made trips to Asia every summer for five years), and has "written a lot about people you've never heard of — the one-dance choreographers where that one dance is often very important to write about even if they never produce another good dance — because this, too, extends the possibility of dance writing."[31]

"Critics," says Siegel, "need to change format, jobs, to side-step, to give up. They can get stuck, locked into attitudes through format."[32] Clearly, the rich variety and rigor of Siegel's' career in dance criticism attests that she has put that philosophy into action. Besides completing two other books on dance, *Days on Earth – The Dance of Doris Humphrey* (1987) and *The Tail of the Dragon — New Dance 1976–82*, Siegel has also lectured and taught dance criticism and history extensively and internationally. She has served at many conferences as speaker and panelist. In 1980 Siegel gave a lecture series on Dance Modernism at the Walker Center in Minneapolis which was the start of a history career as a teacher for her and has fuelled her historical approaches in dance criticism ever since. All four critics of the New York School describe similar cross-fertilizations of material and approaches via the teaching/writing career combination. The teaching of dance criticism is, however, one of the most powerful sites of influence in the School's collective impact on the discipline and  Marcia Siegel's activities, along with Deborah Jowitt's have been the most systematic and far reaching in this regard. Siegel's other activities have included script writing for television dance series such as "Live From Lincoln Centre"( on "Swan Lake" and "Giselle"), acting as Advisor to the New York State Council on the Arts, serving on the Board of Directors for the Dance Critics Association and acting as Consultant to The Dance Project, Channel 13. Currently, Marcia Siegel is Associate Professor of Performance Studies, Tisch School of the Arts, New York University.

Her notion of the American dance as a cultural artifact in need of a curatorship and her consciousness as a teacher of criticism and history secure her place in the New York School. "I have tried hard" says Siegel, "to write penetratingly about one person's reactions and to bring off *the way it is possible to get into a dance.*"[33]

---

[31] Interview with Marcia Siegel, September 1994, New York City.

[32] Ibid.

[33] Interview, June 1985, New York City.

**Plate 17**  Marcia Siegel, July 1994. Photograph by Hsü Pin.

# 5

# THE ARLENE CROCE FILE

Arlene Croce was born in Providence, Rhode Island, in 1934. She came to New York in the 1950's to attend Barnard College where she was an English major. From the late 50's to the mid-60's she wrote film criticism for specialist magazines: *Film Quarterly* (Croce's first article appeared in the 1958 winter issue); *Film Culture* (a quarterly featuring Croce for the first time in the 1959 winter issue); and *Commonweal*, a weekly review of public affairs, literature and the arts, edited by Catholic laymen, and describing itself as "liberal against the ultra-conservative revival," "anti-communist," and for "human rights and equal rights." Croce's first article as film critic in *Commonweal* appeared on January 23rd, 1959.

During these years Croce also began to watch some professional dance performances and kept notebooks for six or seven years before publishing anything on dance. Although she had seen some of Balanchine's repertory such as *Symphony in C*, works by Graham, and performances by the Royal Ballet, dance on film had been her main experience. Her most notable interest was with the dancing of Fred Astaire and Ginger Rogers, leading eventually to her first major dance book, *The Fred Astaire and Ginger Rogers Book* in 1972.

Croce describes herself as being "a writer in search of a metier."[1] She found her metier on December 1, 1957 when she saw Balanchine's *Agon* and *Apollo*. Croce claims that this particular experience of seeing Balanchine's program was a transforming one, explaining it by saying that "what was borne in upon me that night was a sense of the morality of art — some feeling akin to Rilke's "you must change your life."[2] Furthermore, a discovery that night of a "Balanchine principle"[3] would become the aesthetic code to inform the majority of her writings on dance, and lead her to a professional lifetime of critical investigation into the ballets of George Balanchine.

---

[1] Interview with Arlene Croce, June 1985, New York City.

[2] Ibid.

[3] Ibid.

In 1965 Croce founded *Ballet Review* which "consciously aimed to show that dance was as worthy of serious critical interest as other art forms" and that "the seriousness of dance and its literature needed to be emphasized"[4] This editorial philosophy reflected the same concerns as that of her editor at *Film Quarterly*, Ernest Callenbach, whose aim for that Magazine, started in 1958, was "dedicated to film criticism as a discipline" and the need to "develop new critical vocabularies and methods to cope with styles that cannot be dealt with in old terms." Another editorial influence on Croce's *Ballet Review* was, evidently, *Film Culture's* featuring of critics' ratings of current films. This rating "graph" first appeared in *Film Culture* in the winter 1962–63 issue. Films were listed in the order of their New York openings, by title and director and were rated by the critics from 0 (poor) to 5 (exceptional). This same critics' rating feature appeared in *Ballet Review* for the first time in 1969 (vol. 1, No. 5). The key to the rating system was based on F (insufferable) to A (masterpiece). Participating critics in that first rating system were Jack Anderson, Patricia Barnes, George Dorris, Robert Kotlowitz, William Livingstone, Don McDonagh, Patrick O'Connor, David Vaughan, James Waring, and of course, Arlene Croce. Rating a selection of works in that Winter Season of 1968–69 in New York by Ballet Theatre, Harkness Ballet, New York City Ballet, José Limon, Alvin Ailey and Murray Louis, not one "A" appeared in the chart and Croce's' "column" had more "F's" than any other critic's. The pursuit of the exceptional in art has characterized her entire critical career.

In 1973 Croce began writing dance criticism for *The New Yorker* and these pieces largely form her collections published as *Afterimages* (1978), *Going to the Dance* (1982), and *Sight Lines* (1987). These lengthy, "review-essays," though written for deadlines, were not daily ones. The extra time for editing that went into these pieces gives Croce's dance criticism a "literature status or tone" that sets it apart from other dance critics, including, at times, the other critics from the New York School.[5]

Croce has also been a television writer for the *Dance in America Series* on WNET Channel 13 in New York (Public Broadcasting System) on such scripts as "Sue's Leg — Remembering the 30's" (March 24, 1976) and "Choreography by Balanchine" (December 14, 1977). She has also served as a dance advisor to the PBS. Many dance conferences and symposia have featured Arlene Croce as keynote speaker or panelist. Perhaps a more controversial aspect of Croce's critical career has been her service as

---

[4] Ibid.

[5] In discussion with George Jackson, Washington D.C., March 1991.

panelist on the Dance Panel of the National Endowment for The Arts. In this capacity, the impact of her views as a critic on "artists, audiences, entrepreneurs and funding sources" has been challenged by some.[6] A final credit to her list of accomplishments, is as a recipient of the American Institute of Arts and Letters Literary Award. Currently, she is completing a critical study of George Balanchine.

Reading Croce's film criticism provides a vital insight into her key characteristics as a dance critic. They are located in the ways in which she handles the challenge and the emotion of discovery within the framework of her medium. Writing in *Film Quarterly* in 1960 on Truffaut's first feature film *Les Quatre Cents Coups (The 400 Blows)* Croce's tone and techniques read with memorable parallels to her pieces on seeing the choreography of Twyla Tharp for the first time or her piece on Balanchine's *Four Temperaments* in which she engages a most vividly cinematic style in describing the effect of particular dance passages. Describing Truffaut's film as "one of the few masterpieces of its kind granted to the cinema in recent years" Croce launches into an analytical description of the film. I quote it here in considerable length in order to convey the impact of her way of accumulating the technicalities of the director's style into a statement, ultimately, on meaning. As in her dance criticism, the method employed here is that of "telling the story of the film" not through actual narrative as much as through the means and effects of the medium:

> The 400 Blows *is a film about freedom. Its metaphor for freedom is space... The most original feature of Truffaut's beautiful, obligue style of commentary is his by-now famous use of protracted sequence accomplished through the sustained single shot and through a minimum of cutting: the scene in the revolving door, the long ride in the paddy wagon which encompasses the boy's whole descent from innocence, and which I recall as one long close-up alternated with a single reverse-field shot: the extraordinary interview with the (offscreen) psychiatrist in which there are no cuts, merely a series of unsettling dissolves; and the long tracking shot of the stupendous finale. Since cutting is a director's chief means of comment, the effects Truffaut obtains in these sequences depend on the progression of meanings in the frame....[7]*

In the same way that Croce uses the language of the cinema in her film criticism and yet manages to make this language *seem* accessible so she uses the technical vocabulary of ballet in her dance writing. Substituting cinema shots and angles for ballet steps, one can read, for example, one of her

---

[6] Zita Allen, "Arlene Croce Re-writes Dance History," *The Village Voice*, Ag. 13–19, 1980, Vol. XXV, No. 33, p. 66.

[7] Arlene Croce, "Les Quatre Cents Coups," *Film Quarterly* Spring, 1960, Vol. XIII, No. 3, p. 35.

descriptions of Baryshnikhov's dancing and experience that same sense of being pulled into Croce's way of seeing, of being, finally, persuaded that the language of the dancing has so much to show you, so much to say to you directly. There is almost an urgency in Croce's insistence that we look and look again at the dancing on its own terms:

> *Baryshnikov crams traditional roles with new vitality, and in them he seems literally to be flying out of the nineteenth century into the twentieth century... For Baryshnikhov, a double pirouette or air turn is a linking step, and preparations scarcely exist. In the Bayadère variation, he turned a grande pirouette in second, in passé, in attitude — nine or ten revolutions in all and all from one preparation. His finishes are achieved in a faultless diminuendo or a sudden clean stop. He gives a new urgency to commonplace allegro steps like brisés (in the two speeding diagnols of Giselle), and an ordinary jump appears in all its compound splendour as grand jeté dessus en tournant battu — redefined almost past recognition, and about a mile off the ground too.... Baryshnikhov's promise lies not in novel steps but in his power to push classical steps to a new extreme in logic, a new density of interest. He is a modern classical dancer.*[8]

Croce, like Denby, "lets her love show" and in the process arouses our excitement to a level that hovers around live performance pitch. Here she achieves her effects by using the vocabulary of ballet itself. This may be seen as an elitist style of writing by some, but it is, I believe, Croce's quest for accuracy rather than an elitist attitude that is the issue here. Croce is a committed classicist. The thrust of her critical viewpoint is that classical technique speaks for itself and speaks more clearly and more eloquently than any other vocabulary. Since ballet technique is a complete language, each step expressing a clear line of thinking, it is logical that she use that language and not compete with it. Admittedly familiarity with the ballet vocabulary helps the reader towards a fuller appreciation of Croce's portraits but Croce is not one to compromise. In this case, she is probably right. To describe in lay terms what each ballet movement looks like would disrupt the momentum of her description. The ballet vocabulary is appropriate to her tone and it economically clinches the visual and kinesthetic image of the dancer in motion.

Croce's remarkable powers of illuminating dance can be attributed to the fact that she is a writer first and dance happens to be her subject. This literary basis is what gives Croce's dance criticism such range and such wide appeal. As Mindy Aloff describes her, "she sounds like a generalist who has happened to dwell on dance, although if you examine her views you may find that in the manner of specialists and artists, she harnesses the universe

---

[8] Arlene Croce, "Baryshnikovs' Day," *Afterimages*, New York: Alfred A. Knopf, 1978, pp. 74–75.

to her subject."[9] One of her meatiest essays from the collection *Going To The Dance* called "News from the Muses" is a dense dance tale of Balanchine's *Apollo*. The mythology, the score, Stravinsky's notes, the production history, interpretations of dancers through generations and the analysis of Balanchine's steps are all encompassed here. Poetic imagery, intricate scholarship and cross referencing to past and current works weave together for twelve pages. Yet one never gets the sense that the pages are crammed with information. For all its density there is constant movement in this "harnessing of the universe." In Croce's hands text seems literally to dance, to be a choreographic construction.

> *Apollo has been a classic of our theatre for so long that no one stops to think any more how difficult it must have been to create Terpsichore and make her special in a ballet. And on Stravinsky's terms! Balanchine had to invent a mistress of classical dancing — one whose natural ease of expression was beyond question. He had to convey that dancing is the finest of the Muses' arts, because it is the closest to Apollo's art, music, yet the sister variations could not be unmusical. To make matters worse Diaghilev had decreed that Balanchine give the role to Alice Nikitina instead of Alexandra Danilova. The men compromised, and the two ballerinas alternated in the role. There appear to have been differences between Nikitina's and Danilova's versions of the solo, and periodically since then Balanchine has made slight changes in the choreography to suit different interpreters. Nikitina, the first Terpsichore, was a long-legged, cat-eyed woman with an elegantly boyish body. Danilova, an enchantress even then, recalls that Balanchine put more airwork into her version including some large sissonnes that have since disappeared. The ballerinas of the New York City Ballet have always danced the same choreography, although Suzanne Farrell's grand-scale reproportioning of it in 1963 was in Polyhymnia's characteristic backward-tilting stance, its legginess emphasised by point tendue, seems in one version or another, to have stamped itself in the annals of ballet. Felia Doubrovska says that Balanchine originated it for her in Le Pastorale, in 1926. In écarté straddling a recumbent Prodigal, it is viciously and famously triumphant. But is there not some relation here to the Hostess in Nijinska's Les Biches, of a few years before? In Apollo's role, notably in his stealthy sidewise approach to the Muses at the end of the pas d'action there are traces of the faun.*[10]

Again, as Mindy Aloff comments, "there are more linking steps in her arguments than in many contemporary ballets."[11] A very distinctive feature of Croce's work which can be gleaned from the passage above is her "journalist-historian" stance. It manifests itself in an almost seamless interweave of her personal viewing history and her investigative research, resulting in a uniquely swift-paced erudition and vivid subjectivity.

---

[9] Mindy Aloff, on "Arlene Croce," in *Dance Magazine*, November 1982.

[10] Arlene Croce, "News From the Muses," *Going to the Dance*, New York: Alfred A. Knopf, 1978, p. 113.

[11] Mindy Aloff, "Arlene Croce," *Dance Magazine*, November 1982.

An April 1971 essay appearing in *Afterimages* called" "Balanchine's Girls: The Making of a Style" is another example. She selects features of several major female dancers in the New York City Ballet which both inspire and are shaped by Balanchine and recalls their approach and effect within various works in the repertory. Croce's seemingly inexhaustible supply of ideas and observations and the pace at which they are delivered, would give Camille Paglia pause. A brief example from this eleven page-strong "review" goes like this:

> *Balanchine uses whatever his good dancers can give him. As he used Kent's feyness, Haydn's swagger, Verdy's rhetorical drive, Adam's dignity, Farrell's creaturely impact, he seems to have admired and drawn upon McBride's purity of conscience as a classical dancer... In one sense, New York City ballerinas* are *like nuns: they're a sisterhood. They survive in the atmosphere of an aesthetic style that happens to exist nowhere else in the world, that absorbs modern tensions and transcends them...*[12]

Another review essay, called "Love's Body" written in July 1981 and included in her *Going To The Dance* collection is a relentless surveying of Kenneth MacMillan's choreographic "offenses" against taste and meaning in his ballets, *Gloria, Isadora,* and *Meyerling.* "Swan Lake and its Alternatives," written in May 1979 and appearing in the same collection, provides a kind of consumer report of recordings of ballet music, documents the revisions and revivals of musical scores for *Swan Lake,* compares various productions of the ballet, both conventional and experimental, and ends with an examination of Balanchine's one-act version of *Swan Lake,* saying

> *Balanchine's ballet is a* Swan Lake *rhapsody; I am caught up in it as in no other version of the ballet, because, although it isn't the traditional* Swan Lake, *it's the essence of what attracts me in* Swan Lake*... Balanchine has produced several other essays on* Swan Lake*... the great adagio in* Symphony in C*... the second movement of* Diamonds*... Tchaikovsky* Piano Concerto No. 2*...*[13]

In these essays, cross-referencing among productions, performers, music, style and choreographers abound. Another piece, "Higher and Higher" is a graphic example:

> *It was a time when one could see a better* Evening's Waltzes *than* Liebeslieder Walzer, *a better* Suite No. 3 *than* Serenade*.... Balanchine made* Chaconne *and* Union Jack *during*

---

[12] Arlene Croce, "Balanchine's Girls: The Making of a Style," *Afterimages*, New York: Alfred A. Knopf, 1978, p. 424, 426.

[13] Arlene Croce, "Swan Lake" and its Alternatives," *Going to the Dance*, New York: Alfred A. Knopf, 1982, p. 187.

*this period, revived (or revised)* Square Dance *and fiddled with a number of repertory pieces. ...In Washington I saw Merrill Ashley's debut in* Square Dance*.... The old version of the role was more complex than the version Ashley had been given to do; she could be the one to restore the exploding passage of beats in the finals... Balanchine's tinkerings have effected some changes in the Elegy of* Serenade, *none of which strike me as happy ones. ....The sisterhood of the corps in* Serenade, *which has expanded through the years as Balanchine expanded the choreography, is in its anonymity one of the most moving images we have in all ballet, and the three new heads of hair in the last movement violate the image...*[14]

By the time Croce published *Going To The Dance* this aspect of her style of dance criticism was formally articulated as a method of "critical repertory" and cited by her as "the same way of working in other art literatures."

*The pieces in this book were all written during a period when going to performances, for me, took on some of the ritual intensity of performance itself. It seemed to me that I was developing a repertory as a critic — isolating and concentrating on certain recurrent themes, much as dancers do when given the same roles season after season. I think, too, that unconsciously I was trying to approach in my writing the conditions of performance, trying not to let the repetition show too much, trying again and again to view dances that had become an intimate part of my life as fresh experiences. Many of these reviews were written in what was, for me, record time. I found I could write as much in two days as in pre-New Yorker times I could write in two weeks. Speed helped resolve the difficulty of writing "in repertory." But what helped more was the performance of the dancers. Compared with a singer's or an actor's, a dancer's repertory is small. Therefore, the capacity for repetition and renewal must be great. When dancers are able to perform old roles as if they were new, my job is all but done. When a classic is interpreted with new vitality, it constitutes for me a new ballet — a new subject to write about.*[15]

Of course, the one great advantage for Croce in adopting this method is the New York dance environment itself. From her vantage point of having access to the *repertory* of major dance companies and to the volume of performances of those repertories, Croce has had the luxury of repeated viewings of performances and the opportunity to document the changing conditions and contexts of those performances such as casts, theatres, companies or rehearsal processes. The rigors of Croce's responses to her dance beat assume the stature, the sense of purpose, of one who believes that with privilege comes responsibilities. Her writings reflect the sense of repertory as a living process about performance itself. She observes minor and major revisions in ballets, re-explores themes of ballets through different performance treatments, and so on. Talking about Balanchine, for instance, Croce scrutinizes a particular episode in his career saying,

---

[14] Arlene Croce, "Higher and Higher," *Afterimages*, New York: Alfred A. Knopf, 1978, p. 268.

[15] Arlene Croce, "Introduction," *Going to the Dance*, New York: Alfred A. Knopf, 1982.

> *musically overconditioned by 12-tone scores, Balanchine returned to Glazounov and School of*
> *Glazounov, first via Petipa, then Fokine. Like a spring uncoiled, the court dances in Act II of*
> *Don Quixote, the variations, lock-linked poses and groupings of Act III, stretch away from*
> *Agon as Agon does from Apollo, not reversing the former work but reconstituting it in a*
> *new, different loveliness.*[16]

With each viewing the "renewed response," the "fresh experience" that Croce has of ballet materialises into not only another dimension of the work, but into an examination of the accuracy and consistency of her own responses to the work. And her responses are of a very catholic construction, drawing upon literature, philosophy, history, music, cinema and painting which all coalesce on the pages of this prolific, once film, now dance critic.

Of the four critics comprising the core of the New York School Croce is perhaps the dancer's greatest pen portrait artist. For Croce the dancer and the dance are as inextricably bound as form and content. The dancer and the choreographer mutually reveal each other's value. Reflecting a strikingly Mallarmé-influenced tone (who is according to Croce "the critic Balanchine deserved") she wrote:

> *In the performing arts, there is generally some contest between the performer and the thing*
> *being performed.... Yet nothing is more exciting to an audience than performing that is so*
> *far out of itself and into the subject of the performing that the two can't be separated. When*
> *that happens, we have the illusion of absolute art, though we know it is only an illusion...*
> *occasionally, as we watch one of these girls moving with brilliant clarity, the thought "She*
> *doesn't know what she's doing" occurs to us. If she did, though would she do it better? The*
> *question has never been answered, it isn't mindlessness but the state beyond mind that moves*
> *us in perfect dancing. It's what moves the dancer too.*[17]

Combining an almost clinical capacity for kinesthetic and anatomical detail and active imagery, Croce not only distinguishes between one dancer and another in performance but also conveys the impact of their performance and most importantly, the ways in which the dancer discovers the choreography in performance. Some of Croce's most potent writing is in her descriptions of dancers. As susceptible to some dancers as an "over fond lover" Croce's portraits are as subjective as is, she claims, the act of criticism, arguing: "many critics think reviewing dancers just isn't good form because it may get personal, but surely criticism is a personal act, intimately personal, just as dancing is."[18]

---

[16] *Ballet Review*, Vol. 1, No. 1, 1965, p. 5.

[17] Arlene Croce, "Balanchine's Girls: The Making of a Style," *Afterimages*, New York: Alfred A. Knopf, 1978, p. 420.

[18] Claudia Pierpont, "Arlene Croce's *Sight Lines*", *Ballet Review*, Winter, 1988, p. 39.

One dancer who has dominated Croce's critical attention throughout her career is Susanne Farrell, Balanchine's "muse" at the New York City Ballet for many years. And it is with the vast "critical repertory" of Farrell-watching that one can also read the greatest extremes in Croce's observing temperament. On one end of Croce's extreme is the critically profound "proclamation" such as:

> *Farrell was the first ballerina in our time to announce herself to an audience wholly though her dancing: she made no appeal on the basis of personal charm, acting ability or resemblance to a known ballerina type. Her technique was and is the definition of her personality.*[19]

At the other extreme is Croce's extravagant anatomical dissection of the dancer. The focus veers from a telescopic inventory of Farrell's body to a flood-lit exposé of the dancer's performance qualities.

> *....the impact of the long, full legs was different, too. If anything they're more beautiful than ever, but no longer so impressively solid in extension, so exaggerated in their sweep or so effortlessly controlled in their slow push outward from the lower back. The largesse of the thighs is still there, but in legato their pulse seemed to emerge and diminish sooner than it used to, and diminish still further below the knee in the newly slim, tapering calf. Yet the slenderness in the lower leg gives the ankle and the long arch of the foot a delicacy they didn't have before. And it shaves to a virtual pinpoint the already minute base from which the swelling grandeur of her form takes its impetus. Farrell is still broad across the hips (though not so broad as before), in pirouettes she is a spiralling cone. But it isn't that Farrell is so terribly big; it's that she dances big in relation to her base of support. The lightness of her instep, the speed of her dégagé are still thrilling. You'd think a dancer moving that fast couldn't possibly consume so much space - that she'd have to be squarely planted. Farrell defies the logic of mechanics, and in that defiance is the essence of the new heroism she brought to Balanchine's stage a little over a decade ago.*[20]

For all my admiration of Croce's powers of recovery, this essay always makes me suspicious. How can anyone see all that? At this extreme end of the scale Croce seems to push too insistently on physical "documentation." For all its information overload it is less persuasive than the technically factual yet passionate piece on Baryshnikov cited earlier. Who would not be compelled to follow the course of her criticism with opening lines like

> *To watch Baryshnikov dance for the first time is to see a door open on the future — on the possibilities, as yet untold, of male classical style in this century. The second time, and the third and the fourth, it's the same — that same dazzling vista, crowded with prophetic*

---

[19] Arlene Croce, "Farrell and Farrellism," *Afterimages*, New York: Alfred A. Knopf, 1978, pp. 120–2.

[20] Ibid.

*shapes and rhythms; we see it clearly in a flash, and then it's like trying to recall the content
of a dream we only feel the emotion of: we get the same ache…*[21]

Here, Croce may have been influenced by her admired Agee's writing in
*The Nation*. Agee's sweepingly majestic and heroic tone in writing about
D. W. Griffith's film, *Birth of a Nation*, proclaimed:"to watch his work is like
being witness to the beginning of melody, or the first conscious use of the
lever or the wheel; the emergence, co-ordination, and first eloquence of
language; the birth of an art…."[22]

Often in Croce's criticism, the more passionately she feels about
the worth of an artist's work, the more protectionist an attitude she assumes.
Nowhere is this precious protectionism more evident then in her writings on
Balanchine. At times it assumes mythic proportions. Take for instance her
commentary on Balanchine's early days in the City Center in New York.

*Ballet in this country is an island paradise occupied by Balanchine in a sea of resentment.
From his $8 million Ford Foundation estate Balanchine dispenses patronage and pedagogy
like an active missionary colonising a wilderness.*[23]

She even goes so far as to indicate, in another essay, that the erstwhile
muse-of-all-time for Balanchine, Susanne Farrell, was civilized into her
Balanchinian muse-hood by the choreographer and would have otherwise
been as rawly expressive and unrefined as the entirely un-balletic Isadora
Duncan: "Who is to say that what Farrell gave Balanchine was not self-
expression? But for her meeting with Balanchine, might she not have been
another Isadora?"[24] This attitude, purist and "we know better" in tone, is
based on her personal taste and the view that the *popularization* of major
artistic values erodes and deforms those values through a misunderstanding
of what they are and how to use them. One of her most memorable essays,
"Ballet without Choreography" chronicles what Croce perceives as the
world's choreographers' mishandling of the "Balanchine's principle"
resulting in what she describes as "vulgar and rampant dance totalism"
(plotless ballets) being offered by choreographers to an audience incapable
of knowing the difference.)[25] This essay indirectly transfers a victim status

---

[21] Arlene Croce, "Baryshnikov's Day," *Afterimages*, p. 74.

[22] James Agee, "Birth of a Nation," *The Nation*, 1948.

[23] Arlene Croce, "Sylvia, Susan and God," *Ballet Review*, Vol. 1, No. 1, 1965, p. 3.

[24] Claudia Pierpont, "Arlene Croce's Sight Lines," *Ballet Review*, Winter, 1988, p. 41.

[25] Arlene Croce, "Ballets without Choreography," *Afterimages*, New York: Alfred A. Knopf,
1978, p. 328.

onto Balanchine, that of a genius whose legacy is made impure by populations of audience and artist abusers. She transferred a similar victim status to Bergman in an early film review, "The Bergman Legend" in *Commonweal*. Croce, after so poetically and actively analysing Bergman's impact as a film director commented:

> *Persistence without certitude, then, is the quintessence of Bergmanism. The difficulty that arises in the quasi-cabalistic atmosphere of the expresso-lounge seminars is in distinguishing Bergmanism from Bergmania.*[26]

This tone is a feature, too, of Croce's first article as editor and founder of *Ballet Review* in 1965. Her opening paragraph in an essay called "Sylvia, Susan, and God" reads:

> *In a recent and magnificently loathsome movie called* Sylvia *the heroine is a prostitute who writes poetry. In this way she keeps body and soul apart.... you have only to compare Sylvia with Lorenz Hart's Stripper in* Pal Joey.... *to see what the mass distribution of culture has come to in the last 25 years.... This is nothing new; only the anxiety is new. By eliminating the borders between styles and levels of expression, hip art traduces the sense of Cocteau's marvelous games, Eliot's masks.... Is it camp? Is it put-on? With nothing to do but astonish each other, hip connoisseurs can only mount freak shows. Their jumpy opportunism precludes sophistication...*[27]

Croce's protectionism doesn't stop with the role of intermediary between audiences and those artists she annoints with hero status. Her protectionism, like that of her fellow critics discussed in this book, most notably Marcia Siegel, is also about claiming and maintaining for American artists the status of "being first" to establish genres and vocabularies. In Jill Johnston's words, the need to possess and stake out "territory" for American identity inspires her to extreme stances. Again, as with her fellow critics, this quality ignites most hotly on the subject of European dance. In her piece called "Bad Smells" from the *Sight Lines* collection, Croce writes about Pina Bausch and other "European theatricalities":

> *It is hard to believe in... audience involvement techniques fifteen years after the Living Theater; in bleak despair.... and in all the affectless contrivances of avant-garde fashion which Bausch puts on stage after two full generations of American modern dancers have done them to death... she is a force in European theater, and perhaps that explains everything...*[28]

---

[26] Arlene Croce, "The Bergman Legend," *The Commonweal*, March 11, 1960, Vol. XXI, No. 24, p. 649.

[27] Arlene Croce, "Sylvia, Susan and God," *Ballet Review*, Vol. 1, No. 1, 1965, p. 1.

[28] Arlene Croce, "Bad Smells," *Sight Lines*, New York: Alfred A. Knopf, 1987, p. 218.

The irony of Croce's arguments in these instances is with her very question, "how can we continue to look at something after it has already been done?" Quite apart from the case she is making that such and such has already been achieved or explored in America, the issue of "renewed seeing" (so much a part of her principles) is left exposed most vulnerably or at least selectively. The same question does not seem to trouble her when looking at Balanchine's ballets, for example, where her capacity to look and look again is stunningly prolific. Her morality and outrage, passion and protectionism are akin to the qualities Croce describes of Agee in her homage to him in her essay "Hollywood the Monolith" in 1959 in *The Commonweal*, saying he had

> an almost evangelical sense of obligation to the public whom he sincerely believed to be "diseased chiefly with passiveness" and therefore "teachable"… In Agee's view a bad film, was more than a violation of the public trust, it was a criminal abuse of a noble, and ennobling art form.[29]

Likewise, for Croce, the "ennobling" capacity of dance needs critical safeguarding from bad choreographers! Croce is often struggling to reunite two different positions about dance. On the one hand she often plays guardian to an elite and esoteric art form promoting its intellectual challenge, trying to create serious attention for it and not suffering audiences who respond only to its immediate sensation value. In the first issue of *Ballet Review* she says:

> It's significant that intellectuals have not in 40 years dealt successfully with the ballet…. it is not a world in which verbalists can feel comfortable, nor does it yield easily to evaluation and analysis… Ballet is high art that has stayed high art…. but most people enjoy it as undifferentiated sensation.[30]

On the other hand Croce pleads for "suspension of disbelief" on the part of audiences in looking at dance, for a willingness to look at what is before them in the dance rather than to ask what it means. Again, in *Ballet Review* she writes in a discussion of Astaire and Rogers dance musicals on film:

> This way of dancing up to a song, rather than down to a plot, is what takes you by surprise; that, and the way they would give each song all the emotion that belonged to it, even if it was deeper than a surrounding shallowness of plot and characterization could allow for… Audiences no longer know how to "read" Astaire's' kind of musical; they are depressingly literal-minded. All that should matter in Carefree is that a dance emerge…[31]

[29] Arlene Croce, "Hollywood The Monolith," *The Commonweal*, January 23, 1959, p. 431.

[30] Arlene Croce, "Sylvia, Susan and God," *Ballet Review*, Vol. 1, No. 1, 1965, p. 2.

[31] Arlene Croce, "Notes in la Belle, La Perfectly Swell, Romance," *Ballet Review*, Vol. 1, No. 1, 1965, p. 24–25.

**Plate 18** *Carefree*, with Fred Astaire and Ginger Rogers (1938). © Arlene Croce. Courtesy of the Dance Collection, The New York Public Library at Lincoln Center.

Perhaps the link between these two poles is the role of a critic in teaching an audience how to look at dance and how to acquire two essential qualities when looking: taste and imagination. Croce has never had to address the issue of critic-as-consumer-index because all of her dance criticism has been written for specialist publications whose objectives have been about literary structure rather than building audiences. Croce's strong biases against popular culture and mass audiences is always counter-balanced with her unabashed enthusiasms, passions and subjectivity, "making good or bad art a personal matter" as George Bernard Shaw remarked in defining a critic. It is this quality that in fact communicates with and builds an audience for dance. You may not agree with her opinions but her thinking process in itself creates a new experience of dance, often a revelatory one for the reader, about what is possible subject matter for dance and for dance writing.

Whether the dance subject is in fact "popular" (such as musicals, of which Croce is an ardent fan like the "classics" of Astaire and Rogers) or the "high" (such as major choreographic works of concert dance by George Balanchine), Croce is willing to empower dance with "ennobling" qualities: sustaining aesthetic, emotional, and expressive values. This is true particularly if the dance arrives at *meaning* through a "purity" of means. In her essay "Notes on La Belle, La Perfectly Swell, Romance" surveying Astaire and Roger's dance films, she asserts:

> *Yet while there is a great deal being said in these dances Astaire never changes his choreographic style.... nor do he and Rogers ever appear to be acting out meanings... And since the weight of gesture seems no more than what the music of the moment deserves, one is free to enjoy dancing unpossessed by extravagance. This is, of course, the classical view, presupposing mastery of design.... It's the difference.... between Astaire and Kelly. Where Kelly has ideas, Astaire has steps.*[32]

But *steps* according to Croce in a much later essay from *Going To The Dance*, "no matter how inventive or ingeniously combined, have in themselves no power of poetic suggestion." Rather, it is "dancing, by the alchemy of its rhythm" that "transfigures life" — choreography that has "elastic scale and tension" and keeps "moving and changing in ways you feel but don't see."[33]

The manipulation of the medium, adherence to codes of style, the trust in the inherent values of an enduring, classic dance vocabulary and the taste to know how to probe that vocabulary for freshness and appropriateness rather than novelty or "undifferentiated sensation," are the terms by which Croce recognizes a dance language. This "classical" point of view that she asserts is in itself an almost sacred and mystical value. It provokes in her the same sort of protectionist and moralist sentiment that she engages in her writing about certain choreographers or dancers, "claiming" them for her critical territory and acting as intermediary between them and the world of mass audience.

The following passage from her first collection *Afterimages*, taken from an essay called "Ballets Without Choreography" (originally appearing in *Ballet Review* in 1967) is the closest she ever gets to defining this classical sensibility. I quote it at length to illustrate the full attention she gives it, the force of conviction with which she trusts it to serve her understanding and appreciation of dance and the nevertheless elusive conclusion.

> *I think you cannot exaggerate the necessity of maintaining seemliness in the classical tradition once it is invoked. Much of what seems to have been derived from convention and expediency in the classical tradition is in fact a profound honoring of a certain philosophy of life, a way of looking at the world. So the difference isn't technical; it's philosophical — a question of attitude. And you can have the attitude without the technique. Why should Merce Cunningham, for example, while venturing as far as anyone has from the matrix of conventional ballet technique, still express (as clearly, sometimes, by negation and*

---

[32] Ibid, pp. 25–26.

[33] Edwin Denby, "Move By Move In Black and White," *New York Times Book Review*, 1 August, 1982, p. 26. (Review of *Going to the Dance*, New York: Alfred A. Knopf, 1982)

*indirection as by affirmation) a sense of connectedness, of philosophical engagement with classicism — while Gerald Arpino, who works from the conventional classical syllabus, creates ballets which are philosophically deranged? Is it because Cunningham is a master and Arpino a novice at best? If so, what is there that the novice must learn?*

*Seemliness is a poor word by which I fear I have unintentionally conveyed a prudishness insisting on nicety. I mean this: seemliness is what you feel is right. It is a tragedy of the modern sensibility that no one dares suppose he knows what is right or, knowing, dares think someone else may spontaneously agree. Thus I work and overwork childlike distinctions, distinctions we are not even aware of in authenticated works of art which give us joy but which, it seems, cannot be presupposed in our experience of what we are seeing for the first time. The first effort of art is an ordering of our sensations; perception begins when we have confidence in that order, and that is what we mean when we say an artist draws us into his world... This is what I find uniquely unpleasant in Arpino's work — its arrogant assumptions in regard to classical style... like Plisetskaya, Arpino wants to make the style do MORE... the only subject of classical dancing is classical style. It is the thing that is not insisted upon and that anyone clear of eye can see...*

*I don't suppose that, beyond protesting its absence or its mishandling, there is much that one can do toward defining classical style, it is so nonrational a thing. Perhaps Denby knows that you can't hit the point without crushing it... The beauty of Denby is his beauty of inference. He assumes people know in advance what he is talking about. But I wonder if they do...*[34]

This passage reaches the heart of Croce's attitude, objectives, philosophy, and style. It tells us that Croce is, first and foremost, a classicist; that classical style represents a viewpoint about a particular sense of order, structure and relationships and that it is its *own* dance subject — purity of expression. We see that Croce is intensely focussed on the value of choreography as the life of the art of dance and that she is not afraid to measure one choreographer against another. She posseses a grandeur of vision about the ideals, the possibilities of what dance can be. One of the things that will be seen over and over in Croce's writing (and, for that matter, in the works of the other New York School critics) is the way in which it pushes dance into a more universal sphere, how it shows that the subject of dance releases images and issues that are relevant outside the domain of dance and, of course, how issues of the arts outside dance are relevant to *it*.

All the values that Croce considers in the above quote, the philosophical and technical values of classicism, were formed in her consciousness and sensibility largely through her 'discovery' of Balanchine. The values of classicism that she describes are the values she believes he manifested more than any other choreographer of this century. As

---

[34] Arlene Croce, "Ballets without Choreography," *Afterimages*, New York: Alfred A. Knopf, 1978, pp. 327–328.

established earlier in this chapter, the Balanchine canon has informed Croce's dance writing from her first published piece and has remained as ever-actively investigated through her career and since Balanchine's death in 1983. Her first published dance writings are infused with the revelation of this canon and her last published collection, *Sight Lines*, is philosophically centered on Balanchine's death and the weight of that loss in a "post-Balanchine" age of dance. "There is no end to the depth of Balanchine's work and to what his work shows me in other dance works and in other works outside dance" said Croce in an interview a couple of years after his death.[35] As Claudia Ruth Pierpoint commented in her review of *Sight Lines* "this is no simple preference or bias toward a preferred style but the result of an unwavering recognition that great choreography can fully engage the intellect, the imagination, and the emotions!"[36]

Croce created a "Balanchine era" and with it some of the most powerful dance criticism in the history of the discipline. It has shaped the attitudes and appetites of a generation of dance audiences with a creative force answering to the very stature of Balanchine's own genius in shaping the face of dance in a particular time and place. On the other hand the Balanchine canon may have incapacitated Croce's vision of the post-Balanchine era. In her own words, referred to in Chapter 2, "Balanchine's progeny... can add nothing to what he has said."[37]

Arlene Croce brings to her dance criticism a heritage of viewing power and sensibilities influenced by her film criticism, the style of a highly disciplined essayist, and a philosophy of criticism as an evaluative and taste-setting task. She supports her evaluations with highly rigorous analysis and persuades the reader of her discoveries by means of powerfully poetic, political and passionately personal writing. Her aesthetic code is that of the classicist who recognizes the enduring and defining principles of classical style to create meaning in dance. Her Balanchine principle provides the standards of classicism through which much of the dance of her writing career is measured and she investigates Balanchine and her other subjects with both a scholarly scrutiny and a momentum-gathering subjectivity. She is a moral critic driven between extremes of lofty spiritualism where she can inform us that "it isn't mindlessness but the state beyond mind that moves us in perfect dancing,"[38] and street-wise (or unwise) ruthlessness

---

[35] Interview with Arlene Croce, New York City , June 1985.

[36] Claudia Ruth Pierpont, *Ballet Review*, Winter, 1988, p. 32.

[37] Arlene Croce, "Postmodern Ballets," *Sight Lines*, New York: Alfred A. Knopf, 1987, p. 319.

[38] Arlene Croce, "Balanchine's Girls: The Making of a Style," *Afterimages*, New York: Alfred A. Knopf, 1978, p. 420.

making for highly controversial stances on victim art. Her notorious "review" of a Bill T. Jones work that she did not see is one such extreme. (Her stance within this review was no less momentous, saying, "By working dying people into his art, Jones is putting himself beyond the reach of criticism."[39]) Critical repertory is the method of her dance beat: the isolating of themes, the cross referencing of productions and performances, and the momentum-gathering politics of her perceptions. The understanding of what is essentially American style dance by a leading American critical stylist is the result.

**Plate 19**   Arlene Croce. New York, May 1995. Photograph by Israel.

---

[39] Arlene Croce, "Discussing the Undisscussable," *The New Yorker*, Christmas Issue, 1994.

# 6

## THE DEBORAH JOWITT FILE

Deborah Jowitt was born in Los Angeles, California in 1934. After attending UCLA for one year as a Theatre Arts major she left for New York in 1953 to dance professionally with the Harriete Ann Gray Company. As a dancer her concert performing expanded to include the companies of Mary Anthony, Valerie Bettis, Pauline Koner, Pearl Lang, Sophie Maslow, Joyce Trisler and Charles Weidman. From 1957–1959 Jowitt became a member of the Juilliard Dance Theatre, performing works by some of the American modern dance pioneers, Doris Humphrey, José Limón, Anna Sokolow and Helen Tamiris. From the late 60s through the early 70s she was a member of the core company of Dance Theatre Workshop and performed works by Art Bauman, Jeff Duncan, Jack Moore and John Wilson. She also performed as a guest dancer with the companies of Frances Alenikoff, José Coronado, and Elina Mooney, and in 1990 she was a guest performer with Marta Renzi and Phyllis Lamhut. Other dance performance includes companies featuring Asian styles and in musical comedies. Jowitt's performing career also included acting and more extensively, choreography. As a choreographer she showed work in shared concerts of *Dance Theater Workshop*, in New York and on tour, and was a commissioned choreographer for *Dance Uptown, Choreoconcerts* and *New York University's Tisch School of the Arts* (1978–1989). Acting roles included television appearances such as the ABC network *Christmas Special* and "Lamp Onto My Feet" in 1966, the role of Lesbia in Shaw's *Getting Married* at the Equity Library Theatre, and parts in experimental one-act plays at the *Cubiculo* theatre and the Judson Church including Jean Cocteau's solodrama *La Voix Humaine* at the Cubiculo.[1]

Most clearly established amongst the four critics being discussed, as the "doer and viewer" of dance, Jowitt has always claimed that she fell into dance criticism by accident. In 1965 radio journalist Baird Searles

---

[1] Deborah Jowitt's performing career, covering a greater spectrum of dance companies and theater genres than mentioned in the chapter, was operative mainly from 1953–1982. However, she has continued to perform from time to time.

put together a programme on WBAI New York radio called "The Critical People," gathering a panel of critics on Art, Architecture, Music, Film, Theatre and Dance. "The programme arose" explained Jowitt, "from his dissatisfaction with journalistic criticism." Each panelist was given five minutes to speak about their art form. The music panelist was Murray Ralph, Jowitt's husband, who encouraged her to air some views on dance. As Jowitt acknowledges in her dedication to *Dance Beat* Murray Ralph and Baird Searles (and Letitia Kent) made her a dance critic in spite of herself.

"The show became so popular" as Jowitt described it, "that it got an 'alternate' cast. Denby sent a strong letter of praise and encouragement to the program. Marcia Siegel, then editor of *Dance Scope* heard the program and invited me to review Denby's book for *Dance Scope*." This review of Denby's *Dancers, Buildings, and People in the Streets* was Jowitt's first published dance piece, appearing in *Dance Scope's* Spring issue, 1966.

Jowitt continued as panelist for WBAI — FM's *The Critical People* until 1968 and also continued writing for *Dance Scope*. Starting in 1967 she wrote her first review for *The Village Voice*, under the two titles "Spoiled by Success?", about Paul Taylor's *Agathe's Tale and* "Joffrey Postscript" about Robert Joffrey's ballet *Astarte*. That is where she established her greatest 'beat' and reputation as a dance critic, contributing a very long weekly column to *The Village Voice* in which she still writes today. She describes her early years in dance criticism as having been highly influenced by the radical critic Jill Johnston, whose "Dance Journal" column in *The Village Voice* (1960–1970) addressed dance, painting, sculpture, happenings and all multi-media art. "She was juicy like Denby but she was also slangy *unlike* Denby and I strained to get that same tone myself," recalls Jowitt.[2] Compared to the quirky stream-of- consciousness style of writing employed by Johnson, Jowitt's writing appears lyrical, elegant and logical. But Johnston's influence can be felt in Jowitt's signature trait of rhythmic colloquialisms in her description and analysis of dance.

When Jowitt began writing dance criticism she believed that the process of description was her most important task. "Really seeing" dance was, according to Jowitt, the only way one could really confront it. And to improve upon her ability to "really see" she, like Siegel, started "vision therapy" training with Dr. Richard Kavner.

Jowitt's dance criticism career expanded from her early *Village Voice* days to include regular contributions to *The New York Times Sunday Arts and Leisure Magazine, The New York Times Book Review, Dance Magazine, Mademoiselle, Dance Research Journal, The Drama Review, Ballet International,*

---

[2] Interview with Deborah Jowitt, June 1985, New York City.

German *Geo, Ballet Review, Art in America, Artscanada,* the *Miami Herald,* the *Detroit News* and the *Chicago Tribune,* throughout the 70's and 80's. She has also contributed major dance essays to anthologies such as *Contemporary Dance* and *Ballet and the Arts.*

Her first book, *Dance Beat* was a collection of reviews, mostly from her *Village Voice* column, and appeared in 1977, the same year as Siegel's second collection: *Watching the Dance Go By.* A second, very different book, was published in 1985. Called *The Dance in Mind,* this book focussed on selected choreographers and dancers — in the rehearsal studio, in performance, through reviews and interviews — and plotted their course of achievements and traits and relationships in the context of American dance history-in-the making. Her third book, *Time and the Dancing Image* published in 1988, was a series of essays on the changing image of dancers from the Romantic Ballerina to the post-modernist. This book won Jowitt the De La Torre Bueno Prize, the most prestigious award in dance publishing and scholarship. Jowitt is also the winner of a "Bessie," an acclaimed New York Dance and Performance Award. Like Siegel, she has also been an active member of the Dance Critics Association (Treasurer and, as of 1992, Co-Chairman) and like Croce, she has been a member of the advisory Dance Panel to the National Council on the Arts, and later, Co-Chairman. Jowitt's career as a writer has also flourished within the entirely separate field of Spanish translation. Writing under the pseudonym of Rachel Benson, she has translated articles and essays for *Atlantic Monthly, San Franscisco Review* and *Dance Perspectives* and translated and wrote the biographical essays for *Nine Latin American Poets,* published in 1968 by *Las Americas.*

As a teacher, lecturer and speaker Jowitt's experience is vast and varied. A few of her affiliations include *Jacob's Pillow, Princeton University, Temple University, Mills College, New York University, Pratt Institute, American University, George Washinton University, Swarthmore College, Harvard Summer Institute for the Study of Avant-Gardes,* the *London School of Contemporary Dance* and the *Laban Centre.* And, in company with her fellow critics Siegel and Goldner, Jowitt directed the Critics Conference at the American Dance Festival (1973–1980).

The role of teaching in dance criticism and history has been for Jowitt, as it has been for Siegel and Goldner, a major force in the conscious task of creating a dance criticism discipline that can begin to become a tradition, drawing from this newly rigorous and investigative body of dance "text."

Seeing *what is there* motivates all of Jowitt's criticism. In the transition from watching to writing, Jowitt retains that sense of performing immediacy and the *activity of her viewing.* She is a colloquial stylist. Her writing has a conversational ease about it that resembles a vivacious personality issuing clear, polished gems of thought. One never gets the impression that Jowitt has struggled to organise her perceptions of a dance into any particular sequence or definite categories. Just as she is willing to look at all kinds of dance, she appears equally willing to allow the rhythm of her impressions to guide her through her analysis. This gives Jowitt's criticism an unique shapliness, the analysis being filled with lively description and insightful summations of traits and trends.

Her entrance into the profession of dance criticism was, as she described at the beginning of this chapter, uncharted. Jill Johnston's collected criticism *Marmalade Me*, published in 1971, which read like an "event," and the daring and irreverent stream of consciousness style that Johnston characteristically adopted, was seductive. It influenced Jowitt's work in spirit and energy. Johnston, writing about Martha Graham in 1968 for example, radically and graphically emphasized sexual politics much more than she described or analysed choreography:

> *I want to spit out a few more speculations on the lady Graham. Brilliant beautiful unhappy lady. Does she relate to Sarah Bernhardt and chicks like that? In the tradition of great ladies I think of Gertrude Stein as a kind of counterpart to a Cunningham. Certainly Stein wasn't hiding in the attic or sweeping the pieces of her broken heart into a dust pan like Emily Dickinson (Letter to the World).*
>
> > *I'm delaying the issue. I'm feeling presumptuous. I could say that the way she's been depicting herself in her works all these years is clearly as an inverted homo hetero sado masochistic sodomist Why not? It doesn't matter. My point is she never got what she wanted, whatever the fantasy. If she had, all that phallic insanity would have come over as a giant surrealist pun. That's what we're missing in our ballet-modern dance tradition — a stunning surrealism. That's one way of making psychology into an erotic amusement park. Who was the lady kidding? She's an incredible ball-breaker. So bloody serious. So hell-bent for leather, etc. On purpose she set up all those handsome brave-looking gods and snapped off their heads with her bare hands and her décor weapons and her dragon-claw feet. And then had the curtain come down on her alone exclusively usually and she might's well have stood there with a dripping red penis hanging out of her mouth. We know that Salome didn't know a head from a penis. That's what a head is, or vice versa (Herodiade). She's something else, this Graham lady. Where'd she go when the show was over?*[3]

Unlike the larger political statements that Johnston engages in, Jowitt's works are still anchored to the *dance* she is viewing. But in the example below, written for the *Village Voice* in 1971, a very jaunty and liberated Jowitt lets loose on a narrative classical ballet. The review is probably closest to a kind of sisterhood of style with Johnston. Describing a ballet to Bartok's *The*

---

[3] Jill Johnston, "Martha Graham: An Irresponsible Study… The Head of Her Father," *Ballet Review*, Vol. 2, No. 4, 1968, p. 11.

*Miraculous Mandarin* by Swedish choreographer Ulf Gadd, Jowitt has a great deal to say which, although quoted in some length, represents only a portion of the full treatment this ballet gets from her.

> *Everything is a little illogical… The three robbers are far too randy to make efficient pimps; they'd wear the girl out before she could get started. The drunken sailor stays drunk for about eight bars, then bangs the girl competently and escapes the three toughs with absolutely no trouble. The program says that they chase him away because he has no money, but I don't think this happened either. They just make ineffectual grabs at him as he whisks into the wings and then climb sulkily back up their ladder. The young boy is too tender and sweet to take quick advantage of the girl, but after the thugs let him escape too, they unfairly beat her up. Another example of what efficient pimps they are. The Mandarin is mysterious from the start; he just stands there in profile while she does a long tired solo around him. In this ballet, he doesn't get much chance to show how savage his nature is, because the three thieves for once pull themselves together and attack — even though this one obviously knows a bit of karate. Well, they really maul him, carry on in a most unpleasant manner. And each time they leave him for dead, he slowly rises and heads for the girl. The most persistent erection in stage history.*[4]

Other than a few extreme examples such as the slangy yet lyrical passage above showing Johnston's influence, a much more characteristic colloquial style in Jowitt can be found, for example, in her first viewing of a Tharp ballet in 1973.

> *Oh, Twyla, what have you done? Finally stunned me into wordlessness, I think. Here I sit, staring at the rows of mint-green letters on my Hermes, wondering how I can possibly hit them into sentences that will suggest the liveliness, the complexity, the marvelous ease of "Deuce coupé"…*[5]

Jowitt's colloquial style releases a sense of self-granted permission to write about dance within many modes, temperaments, sentiments and intentions; to liberate the review format and open the *style* of dance literature to encompass rigorous accuracy and subjective fancy.

In the Preface to *Dance Beat*, and *The Dance in Mind*, Jowitt explains how her experience as a dancer and choreographer influences her view of the critic's task. Her's is a non-evaluative position in the context of critic as *consumer index*…[6] "I'm not in the business of rating or ranking" she says in

---

[4] Deborah Jowitt, "Sour Notes in the Ballet Season," *Dance Beat*, New York: Marcel Decker, 1977, pp. 5–7.

[5] Ibid, p. 162.

[6] It is essential to note that Deborah Jowitt does indeed respond evaluatively to dance. As I hope this book has shown her work possesses dinstinct aesthetic values and points of view. However, as Jowitt says, it is the "rating and ranking" context that often places critics in the task of consumer guiding that Jowitt resists.

**Plate 20** *Deuce Coupé*, choreography by Twyla Tharp (1973). The Joffrey Ballet, NYC, 1973. Photograph © Herbert Migdoll. Twyla Tharp Archive, The Jerome Lawrence and Robert E. Lee Theatre Research Institute, Ohio State University.

one of her reviews. She has remained consistent in this through the span of
years separating the collections.

> *That I didn't stop choreographing and performing when I began to write criticism has*
> *disturbed other critics, but dancers don't seem to find it particularly odd. Perhaps they know*
> *that while fair-mindedness can be achieved, objectivity is a fallacy. Perhaps, too, having seen*
> *me sweat and heard me curse, they know that.... I can never forget how much thought, care*
> *and work goes into the making of a dance. That is I'm interested in thinking about bad*
> *dances — although I'd rather think about great ones — rather than simply stamping on them*
> *and sweeping them under the rug.[7]*

In *The Dance In Mind*, she writes "it may be my background, it may be my
behaviour, too, that encourages me to try to consider a work on its own
terms, rather than to refer to an absolute scale of values..."[8]

In this position Jowitt sits farthest apart from Croce who, according
to Jowitt does not want to discuss bad work. "Arlene Croce never
compromises her writing standards. I compromise a lot — often my
description is overwritten.... She has very high personal standards... and
she does not have the battery of anxieties about dance that I do."[9]

As a dancer-critic Jowitt has perhaps, inherited a vice and a virtue.
Her kinesthetic sensitivity, so alert and alive to the feeling of experience of
movement, enables her to describe dance with acclaimed vividness and
accuracy. However, this same descriptive approach has sometimes
frustrated dancers who say they want more *opinion*. Of the four critics
discussed in this book, Jowitt has had a reputation as describer rather
than as value-setter. However, her pieces of pure kinesthetic recall act in
themselves as a kind of "accompanying text" for the dances viewed. This
text records the very process of a critic making sensual and intellectual
sense out of a dance she has viewed and it activates at times more objective
writings on choreographers. In a review called "When is Not Enough Too
Much?" Jowitt incorporates her kinesthetic involvement with the dance into
her criticism thus:

> *Certain minimal dances loiter in my memory long after I've seen them. By minimal, I don't*
> *mean just dances that make a point of everyday behaviour and any-old movement, but dances*
> *tenanted by one plain, vivid movement image or dances, in which a few sturdy patterns are*
> *repeated so many times that the viewers' muscles begin to flex in response.*

---

[7] Deborah Jowitt, *Dance Beat*, New York: Marcel Dekker Inc., 1977, "Preface", p. v.

[8] Deborah Jowitt, *The Dance in Mind*, Boston: David Godine, 1985, "Preface", p. x.

[9] Interview with Deborah Jowitt, June 1985, New York City.

> *When I got home from Lucinda Child's concert at her bare white-walled loft with its new golden wood floor, I tried to do her* Reclining Rondo *as smoothly and flatly as Susan Brody, Judy Padow, and David Woodberry had performed it. I'd liked watching it and I liked doing it. Doing it emphasised the ever, easy-going bending and stretching of the body as it moved through the carefully arranged pattern of sitting, crouching, and lying. Watching it, I had, of course, seen also the ingenious permutations of patterns created by three bodies performing in unison and had sometimes tried to anticipate the changes of direction or spacing that the pattern's occasional asymmetries (e.g. a quarter roll right or left) would produce.[10]*

This very internalising of Child's choreography actually leads Jowitt to more objective rather than subjective commentary on the effects of that choreography and how they are achieved. It is the process of a critic, uniquely, both de-mystifying and celebrating a dance — viewing the dance imagistically and experientially. This passage is not typical of Jowitt in that she does not frequently tell us about her physical re-enactments of dances viewed. But the process of dance-making and dancing seems very much in evidence by the way her descriptive writing so often suggests that she is *inhabiting* what she views.

In another piece of descriptive writing, Jowitt still harnesses her strength of kinesthetic sensitivity and recall to analyze identifying characteristics in the work of choreographer Jeff Duncan.

> *His movement is partially a spin-off from his own tall, columnar body. He enjoys the feel of verticality — body pulled straight and high, arms hanging at the sides — and also the plunging away from it into falls and crouches. Sometimes the verticality is re-stated by alert drops to one knee or shoulder-stands. Thus the ground becomes charged in his dances: in his nature pieces, it is benevolent, magical; in his violent or unhappy pieces, it often appears to be jolting or shifting... Just recently I noticed an interesting point: this energy is almost always the same for everyone within the group. They all feel it. Even though specific movements may be different, it is as if the same tide has them in its grip. This, I think, is what gives the humanity-hordes effect — a metaphor for the human condition that we all share.[11]*

It can be seen, in both the above passage and in the earlier one on Lucinda Childs that entire facets of Jowitt's criticism *resist* rather than avoid evaluation. In the above passage she edges towards a statement on the significance of Duncan's choreographic characteristics. However, the main thrust of the piece is decidedly contained in her alertness to the physical

---

[10] Deborah Jowitt, *Dance Beat*, New York: Marcel Dekker, Inc., 1977, pps. 119–20.

[11] Deborah Jowitt, "From the Inside," *The Village Voice*, October 22, 1970.

facts of the movement and (characteristic of the school of critics) in her ability to relate those facts in dramatically active and readable terms. Jowitt also reveals her aesthetic values as a critic in the context of cultural history. Sometimes these views are inferred through her descriptions and at other times she is more forwardly and formally analytical.

*Dance Beat*, covering the years 1967–1976, is organised mostly according to ballet, modern dance, the "rebels" and alternative genres. Within those broad categories certain treatments of the subject come into focus. Major themes are pursued, one per essay in some cases, such as male dancing, the choreographer's use of spaces, the content of new dance and so on. The material in the collection, whether thematic essay or the single dance review almost always incorporates movement description, imagery conveying the dance's expressive impact, cross references to other dances and a summation of identifying characteristics and trends which the dance reflects or instigates. Sometimes Jowitt investigates the works of one choreographer over several pieces, as in her trilogy on Martha Graham called "Monumental Martha" or in her studies of the post-modern choreographers later in *The Dance In Mind*. This book takes on as original a structure for dance criticism as *Shapes* by Siegel. Here, Jowitt combines interviews with choreographers and dancers with her own analysis of works: describing individual works; plotting the development of a choreographer's repertory and style; establishing a choreo-historical context of which the dances are a part and, as in the essay on dancer Martine van Hamel, creating a portrait of individual dancers through interviews and on-the-spot performance and discussion. She pieces her thoughts about a dance together with the dancer moving before her in the studio space. This combination of scholarship and involvement with the subject creates a truly unique brand of critical literature in dance.

Siegel has referred to Jowitt as "my alter ego" — a critic who shares many of the same views and concerns about dance. Both critics are particularly tuned to the American modern dance heritage and both are concerned for the preservation of that heritage. Siegel admonishes dancers about "mucking around with their posterity," Siegel and Jowitt refer to "choreographers... collecting those shrouds of past conventions which they consider still useful," and "throwing out everything else with the requisite blithe arrogance of revolutionaries." Siegel devotes whole essays to the subject of historical consciousness-forming, appealing and urgent. Jowitt's pieces are insistent too, but she takes it more in her stride. Within her casual tone though, she establishes precise observations about style and snaps us to attention.

"Marcia and I have been very involved in dance history and cultural history. Too often dance is seen in a vacuum"[12] says Jowitt. Again, like Siegel and like Croce, two issues in the cultural-historical view of dance are a particularly strong feature of Jowitt's criteria. One is the issue of preserving and safe-guarding dances and the other is the clarification and differentiation of style. In *Detective Story: Find the Work* we see a good example of attention to physical details of preserved works and the problems of fidelity invited by revivals.

*If you ask, "What is the work?", about a piece of choreography, things immediately become stickier. Sometimes you find that it no longer actually exists; it's no longer performed, was never filmed, can't be found among the Dance Notation Bureau's small but growing library of scores. All that remains of such a dance are photographs, reviews, choreographer's notes — if he or she took any — perhaps the musical score, costumes, sets. Small chunks of dancing or stage patterns may remain in the minds of those who once performed the dance or those who saw it — if they're still alive...*

*...It's just possible that nobody cares, either. Most people, consciously or unconsciouly, accept each performance of a dance they're watching as The Work itself; if they see it again, they may adjust their mental picture. It's only in discussion or critical writing that you become aware of the ephemeral nature of even a frequently performed work.*

*Alvin Ailey's classic* **Revelations** *is a bigger, splashier dance than it was 10 years ago, because of gradually accumulating changes, planned and unplanned. Members of the Royal Danish Ballet for years have boasted of their unboken Bournonvillle tradition, yet there exists in Copenhagen a 1904 film which, compared with the Bournonville style of today, clearly demonstrates how much that style has altered as it has been passed on from dancer to dancer...*

*...Naturally, more people are excited about dancing and making dances than about chronicling or preserving them. This is particularly true in the field of American modern dance, wherein the deplorable lack of history may be the result of its own rallying cry: "Down with the old, up with the new!"...*

*...Still, when I think of the several films, the notation score, the frequent performances of Doris Humphrey's* The Shakers *(1931), I think that our pride in dance's ephemeral nature may be a trifle defensive. Many young contemporary dancers have learned* **Shakers** *the way ballet students learn variations from* **Swan Lake***; they can argue happily about the correct interpretation of the 9-count phrase. I can think of very few modern dances you can treat in this way. When I speak of* **Shakers** *as The Work, I may even know what I mean...*[13]

---

[12] Interview with Deborah Jowitt, June 1985, New York City, and correspondence over 1985–1991.

[13] Deborah Jowitt, "Dectective Story: Find the Work," *Dance Beat*, New York: Marcel Dekker, 1977, pp. 47, 48, 49, 50.

For Jowitt the work is not to be valued as the single-viewed performance but rather as an enduring entity, with a stylistic tradition and social/historical/aesthetic context. And in the last paragraph of the above passage, where she rallies to the notion of authenticating dance text she is arguing for a formality of definition in the modern dance which would ultimately allow for performances of a dance to be interpretive instances of a work rather than be viewed in the "safely" non-evaluative, non-contextual and ephemeral performing present. For all her immediacy of descriptive writing and her seemingly non-evaluative descriptiveness, Jowitt fully embraces the rootedness of dance within a cultural and historical context. While she and her fellow critics are exceptionally alert and responsive to *the new* in dance development and movement to the point at which *the new* is in itself an aesthetic value, clarification, regard, and accuracy in the matter of style and posterity is still paramount.

> *I'm terribly pleased that so many important ballet companies are mounting works by some of the dead geniuses of modern dance, but my pleasure has made me all the more edgy and critical. I see that care and expenses have gone into the staging; I see the dancers trying hard to capture the style; but what's missing in most cases is the specific dynamics of the dance style.*

> *Dancers tend to think a lot about the shapes their bodies are making, probably because of the strain and skill involved. Dancers these days are very versatile about shape-making, but in concentrating on* what *gets done they don't always remember to think about* how *it gets done...*[14]

By insisting on the value of dance history and posterity, by clarifying and re-working observations on links, differences, or influences between choreographers, and by exercising alert instincts and attitudes, Jowitt, like her colleagues, seems always "ready at the scene" of any currents or trends and forecasting their implications.

In looking at individual dances Jowitt's work pinpoints the telltale mechanisms that make a dance function and give it its special impetus. Through her writings a consistent pattern of response emerges. She weaves together description of the specific moments of movement that are essential to it in some way, imagery which conjures up the expressive effect of the dancing, and identifying characteristics of the work of the particular choreographer. Her review of Balanchine's *Chaconne* (1976) is a typical example of this treatment.

---

[14] Deborah Jowitt, "Allies of the Ground, Eye in the Sky," *Dance Beat*, New York: Marcel Dekker, 1977, pp. 47, 48, 49, 50.

*The extraordinary duet that Balanchine has made for Suzannne Farrell and Peter Martins also seems to be happening in a dream. They dance slowly and delicately, almost as if trying to remember how to dance together. Their energy is like that used by dancers when they mark quietly through a dance, humming to themselves, barely indicating some of the steps. They seem to hear or feel, more often than, see, each other. You're scarcely aware of choreography, only of tendrils of movement the dancers curl around each other. A couple of times, as I remember, he dips her down and slides her along on her toes, but instead of immediately swooping her up again, he pauses, leaving her almost horizontal to the ground for a second before helping her to twine around and rise. Moments like this, that you can almost read as awkward — or perhaps tentative — make the dance seem not only tender, but ineffably poignant… Nothing really prepares you for the second duet of Farrell and Martins. Martin's solo passages are full of smooth, dexterous footwork, and the way he keeps shifting his focus gives you the illusion of seeing many facets of the movement. Farrell's solos involve curious relevés on one toe, in which her gesture-leg flicks softly out in unpredictable directions while her arms or body curl into positions so extreme that you wonder how it is that she isn't pulled off balance. As in much rococco art, the skeletal structure is so slim it almost vanishes, and you simply see dancing unfurling in scrolls and tendrils and sprays. The dancing for the corps de ballet frames this, but cannot quite match the flexibility, the radiant vitality of the dancing for Farrell and Martins. It's as if triumphant love (and choreographic inspiration) had made this Orpheus and Eurydice more luminous than the rest of humanity.[15]*

The writing here is as delicate and suggestive as the choreography it describes. It reflects not only the nature of the movement in terms of steps but the temperament of the dance in terms of performance energy and mood. The phrase "as if trying to remember how to dance together" immediately conjures up the tentative intimacy of the pas de deux. The effect of the choreography that "you're scarcely aware of" is what Jowitt attends to almost as if instictively knowing that to describe movements in full detail would be too heavy-handed for this genteel rococo dance. Within this deliberate restraint a poetic dialogue between creation and creative response emerges non-insistently but utterly authoritative by the very nature of the description itself.

At the other end of the spectrum — *the new* — Jowitt exercises this same descriptive ease, this instinctively perceptive energy sense that captures the particular challenge of the choreography. In the following passage, taken from her essay called "Pull Together in These Distracted Times," (1975) in *Dance Beat* Jowitt writes about a post-modern company called Grand Union. This is a spontaneous, gut-level response of an involved viewer — a viewer who feels comfortable with the shape of the new and as yet unformulated possibilities of dance and someone sensitive to the atmosphere transmitted by the performance act. There is a feeling of

---

[15] Deborah Jowitt, op. cit., pp. 30–31.

"discovery" about the performance in the writing, which allows the event to unravel. Her language clinches this raw, improvisational aspect of the performance:

> *I spend two evenings at* La Mama... *thinking that if I stuck my head out the window and yelled to the street below, "catch me," maybe, just maybe, someone would..." It's easy to remember a Grand Union performance in terms of its highlights and its low points or to talk about one performance that "worked' and one that didn't. But I find that the most important thing the group's performing does is to articulate for us, in a particular way, the shifts of equilibrium, the spurts of directed tension, the changes of focus that we're all constantly engaged in — alone or in groups. The particular way the Grand Union does this emphasises — I can't think of a pithier word — coping. I like to watch the way a Grand Union person will try to see through something he or she has started — patiently, at times gallantly, even though whatever it is may have become unwieldy or painful — but then finally, drop it without regret. I like the way they all help each other out of difficulties or lend their weight to accomplish some group purpose, or the way they fit themselves into something that may not be their bag. In the deepest and best sense of the word, the are polite — however vigorous, raunchy, aggressive or noisily eccentric they may allow themselves to get.*[16]

As I have mentioned, all the critics in the New York School are alert to innovation and are willing to embrace the new. Perhaps, Jowitt, with her particular regard for and fascination with experimental dance, is the brightest light beckoning them forward where she will be ready, and with her eyes open.

> *It's the business of the avant-garde to be astringent and uncompromising to keep us from getting too comfortable with the old forms. The rest of us may never reject all our ideas about dance, but we'll sure as hell re-examine them. We may even follow wholeheartedly in the new direction; then after 10 years or so, the new avant-garde will revolt against us.*[17]

Re-examining her ideas on dance again and again; thinking as much about why dances don't work as much as why they do work; kinesthetically re-living dances through her dancer's perspective; attending to dances with a descriptive response which reflects the rhythm of her discovery in viewing; exercising not so much an evaluative framework as a critic but rather an "equal rights" attitude towards dances from all extremes of the spectrum, offering something of value or interest for her viewing investment. So Jowitt, ever alert to and fierce guardian of styles and the place of dance in America as cultural heritage, takes her place amongst the New York School.

---

[16] Ibid, p. 132.

[17] Ibid, p. 116.

**Plate 21** Deborah Jowitt. Photograph by Lois Greenfield.

# 7

# THE NANCY GOLDNER FILE

Nancy Goldner was born in Queens, New York, March 19, 1943. As a young girl she trained at the School of American Ballet for seven years, dancing in the premiere of Balanchine's "Nutcracker" in 1954. Then "adolescence happened" and an intended career in dance performance ended. She graduated from the University of Michigan in 1964, majoring in Literature, Philosophy, and History. Her first professional work was in publishing, working as an editor for two publishing houses in New York: Macmillan and then Crowell. Her first regular professional dance writing began in 1969 for *Dance News* in which she was featured until it folded in February, 1983. Throughout the 1970's and 1980's Goldner wrote dance criticism on a regular basis for many publications including *The Christian Science Monitor, The Nation, The Soho Weekly News and Les Saisons de la Danse*. She has taught dance history and criticism at New York University, York University in Toronto and at the Critics Conference at the American Dance Festival at Duke University, North Carolina, where she also served as director from 1980–84. She is the author of *The Stravinsky Festival of the New York City Ballet* (Eakins Press, 1974) and the recipient of a grant from the National Endowment for the Humanities for research on the Bennington School of Dance. She is also on the editorial board of the International Encyclopedia of Dance, to be published by Oxford University Press.

 *The Nation*, a weekly magazine, featured criticism fortnightly. Goldner describes her work there as being "long, detailed pieces with a freedom of subject matter." These dance pieces were about 1500–2000 words and Goldner was able to operate on an assumption of readership interest in the subject of dance. As she describes it "I did not have to cover all bases but could be as idiosyncratic as I felt like being and there was no editing." Her writing for the daily, *The Christian Science Monitor* from 1970 to 1984, appeared on a regular basis, though with much less luxury of space (approximately 700 words). She describes these pieces as being "more informative and more balanced." From 1980–1983 Goldner contributed lengthy dance pieces (approximately 1,000 words) to the *Soho Weekly News* on alternate weeks. Here, too, she had a readership who were very interested in the arts. In competition with New York's *Village Voice*, the *Soho Weekly News* "tried to be off-beat." Goldner says that although there was only sporadic editing of her work at this paper her pieces were assigned. This was unlike *The Nation* where she made all her own choices of what to write about, when to write, and the lengths of the pieces. *The Nation* offered a rare opportunity as neither she nor her editors there had preconceptions of what the column would turn into. "The arts editor at *The Nation*, Robert Hatch, had only one assumption: that the writing was serious criticism." From 1982–1984 she also wrote dance criticism for *Saturday Review*, a weekly national magazine to which she contributed articles once a month. Describing the editor's concern that she "make the arts column more rigorous than in *Newsweek*," Goldner's 1,000 word articles answered the demand with a highly polished writing style. Other dance writing (freelance) included, during the 1970's, the *New York Times Magazine*, the *Village Voice*, the monthly magazine, *The Bennington Review* and the monthly *Les Saisons de la Danse*. Currently, Nancy Goldner is dance critic for the *Philadelphia Inquirer* where she has been a daily contributor since 1984, writing 500–700 word reviews. She also writes major Sunday articles with more space and more commentary or "think piece" style. The arts editor there, Howard Shapiro, practices a policy of full coverage of the New York arts scene (by readership demand as Philadelphia is only 70 miles away) so Goldner's column covers both New York and Philadelphia. Describing her launch into dance writing, Goldner explains that

> After college I went to New York and couldn't "work off" my interest in dance by only talking. My friends didn't share my interst in dance so I had to, really needed to, write about it. I felt secure in doing critical writing, and had a knowledge of dance, a certain authority (versus an interest in music without the real knowledge). I felt there was a real need for decent writing about dance; I felt I could contribute to this field, felt there was room for me.[1]

One of the great motivating forces in Goldner's career was the mystery of Balanchine.

> I watched Balanchine rehearse all the time; I loved watching the process, was fascinated by the fact that what I saw in rehearsal had no bearing on the performance. It was a magical transformation. Watching him make or rehearse a piece was absolutely no preparation for writing about the piece. Sometimes it was a hindrance. Sometimes what worked so well in rehearsal did not work in performance and vice versa. He was the only choreographer I saw working on a continuous basis and sometimes it was so boring, so dry, so nuts and bolts, all logistics. There were no clues as to why Balanchine was so good, there were no explanations for his artistry.[2]

---

[1] Nancy Goldner, discussion, September 1994, New York City.

[2] Ibid.

Goldner's extensive teaching experience in dance criticism and dance history reinforces her critical practice and vice versa. "Things discussed in the teaching process might find its way into writing" she comments. She taught dance criticism, history and Russian Ballet for three years in the early 80's in the Department for Performing Arts at New York University (now called the Tisch School of the Arts, where Jowitt and Siegel also teach). She also taught and occasionally still teaches at York University, Toronto, The New School, New York and other institutes and universities.

Unlike the other critics in this study, Goldner has not published any collections of her dance criticism. She is author of the book, *The Stravinsky Festival of the New York City Ballet* which records the Stravinsky Festival of the New York City Ballet from June 18th to June 25th 1972. In this chronicle she records the ballet program for each evening and then selects from the evening's program a choice of ballets to describe, analyze and comment on. The book is a celebration of Balanchine whereby Goldner points out for us all his most endearing and enduring qualities as master choreographer. It is the work of both a devoted fan and a sensitive, curious and passionate critic, very much in the spirit of Edwin Denby's early pieces on Balanchine, where he insists, through a series of excited questions, that we look and see and share in his revelatory experiences. Goldner here plucks the gems from Balanchine's repertory and asks us "Do you not see how this moment glitters?" "Isn't this passage exquiste?" "How does he do it?" For Goldner the festival and the book that recalls it are occassions for complete immersion in Balanchine's repertory and an opportunity for Goldner to tap into the critical repertory so uniquely available to the New York School — an opportunity for repeated viewings, the viewing of a large body of work, the viewing of different artists in the same roles and the particular stylistic distinctions and questions raised accordingly. Thus her statement in the "Introduction" of the book:

> For the company the festival was an explosion of activity set off by "an atomic pill," which is the way Balanchine once described Stravinsky's music. Statistically alone, it was such a feat of daring that quantity became as important as quality. As such it uncovered the unique beauty of American overabundance. No weeding, no connoisseurship, no waiting for that muse on union time — it threw the bundle at us, junk and all.[3]

"A performance infects you," says Goldner. "It is so moving. There is, then, the necessity of finding out what it is that prompts you to investigate. This need to investigate seriously starts with Balanchine because he is so inspiring…"[4] Immediately, it can be established that Nancy Goldner makes

---

[3] Nancy Goldner, *The Stravinsky Festival of the New York Ballet*, New York: Eakins Press, 1973, p. 62.

[4] Interview with Nancy Goldner, June 1985, New York City.

a natural partner for Arlene Croce, immersed as she is in the "Balanchine aesthetic." Like Croce, Goldner is inspired by Balanchine into a particular way of looking at dance and a means of organizing her perceptions and defining her standards.

In addressing Goldner's criticism here, we can look at some of the ways in which her "Balanchine based" views are applied in her overall criticism. Unlike Jowitt, whose non-evaluative mode of criticism is a product of her "sliding scale" values and openness to all dance experiences, Goldner draws clear evaluative distinctions regarding the types of dance she views and the type of criticism that results.

> *Balanchine made it possible to discuss content in a sophisticated way. With Balanchine you get to the content; by describing movement and structure..." this approach to other choreographers often doesn't work because they're not as good as Balanchine. So you have to relinquish it to find an approach that best elucidates what is there. This takes craft, but it isn't the most fun. With less-than-Balanchine dance, I think a lot about why something does or doesn't work. With the best dance, you think about how it works. Thus, the one kind of criticism is essentially evaluative (and less fun to do); the other kind is analytical (and much more fun to do).*[5]

Elucidating what is there, seeing fully what the dance offers on its own terms, Goldner's eye is like a high powered lens scanning over dance surfaces. "The best criticism is a response to the best work, and historically that is the way it ought to go," says Goldner.[6] Naturally, Goldner's most inspired pieces are responses to those choreographers whose works she most admires.

The style and organising principle of Goldner's criticism is strongly influenced by her literature studies in the "New Criticism," which, according to definition

> *Insisted on close reading of the text and awareness of verbal nuance and thematic (rather than narrative) organization, and was not concerned with the biographical or social backgrounds of works of art. The text existed as a text on a page, an object in itself, with its own structure, which should be explored in its own terms.*[7]

"I was taught to examine text very carefully, taught that the meaning of the thing came from details. It is obvious in poetry (rhythm placement, image)

---

[5] Correspondence with Nancy Goldner, March 1991.

[6] Interview with Nancy Goldner, June 1985, New York City.

[7] Ibid.

but it also happen in novels,"[8] explains Goldner. This exploration of the dance "text" is what Goldner adheres to, perhaps more unwaveringly than her colleagues. "The source of the meaning is what I am looking for through this structure" she says.

> *In books I remembered the things I wanted to use. I realized the things that were significant along the way. There is a memory problem in all media. The fact that I could only see a dance once didn't throw me. I had seen lots of dance. I had a familiarity with the works.*[9]

As with all the critics under examination, the New York dance environment presented special privileges: dance volume; dance dialogue (with other critics); and the phenomenon of critical repertory.

Goldner's special appeal to me is her consistently clear and systematic approach to criticism. One can rely on the format and dance content of her reviews much as a valuable reference source. With variation, of course, the general shape of Goldner's criticism is as follows: the introduction of an issue or question which is pursued via the dance content; a chronological breakdown of the structure of the dance; an analytical summary of the dance or of the choreographer's stage of development as represented by the dance. Within each section of the dance's structure, Goldner recalls incidents and creates images which speak for the essence of what the dance is "about" and for the quality of its visual and emotional impact.

In a review of Twyla Tharp's dance *As Time Goes By* for instance, Goldner introduces the dance as being "about" the elements of composition, a purely formal conception of the work. She then plots out the dance in sequence. First she discusses in detail a solo section; what various steps look like; the aspects of classical ballet vocabulary that Tharp is experimenting with and commenting on; some of the *qualities* of movement which are characteristic of Tharp's choreography overall; and various cross references to other choreographers in relation to what Tharp is achieving in her dance. She moves on to the next section, "a dance for six, compositionally the most brilliant part of the ballet" and focuses this time on the ways in which the dance structure corresponds to the musical structure, describing both as chamber compositions. This she demonstrates by locating five specific correlations between the chamber music and the choreography. Next comes "a series of finales to end all finales" and here Goldner describes the floor patterns; and finally, a "series of trios, quartets and duets that float

---

[8] Ibid.

[9] Ibid.

imperceptibly into a solo. The solo brings the ballet to its finish just as imperceptibly, so that when it's over you feel that a new friend has been snatched away." The review ends with a summation of the intent and effect of the dance;

> *The dancing is a concrete expression of everyman's desire to dance — that is, to float, sway, just move without the encumbrance of steps — because the music is so beautiful. Tharp gets to the nub of that fantasy without sacrificing the choreographer's instinct and duty to invent steps in interesting arrangements.*[10]

In a review of Eliot Feld's ballet *Romance* Goldner again follows the same basic outline, this time showing how each section of the structure metaphorically describes a particular mood or emotional state.

> *...The expression of restlessness and would-be adultery exists in every action, but it comes to fullest realization when the eight people suddenly throw themselves into a grand-right-and-left. This figure, normally associated with the square dance, rather wryly and absolutely appropriately, becomes the overriding metaphor of the ballet. It allows for every person to be tasted. It creates a world that is wide open and in which relationships are fleeting and fluid and still orderly. Since* Romance *is peopled with couples — who will remain so, despite their yearning, unhappiness, curiosity and adulterous imaginations — the grand-right-and-left is both a wistfully symbolic exercise of their collective wish as well as a wickedly delightful capsule of the events of the ballet.*[11]

Her introductory "issue" in this case is about how a choreographer assimilates the work of another and produces an original style and treatment in his own work.

> *He can use fully the ideas of another without becoming imprisoned or overwhelmed by them. He can do so, probably, because he does use ideas, or a set of images, that lie underneath and run through particular steps, and structural devices that might shape movement but are not movements in themselves.*[12]

Throughout this review Goldner, again, describes movement qualities, capturing images that describe the expressive effect of the dance and locating their sources within the action of the dance.

> *...Each dance of* Romance *is an artful manoeuvre by which partners are exchanged or cast aside. Sometimes the exchange is done by glance. A woman is twirled by her partner and then*

---

[10] Nancy Goldner, review of "As Time Goes By," *The Nation*, December 1973.

[11] Nancy Goldner, *The Nation*, May 17, 1971.

[12] Ibid.

**Plate 22** *As Time Goes By*, choreography by Twyla Tharp (1973). Photograph © Herbert Migdoll. Twyla Tharp Archive, The Jerome Lawrence and Robert E. Lee Theatre Research Institute, Ohio State University.

*bends backward as though in a swoon. Another couple finish their little duet standing back to back; indeed, couples stand back to back as often as not. Their hands touch, perhaps, but their bodies slightly pull toward another.[13]*

Again and again we see in Goldner's criticism motivation to locate the source of the meaning of a dance through its structure and how that objective is reflected in the structure of her writing. The strata of her observations are compressed into a tightly framed essay, sharply focussed, while Croce's venture into other worlds before returning. Goldner's observations are symmetrical and chronological while Jowitt's are not strict in proportions; Goldner is almost unwavering from the subject of the dance itself while Siegel opens up the boundaries into history and society. Within the unit of a Goldner review the rational and emotional aspects of responding to dance meet. The structure of the dance shapes the structure of the review and within that structure Goldner pursues movement quality, identifying characteristics, performing differences, objectives of the choreography, images of the dancer's expressive impact and the movement essential to the force of that impact. Poetic imagination and logical intuition working together make Goldner's criticism ring true in terms of both the facts of the dance and the *felt experience* of watching the dance.

*After I have seen a ballet with emotional content, I find myself relating what it was about in an abstract or metaphorical way, because to relate what I actually saw would not account for what I felt. The ballet gives off strong feelings, but choreography is obscure. Mysteriously, the whole becomes larger, than the parts. One is hard put to determine what creates the overall effect because the raw material, the steps, bear no relation to what we experience in our lives. I think of George Balanchine's* Liebeslieder Walzer *and immediately metaphors crowd my mind: nostalgia, the oppressive luxuriousness of dying flowers, a heroic resignation. The ballet is "about" these feelings but I cannot see them on the stage. I do notice, however, that the dancers' shift of weight, their rise and fall, emphasize the low swing of the waltz, that the bodies are more drawn to the floor than to the air. Maybe that is why* Liebeslieder Walzer *is "that" way. In a work by Martha Graham, the connection between movement and emotional content is clearer. One distills a Graham work by saying that it is about fear, and then returns to the source by saying it contains contractions in the stomach muscles. A critic must find the correct metaphors, but is committed not only to describing what ballets make you feel but why they do.[14]*

This feeling that the whole of a dance becomes larger than the parts is the mystery that Goldner seeks to solve in her criticism and it is this, I believe, that accounts for her style of criticism — *the taking in of the whole of the dance.*

---

[13] Ibid.

[14] Nancy Goldner, op. cit., November 16, 1970, p. 505.

Within the spectrum of Goldner's criticism, from inspired poetic language to the nuts and bolts of structure, it is dance on its own terms, as its own subject, that is primary to her critical response. The dance viewed generates its own particular imagery, its choreographic dilemmas and resolutions, its mysteries, its activity. The dance, as a piece of literature, is an intricate text of language and meaning. Goldner "reads" the dance and interprets the intentions of its author via the movement before her, nothing more, nothing less. That is why Eliot Feld is so aesthetically satisfying to Goldner, because his style creates meaning in motion:

> *Mr. Feld knows how to invest each sequence of the ballet with drama and emotional impact with only a minimum of "dramatic" movement. The language is pure dance, carrying the barest suggestion of feeling and yet overwhelmingly emotional.*
>
> *How this happens is Feld's (and Balanchine's and Robbins's) secret, but I suspect that Feld understands the symbolic weight of dance, that one gesture or simply the curve of the spine is worth a thousand dance steps. Feld has the economy of an imagist poet......*
>
> *These moments are not isolated events or high points; they are within the very fabric of the choreography, emerging the way an arabesque does. Personality, situation, story and dance are one and the same to Feld.[15]*

The ballets of Alvin Ailey do not satisfy Goldner aesthetically because he seems not to speak directly through a dance vocabulary but, rather, through associations of emotions. He relies on what we know about emotions rather than on what we see in actual steps and sequences of movement:

> *When watching a ballet by Alvin Ailey, I am always acutely aware of his choreographic limitations. He does not seem to be able to give his dancers a rich vocabulary, relying instead on their emotive powers to fill in the gaps......*
>
> *There are, however, some good aspects to "Streams." Structurally, it is the most formal, or architectural, of Ailey's works. The tight structure imposes an emotional restraint on the dancers, which is very attractive.[16]*

Croce expresses the same sentiment and the same set of values when she describes less-than-great choreographers (who are not, according to Croce, in command of their medium in the way that George Balanchine is or Jerome Robbins is or Martha Graham is) as having "no idea how to achieve

---

[15] Ibid.

[16] Nancy Goldner, op. cit., April 24, 1970.

theatrical reality as constituted in time and space rather than in performing personalities and literary ideas."[17] According to Goldner the whole area of transferring literature to dance (therefore a considerable ballet canon — the narrative) is not an area of interest. "I never thought literature and dance had anything to do with each other. Transferring literature to dance is a waste of time and shouldn't be done. My love of music and of dance go hand in hand… it's the nonverbal of dance as an art that interests me."[18]

When Goldner says "The dancer's personality comes forth in technique"[19] one immediately recalls Croce's comment about dancer Suzanne Farrell of the New York City Ballet that "her technique was and is the definition of her personality."[20] The dancer as revealed through choreography and choreography empowered with value and meaning through the dancer is shared critical territory for the New York School, and Goldner's views here are particularly aligned to Croce's.

What are these qualities of the dancer's personality that are revealed in technique? "It's one of the questions for anyone interested in the aesthetics of dance, and its not knowing the answer to my satisfaction that sustains my interest in dance reviewing" says Goldner. The key element in answering this question seems to be within the properties of technique, the actual way in which a fully realized technique can charge this viewing experience with aesthetic emotion, emotion particular to the dance. Goldner illuminates this idea when she says in one review for instance:

> Gelsey Kirkland, by literally rolling her feet onto and off point in a series of quick releves, the usual hop being replaced by the sinuous curl and uncurl of an elephant's trunk, proved in the Corsaire pas de deux that the dancer's soul isn't in the eyes or heart. It's in the muscles, in technique…[21]

And in another review she treats the subject in this way:

> When Corkle made me feel the power of power held in check, she was dancing in the truest sense, and this interested me more then do triple pirouettes, although they are exciting too. Martha Graham's big, arching leg kicks are more interesting as gusts of energy that quickly die than as analogues of joy or pain, and her dancers interest me not for their dramatic abilities but for their technical prowess in being able to make a gust of energy die quickly.

---

[17] Nancy Goldner, *Ballet Review*, Winter, 1988, p. 7.

[18] Nancy Goldner, discussion, September 1994, New York City.

[19] Nancy Goldner, *The Nation*, February 8, 1975, p. 153.

[20] Arlene Croce quoted by Claudia Ruth Pierpont in *Ballet Review*, Winter, 1988, p. 40.

[21] Nancy Goldner, *The Nation*, February 8, 1975, pp. 154–55.

*The dancer's personality comes forth in technique, specifically those aspects of technique, that cut across all modes of dance."[22]*

In the world of dance, she seems to be saying, a certain "seemliness"[23] and etiquette of behaviour should prevail. This is partly to do with the artists' modesty code that calls for humility in greatness and partly to do with the notion of restraint and control as good taste. But perhaps the most important moral message here is that of the morality of great choreography. Great Choreography is best served, best realized through great technique. Both Choreography, as steps and structures, and technique, as refined dynamics, possess the most inherently powerful expressive content. The dancer's approach to and attitude towards technique is something you can feel and something you can see as the "personality" of the dancer and as a vehicle through which the expressive values of the choreography are ultimately served.

The morality of great dancing is realized through the performance of a dancer who makes the dance and not himself the focus of the experience. And it is this morality, as it were, in dance and dancing that is an essential facet of its aesthetic power. One of Goldner's most explicit statements in this regard can be found in her commentary on the dancer Eric Bruhn in an essay called *"Beyond Technique"*.

> *...The difference between Bruhn and others, I think, is that, instead of going beyond technique, Bruhn goes deeper into it. Through purely physical refinements, he discovers that any movement can have many colorations. But it is not only the depth of these refinements that places Bruhn above his colleagues; it is also his willingness to deal with refinements in technique instead of persona. In* Miss Julie *Bruhn was first a dancer, second, Jean and third, Bruhn. Everyone in the audience knew that his decision to dance again was a great event, but he restricted a truly historic and personal occasion to a dance occasion — no more and no less...[24]*

The four critics under examination largely share an instinct for preservation and protection for the American dance identity. They regard the ultimate value of dance works within their endurance factor, their sustaining of aesthetic importance and significance beyond single performances. However, Goldner strikes out in a different direction from her colleagues in so far as

---

[22] Ibid.

[23] Arlene Croce's term coined in "Ballets without Choreography," *Afterimages*, New York: Alfred A. Knopf, 1978, p. 327.

[24] Nancy Goldner, op. cit., p. 155.

her emphasis is not on how the erosion of style by dancers threatens the preservation of works but, rather, how to re-look at and re-think dances in their changing contexts to *get* at that which endures. While she agrees that the New York School of Critics "want to talk more about the work itself than about cast changes" she strongly contends that great dances survive even poor performances.

> All this hullabuloo about the changes in Graham's company (therefore in the presentation of her repertory) is ridiculous. What does it say about your interest in the work to begin with? To say that Primitive Mysteries is ruined because the dancers don't have the weight they used to have is just nostalgia. It's just an excuse not to probe the choreography. Of course, if you really think that the essence of a work is mangled through bad performance, then nitty-gritty details are necessary. But only details will do. The New York School is trying to look for the things that make permanent values in dance a fact of life. One must look for a way .... to get to the essence of the dance.[25]

The ballets of Merce Cunningham, who, according to Goldner and her colleagues is one of the select classicists of American dance, provide illuminating instances for Goldner's distinct views on re-looking as a means to preserving. One of Merce Cunningham's primary tenets as a choreographer has been his particular response to the ephemerality of dance. His repertory encompasses a deliberate changeability within his dances by means of his early "chance" procedures in creating them and by means of his later "Events" which stick together portions of and references to works from his repertory. Goldner responds to Cunningham's work by means of a philosophical question: Can works of art exist only in the exact context for which they were created? Need a work be so constructed that, if one part be removed, the whole structure topples and the extracted part becomes unintelligible? "Some critics require works of art to be made that tightly. Explications look for the interrelatedness of things."[26] In a review of Cunningham's *Event No. 26* in 1972, Goldner takes the position that "Cunningham… requires that each part, each step be so interesting and self-sufficient, that it can stand by itself."[27] This attitude overcomes for Goldner the hurdle of preconceived notions of structure and allows her to take on the task of seeing Cunningham's ballets through a new criterion — the power of steps to act as a form of structure. Cunningham's method she says "makes

---

[25] Interview with Nancy Goldner, June 1985, New York City.

[26] Nancy Goldner, "Event No. 26," *The Nation*, March 20, 1972, p. 381.

[27] Ibid.

the individual step resonate with importance. It allows for segments to stand by themselves and, as *Event No. 26* proved, to stand alongside others from different ballets to form a new ballet."[28]

Of course it is the integrity and power of Cunningham's step invention that persuades Goldner that it is indeed possible to re-examine notions of structure in ballet. As she comments in interview, "with the best dance you think about how it works." In her review of *Event No. 26* Goldner sets about supporting her philosophical hunch about this power-of-steps as the essence of structure in Cunningham dances by providing the reader with detailed descriptive passages ("only details will do") about the look of those steps and the mood they create. In her descriptive analysis she acts as an intermediary for the accessibility of Cunningham. "This is what the choreographer does" she is saying through her description, and "this is how what he does allows us to re-examine the idea of structure" she is saying through her analysis.

The result of her question and answer format of criticism results in her idea that Cunningham's ballets have several living identities, relating to title, mood, tone, and even families of steps. "*Event No. 26* did not deny the special meaningfulness of whole ballets" she states, "but it proved that other meanings are possible."[29] This question and answer format, repeatedly demands that the dance itself be investigated for the issues that it provokes and for the physical properties it contains (steps, images and so forth) that answer to those issues.

Another facet of Goldner's criticism is the story teller mode. In these types of pieces Goldner does not so much investigate a dance through its steps as through its mood. In a long review of the *Stravinsky Violin Concerto* she sets the scene thus:

> When the curtain rises Kay Mazzo and Peter Martins are standing behind a piano. the pianist, Gordon Boelzner, and the violinist, Lamar Also, begin to play, Mazzo and Martins listen to and watch the musicians, from time to time moving their eyes from one musician to the other. Watching them watch becomes a theatrical experience in itself. Their faces speak a multitude of thoughts unknown, but their intensity and sweet concentration rivet the audience. You find yourself listening doubly hard to the music to get a clue about what the dancers are thinking.[30]

---

[28] Ibid.

[29] Ibid.

[30] Nancy Goldner, Review of "Stravinsky Violin Concerto" in *The Nation*, 1972, and reprinted in Nancy Reynolds, *Repertory in Review*, New York: Dial Press, 1977.

For several paragraphs she continues in the same vein until the dancing actually begins. But already the reader has been infected with the same spirit of anticipation that she has experienced.

> *After listening to the first movement the dancers are literally and figuratively moved to dance. You can see the duet literally take shape, and you imagine you can see the notes enter the dancers' bloodstreams and muscles, gently pushing their limbs and tipping their bodies forward, backward, and sideways.*[31]

After sketchily describing a few of the actual movements she again captures the story of the performance by describing a solo danced by Peter Martins in these terms:

> *Martin tries on steps for size; he is dancing, it seems, only for himself and Mazzo, who is leaning against the piano and watching him. Occasionally the violinist looks at him too. Martins is pleased with the way he can dance to the music, and his steps get bigger and more outward.*[32]

Near the end of the review she comments that "throughout the ballet dancers and musicians have been aware of each other. Their dialogue is more than musical but not much more, and therein lies the extraordinary tension and mystery on the stage."[33]

On the one hand, Goldner, like her fellow critics, has the luxury of expressing her responses to dances through different critical tactics because of the access she has to many performances of a given dance. The story-telling approach illustrated in the above review is one such instance of the luxury and in itself it could be seen as less scrutinizing than her more rigorously analytical and descriptive work. However, when looked at in the context of a whole body of writing on the works of a choreographer it does, in fact, act as a significant genre within the repertory of this critic's writing and provides an essential perspective on the work of a choreographer.

Goldner, dance essayist and philosophical inquirer, is highly motivated and inspired by the notion of classicism in dance. She engages a moral sense about the relationship between great dance and its audience and, like Croce, the ennobling capacity of such dance. Her investigative mind is motivated by the mysteries that inspiring choreography prompts her to solve and she goes

---

[31] Ibid.

[32] Ibid.

[33] Ibid.

about this task of problem-solving in a methodical, consistent manner. The structure of her critiques is often in the format of question and answer and she unravels the mysteries of a dance's effects by locating their source within the dance movements themselves. Through vivid description, provocative questions and highly personal dialogue with the dance she views, Goldner tells us the story of what a dance is about and its place or significance in her critical repertory.

**Plate 23** Nancy Goldner, Central Park, New York City, April 1995. Photograph by Jules Cohen.

# 8

# THE FRUITS OF THEIR LABOR: CONCLUDING REMARKS

In an era that produced the choreographic distinctiveness and brilliance of Balanchine, Graham, Taylor, Cunningham, Tharp and others, surely we can ask, in words echoing the sentiment of Edwin Denby, "is this not enough"?[1] The critics of the New York School, in ways remarkable and resolute, have answered "yes" to that question.

In what was truly a Golden Age of choreography they have viewed dance as a choreographic art[2] and have been taught by that choreography how to see in particular ways.[3] Having encountered this fertile frontier of rich choreographic forms, these critics have thrived in their labors of looking and looking again. In their collective force they have created a literature of stature, a literature in sustained dialogue with its subject. From their luxurious and rarefied vantage point within New York's dance boom generation the New York School took on a conscious mission to create "serious" writing about dance. The spirit of their mission, both celebratory and prudent, has yielded a critical repertory. This "repertory" has been shaped from a unique volume and repetition of viewing. It has isolated themes and issues in choreography and performance, engaged in the ongoing elaboration and clarification of dance subjects and the critical process itself, and constructed an accumulative history-in-the-making of choreography through fluent cross-referencing between productions and performances.

To promote dance, to penetrate dance as deeply as possible, and to perceive dance as a cultural and intellectual phenomenon, has required of these critics a ground-breaking liberation of the single review form. Having made the single review "do all it could"[4] they had to go beyond it and make dance writing do more. By challenging their own notions of what they thought was possible to do in dance writing these critics released a new intellectual and sensual insight into the discipline. Their descriptive

---

[1] Alex Katz, "Denby Remembered Part II" *Ballet Review* Summer, 1984, p. 24.

[2] Arlene Croce, discussion, New York City, September 1994.

[3] Nancy Goldner, discussion, New York City, September 1994.

[4] Interview with Deborah Jowitt, New York City, June 1985.

investigations into dances forged a genre of perceptual writing and a language for locating, rendering and probing the physical facts of dances and their sensuous values. Their passionate subjectivity, woven into provocative analysis and enquiry, has infused dance criticism with the livliness and humanity of story-telling.

As women these critics have responded to notions of style, etiquette, morality, gender relationships, and subject with a sense of the formal and the romantic. A choreographic code of purity of means has informed their sensibility aesthetically and sexually. Their collective conscience about history and heritage, posterity and preservation, has politicized their critical function as interpreters and as intermediaries between dancers and dance, and audiences and dance. And with the politics of their perceptions they have claimed for American dance a family tree of innovation and identity.

Through the work of this school of critics the Golden Age of choreography cross-fades with a Golden Age of dance criticism. The relevance of dance in American culture becomes clearer and more potent as their writing reveals it. Through their committment to teaching criticism (especially within the careers of Siegel, Jowitt and Goldner), they have trained a generation of critics how to be more receptive to dance.[5] The most distinguished critics who have come up through their training will perhaps reinforce and refine the concept of a school of dance criticism proposed in this book.[6]

There can be no question that the New York School of dance critics has created a turning point in the history of dance writing. The field of dance criticism has been empowered to unprecedented levels of enquiry thanks to their powerfully pioneering voices and prolonged loyalty to their task. But after such an extraordinarily vital dance era a tranisition is inevitable. And while "the anti-climate of newspaper coverage in dance"[7] that Siegel currently observes may in part reflect that, the dance culture of tranisition and its critical literature is itself the material of debate and discourse among dance, feminist and cultural theorists and critics.

This book has been a reflection on how the four American women dance critics, Marcia Siegel, Deborah Jowitt, Arlene Croce and Nancy Goldner created, through their unique critical vitality, a moment in time in which American dance was situated as cultural artifact.[8] It reflects on how they have empowered dance as a subject for new forms of enquiry and how they have forged a literacy for dance.

---

[5] Interview with Marcia Siegel, New York City, June 1985.

[6] Interview with Deborah Jowitt, New York City, June 1985.

[7] Discussion with Marcia Siegel, New York City, September 1994.

[8] A term used by Marcia Siegel in interview, New York City, June 1985.

# BIBLIOGRAPHY

Abrams, M. H. (1953) *The Mirror and the Lamp* (Romantic Theory and Critical Tradition), Oxford University Press.

Acocella, Joan Ross (1986) "Andre Levinson", *Dance Critics Association News*, Spring.

Acocella, Joan (1992) "How Critics Work", *Dance Ink*, V. 3, N. 2., Summer, pps. 8–11.

Adair, Christy (1992) *Women And Dance (Sylphs and Sirens)*, London: MacMillan.

Adshead-Landsdale, Janet (1993–94) "Dance and Critical Debate", *Dance Theatre Journal*, V. 11, N. 1, Winter.

Adelman, Katie (1982) *"The English School of Dance Criticism Circa 1930–1950"*, MFA Thesis York University: Toronto.

Agee, James (1950) "The Undirectable Director", *Life Magazine*, Sept. 18.

Agee, James (1941) *Agee on Films*, James Agee Trust, Volume 1.

Aiken, Henry David, "The Concept of Relevance in Aesthetics", *Journal of Art and Art Criticism*, V. 6, pp. 152.

Allen, Zita (1980) "Arlene Croce Re-writes Dance History", *The Village Voice*, V. XXV, N. 33, August 13–19.

Aloff, Mindy (1982) "Arlene Croce" in *Dance Magazine*, November.

Austin, Richard (1975) *Images of the Dance*, London: Vision Press.

Balcom, Lois (1945) "Dance Culture in America", *Dance Observer*, November.

Baldwin, Neil (1988) *Man Ray: An American Artist*, New York: Clarkson N. Potter Inc.

Banes, Sally (1991–92) "Dancing in Leaner Times", *Dance Ink*, V. 2, N. 3, Winter, pp. 8–12.

Banes, Sally (1993) *Democracy's Body — Judson Dance Theater, 1962–1964*, Durham & London: Duke University Press.

Banes, Sally (1993) *Greenwich Village 1963 (Avant-Garde Performance and the Effervescent Body)*, Durham & London: Duke University Press.

Banes, Sally (1980) "Jill Johnston: Signaling Through the Flames", *New Performance*, V. 2, N. 1, pp. 11–17.

Banes, Sally (1994) *Writing Dancing in the Age of Postmodernism*, Wesleyan University Press.

Barnside, Fiona (1991) "In Defense of Dance Criticism", *Dance Theatre Journal*, V. 9, N. 1, Summer, p. 22.

Barrett, John Townsend (1955) *"The Analysis and Significance of Three American Critics of the Ballet: Van Vechten, Denby, Kirstein"*, Masters Thesis: Columbia University.

Beardsley, Monroe C. (1958) *Aesthetics: Problems in the Philosophy of Criticism*, New York.

Beardsley, Monroe C. and Schueller, Herbert M. (eds) (1967) *Aesthetic Inquiry: Essays on Arts Criticism and the Philosophy of Art*, Belmont, California: Dickenson Publishers.

Beaumont, Cyril (1950) "Balanchine's Ballet Imperial" in *Ballet*, V. 9, N. 5, May.

Beaumont, Cyril (1950) *Dancers and Critics*, ed. Cyril Swinson, London: Adam & Charles Black.

Beaumont, Cyril (1947) *The Romantic Ballet as Seen by Théophite Gautier*, London.

Bell, Clive (1958) *Art*, New York: Putnam's Capricorn Books.

Bell, Clive (1973) "Significant Form" in *A Modern Book of Esthetics*, ed. Melvin Rader, New York: Holt, Rinehart & Winston.

Beiswanger, George (1973) "Doing and Viewing Dances: A Perspective for the Practice of Criticism" in *Dance Perspectives*, No. 55, Autumn.

Beiswanger, George (1976) "Rakes Progress or Dances and the Critic", *Dance Scope*, V. 10, N. 2, S/S, pp. 29–34.

Beiswanger, George (1962) "Chance & Design in Choreography", *Journal of Aesthetics*, V. 21, No. 1, Fall, pp. 13–17.

Bell, Clive (1919) "New Ballet", *New Republic*, V. XIX, July 30.

Berger, John (1972) *Ways of Seeing*, Penguin: New York.

Blackmur, R. P. (1955) *The Lion and The Honeycomb*, New York: Harcourt Brace.

Blackmur, R. P. (1935) *The Double Agent*, New York: Arrow Editions.

Boas, George (1968) *Primer For Criticism*, New York: Greenwood Press.

Borek, Tom (1974) "About Critic Clive Barnes", *Eddy*, N. 2, Jan.

Borek, Tom (1974) "Edwin Denby Revisited", *Eddy*, N. 3, April.

Brinson, Peter (1963) "Critics and Criticism", *Dancing Times*, London: August.

Buckle, Richard (1950) Review of *Looking at Dance*, by Edwin Denby in *Ballet*, V. IX, N. 1, January.

Carter, Curtis (1976) "Intelligence and Sensibility in the Dance" in *Arts in Society* (Growth of Dance in America), V. 13, N. 2, S/F.

Carter, Curtis (1976) "Some Notes on Aesthetics and Dance Criticism" in *Dance Scope*, V. 10, N. 2, S/S.

Casey, John (1966) *The Language of Criticism*, Methuen and Co. Ltd.: London.

Cass, Joan (1965) "The Critic as Thinker", *Dance Scope*, Fall.

Cavill, Stanley (1969) *Must We Mean What We Say?*, Cambridge University Press.

Chapman, John (1979) "Ballet Criticism in London 1750–1825" in *New Directions in Dance*, ed. Diana Taplin, Oxford: Pergamon Press.

Cobau, Judith (1992) "Women and a Vision of Dance," review of Deborah Jowitt's *Time and the Dancing Image* in *Dance Chronicle*, V. 13, N. 2, pp. 241–245.

Cohen, Selma Jeanne (1974) *Dance as a Theatre Art: Source Readings in Dance History*, New York: Dodd, Mead & Co.

Cohen, Selma Jeanne (1950) "Some Theories of Dance in Contemporary Society" in *Journal of Aesthetics and Art Criticism*, V. 9, N. 2, December.

Cohen, Selma Jeanne (1988) "The Textures of American Dance," *Dance Chronicle*, V. 11, N. 3, pp. 64–66.

Cohen, Selma Jeanne (1962) "A Prolegomenon to an Aesthetic of Dance," *Journal of Aesthetics*, V. 21, N. 1, Fall, pp. 19–26.

Cohen, Selma Jeanne (1986) *Next Week: Swan Lake*, Wesleyan University Press.

Cohen, Selma Jeanne (1950) "Some Theories of Dance in Contemporary Society," *Journal of Aesthetics and Art Criticism*, V. 9, N. 2, December.

Cohen, Selma Jeanne (1970) "The Critic Prepares," *Dance Magazine*, February.

Conrad, Peter (1977) "The Modes of Writing: Metaphor, Metonymy and the Typology of Modern Literature," *New Statesman*, 94.

Copeland, Roger (1993) "Backlash Against Balanchine" in *Choreography and Dance International Journal*, V. 3, Part 3 (issue: *Balanchine: New Approaches*, ed., Eleni Bookis Hofmeister).

Copeland, Roger (1993) "dance criticism and the Descriptive BIAS", *Dance Theatre Journal*, V. 10, N. 3, S/S, pp. 26–31 and Responses to this article, *Dance Theatre Journal*, V. 10, N. 4, Autumn.

Copeland, Roger (1995) "Not/There: Manipulating the Myth of Victim Art" in *American Theater*, April.

Copland Roger (1981) "The Politics of Perception", *Contact Quarterly*, Winter.

Copeland, Roger and Cohen, Marshall (eds) (1983) *What is Dance? (Readings in Theory and Criticism)*, Oxford University Press.

Cornfield, Robert and MacKay, William (eds) (1986) *Dance Writings — Edwin Denby*, New York: Alfred A. Knopf.

Coton, A. V. (1965) "On Modern Dance Aesthetics", *Dancing Times*, V. 55, N. 657, June, pp. 452–94.

Coton, A. V. (1975) *Writings on Dance 1938–68*, London: Dance Books.

Crabb, Michael (ed) (1979) *Visions*, Toronto: Simon & Pierre.

Croce, Arlene (1978) *Afterimages*, New York: Alfred A. Knopf.

Croce, Arlene (1969) "Dance Books in My Life", *Dance Magazine*, March.

Croce, Arlene (1985) "Edwin Denby Remembered Part 1", *Ballet Review*.

Croce, Arlene (1982) *Going to the Dance*, New York: Alfred A. Knopf.

Croce, Arlene (1959) "Hollywood The Monolith," *The Commonweal*, January 23.

Croce, Arlene (1960) "Les Quatre Cents Coups," *Film Quarterly*, V. XIII, N. 3, Spring.

Croce, Arlene (1965) "Notes in la Belle, La Perfectly Swell, Romance," *Ballet Review*, V. 1, N. 1.

Croce, Arlene (1987) *Sight Lines*, New York : Alfred A. Knopf.

Croce, Arlene (1965) "Sylvia, Susan and God," *Ballet Review*, V. 1, N. 1.

Croce, Arlene (1972) *The Fred Astaire and Ginger Rogers Book*, London: WH Allen.

Croce, Arlene (1978–9) "Writing About the Dance" in *Ballet Review*, V. VII, N 4.

Daly, Ann (1991) "What Revolution?: the new dance scholarship in America," *Ballett International*, Koln, V. 14, N. 2, January.

—— (1982) "Dance On Marcia Siegel," Program from the public access cable T.V. Series "Dance On", taped at E.T.C. Studios, directed by William Hohauser.

Deakin, Irving (1936) *Ballet Profile*, New York: Dodge Publishing Co.

Denby, Edwin (1969) "A Conversation with Edwin Denby," Part 1, *Ballet Review*, V. 2, N. 5, pp. 3–30 and Part II, *Ballet Review*, V. 2, N. 6, pp. 33-45.

Denby, Edwin (1949) "Ashton's Cinderella" in *Ballet*, V. 7, N. 2.

Denby, Edwin and Brodovitch, Alexy (1945) *Ballet*, New York: J. J. Augustin.

Denby, Edwin (1965) *Dancers, Buildings and People in the Streets*, New York: Curtis Books.

Denby, Edwin (1949) *Looking at the Dance*, New York: Curtis Books.

Denby, Edwin (1982) "Move by Move in Black and White," review of Arlene Croce's *Sight Lines*, in *The New York Times Book Review*, August 1.

Denby, Edwin (1936) "Nijinska's Noces," *Modern Music*, V. XII, I N. 4, May–June.

Denby, Edwin (1980) "Reminiscences of A Dance Critic," Interview with Edwin Denby, *Performing Arts Journal*, V. IV, N. 1 & 2.

Denby, Edwin (1974) "Two Conversations with Edwin Denby," New York: Byrd Hoffman Foundation.

Dewey, John (1934) *Art as Experience*, New York: Minton, Bulch.

Doob, Penelope (1975) "Touchstones: Sibley, Park and Makarova at Convent Garden" in *York Dance Review*, Spring.

Ducasse, Curt (1966) *The Philosophy of Art*, New York: Dover Publications.

Dufrenne, Mikel (1973) *The Phenomenology of Aesthetics*, Northwestern University Press.

Eliot, T. S. (1925) "The Ballet," *Criterion*, April.

Eliot, T. S. (1962) *Aesthetics and History*, Purdue University, Open Court.

Esslin, Martin (1976) *Anatomy of Drama*, London: Sphere Books.

Farndale, Nigel (1990) "Against Dance Criticism," *Dance Theatre Journal*, V. 8, N. 3, Autumn, pp. 16–18.

Fenner, Theodore (1977–8) "Ballet in Early Nineteenth-Century London," *Dance Chronicle*, V. 1, N. 2.

Ferdun, Edrie (1967) "On Criticism and Dance," *Dance Magazine*, February.

Fleming, Bruce (1991) "Coming to Terms with Reality: American Dance Criticisms Task for the 90's," *Dance Critics Association News*, Spring.

Foster, Susan Leigh (1995) *Choreographing History*, University of Indianna Press.

Foster, Susan Leigh (1986) *Reading Dancing (Bodies and Subjects in Contemporary American Dance)*, University of California Press.

France, C. E. (1977) *Baryshnikov at Work*, London: Adam & Charles Black.

Franks, A. H. (ed) (1955) *Ballet: A Decade of Endeavour*, London: Burke Publishing Co. Ltd.

Friedman, James (1975) *Dancer and Spectator*: An Aesthetic Distance. San Francisco: Ballet Monographs.

Friesian, Joanne (1975) "Perceiving Dance" in *Journal of Aesthetic Education*, V. 9, N. 4.

Fry, Roger (1981) "Essay in Aesthetics," *Vision and Design*, Oxford.

Gautier, Theophile (1932) *The Romantic Ballet* (1837–1848) trans. Cyril W. Beaumont, London: C. W. Beaumont Publisher.

Gill, Jerry H. (1975) "On Knowing the Dancer From the Dance," *Journal of Aesthetics and Art Criticism*, N. 34, Winter, pp. 125–135.

Goldner, Nancy (1975–77) Reviews in *Bennington Review*.

Goldner, Nancy (1970–84) Reviews in *Christian Science Monitor*.

Goldner, Nancy (1970–80) Reviews in *Dance News*.

Goldner, Nancy (1970–80) Reviews in *The Nation*.

Goldner, Nancy (1983–84) Reviews in *The Saturday Review*.

Goldner, Nancy (1980–83) Reviews in *Soho Weekly News*.

Goldner, Nancy (1974) *The Stravinsky Book of the New York City Ballet*, New York: Eakins Press.

Goldner, Nancy (1979) Criticism Seminar (notes) The University of Waterloo, Ontario, Canada, Winter.

Greenberg, Clement (1973) "Modernist Painting," *The New Art*, ed. Gregory Battcock, New York: E. P. Dutton & Co.

Greene, Theodore (1952) *The Arts and the Art of Criticism*, Princeton University Press: Princeton, N. J.

Guest, Ivor (1962) "Ballet Criticism and the Historian's View," *Ballet Annual*, N. 16.

Haggin, B. H. (1971) *Ballet Chronicle*, New York: Horizon Press.

Haskell, Arnold L. (1960) "On Criticism," *London Dancing Times*, V. 50, No. 596, May.

Haskell, Arnold (1977) *Balletomania Then & Now*, New York: Alfred A. Knopf.

Hatfield, Anne (1980) "Illuminating The Dance: Philosophical Enquiry and Aesthetic Criticism," *Dance Research Journal*, V. 13, N. 1, Fall.

Heppenstall, Rayner (1936) *Apology for Dancing*, London: Faber & Faber Ltd.

Herthal, Thomas Barnes (1966) *John Martin, Dance Critic: A Study of His Critical Method in the Dance as Theatre Art*, Cornell University: PhD. Thesis.

Heyl, Bernard (1971) *New Bearings in Aesthetics and Art Criticism: A Study in Semantics and Evaluation*, New York: Greenwood Press.

Isenberg, Arnold (1949) "Critical Communication," *Philosophical Review*, N. 58.

Jackson, George (1988) "Requirements for a Book about Balanchine," *Washington Dance Review*, Winter.

Jackson, George (1988) "School Ties" in *Dance Critics Association News*, Winter.

Jackson, Graham (1978) *Dance as Dance*, Scarborough: Catalyst.

Johnston, Jill (1968) "Martha Graham: An Irresponsible Study... The Head of Her Father," *Ballet Review*, V. 2, N. 4.

Johnston, Jill (1971) *Marmalade Me*, New York: E. P. Dutton.

Jowitt, Deborah (1976) "A Private View of Criticism," *Arts in Society: (Growth of Dance in America)*, N. 13, N. 2, S/F.

Jowitt, Deborah (1977) *Dance Beat*, New York: Marcel Dekker, Inc.

Jowitt, Deborah (1973) "On Seeing Dance," *Artscanada*, N. 30, Oct., pp. 86–88.

Jowitt, Deborah (1985) *The Dance in Mind*, Boston: David Godine.

Jowitt, Deborah (1988) *Time and the Dancing Image*, New York: William Morrow.

Jowitt, Deborah (1986) "Who Are We When We Write?" in *Dance Critics Association News*, Summer.

Katz, Alex (1984) "Denby Remembered – Part II," *Ballet Review*, Summer.

King, Kenneth (1967) "On the Move, A Polemic on Dancing," *Dance Magazine*, June.

Kirstein, Lincoln (1970) *Movement and Metaphor*, New York: Praeger.

Kisselgoff, Anna (1983) "The Search for New Definitions," *The New York Times*, Sunday, March 13.

Kriegsman, Alan (1979) Panel Discussion at Conference entitled "Illuminating Dance: Philosophical Enquiry and Aesthetic Criticism," Temple University: Philadelphia, May 5th.

Laban, Juana de (1971) "Dance Criticism: What Criteria for Analysis?," *Cord Monograph*, No. 1.

Langer, Susanne (1968) "The Dynamic Image: Some Philosophical Reflections in Dance" in *Aesthetics and the Arts*, Jacobus (ed.), New York: McGraw Hill.

Lahr, John (1972) *Acting Out America (Essays on Modern Theater)*, London: Penguin Books.

Levin, David Michael (1973) "Balanchine's Formalism" in *Dance Perspectives* (Three Essays In Dance Aesthetics), No. 55, Autumn.

Levinson, Andre (1927) "The Idea of the Dance: From Aristotle to Mallarme," *Theatre Arts Monthly*, August.

Levinson, Andre (1925) "The Spirit of the Classic Dance," *Theatre Arts Monthly*, March.

Livingston, Jane (1992) *The New York School Photographs 1936–1963*, New York: Stewart, Tubori & Chang Inc.

Lorber, Richard (1975–76) "The Coming of Age of Dance Criticism" in *Dance Scope*, V. 10, N. 1, F/W.

Macaulay, Alastair (1987) "Notes on Classicism" in *Dance Theatre Journal*, V. 5, N. 2, Summer.

Mallarme, Stephane (1956) "Ballets" in *Mallarme*, trans. Bradford Cook, Baltimore: John Hopkins Press.

Margolis, Joseph (1965) *The Language of Art and Art Criticism*, Detroit: Harvester Press Ltd.

Martin, John (1965) *The Modern Dance*, New York: Dance Horizons.

Maxine Sheets (1963) *The Phenomenology of Dance*, Madison: University of Wisconsin Press.

McDonagh, Croce, Doris (1969) "A Converstaion with Edwin Denby," Part I, *Ballet Review*, V. II, No. 5, pp. 3–19, and Part II, V. II, No. 6.

Moore, Nancy (1974) "The New Dance Criticism," *Dance Magazine*, April.

Osborne, Harold (1955) *Aesthetics and Criticism*, London: Routledge & Kegan Paul.

Pearce, Edward (1994) "Critical faculties and artistic impulses," *The Guardian*, Saturday, December 24.

Peckham Sam (1965) *Man's Rage for Chaos*, New York: Alfred A. Knopf.

Pepper, Steven (1963) *The Basis of Criticism in the Arts*, Cambridge: Harvard University Press.

Pierpont Claudia (1988) "Arlene Croce's *Sight Lines*," review in *Ballet Review*, Winter.

Pridden, Deirdre (1952) *The Art of the Dance in French Literature*, London: Adam and Charles Black.

Quinlan, Laurel (1982) *A Way of Seeing: Edwin Denby's Ballet Criticism*, MFA Thesis: York University, September.

Rambert, Marie (1958) "Diaghileff Teachers in America," *Ballet Annual*.

Reynolds, Nancy (1977) *Repertory in Review*, New York: Dial Press.

Salmagundi (1976) "Special Dance Issue," *Arts and Humanities Quarterly*, V. 33–34, Spring-Summer, Skidmore College.

Scotillo, Christina Mary (1978) *The Role of Movement Description in Criticism as a Significant Factor in Developing a Dance Literature*, M.S. Thesis: University of Wisconsin.

Sheldon, Elizabeth (1935) *The Dancer's Quest* (Essays on the Aesthetics of the Contemporary Dance) Berkeley, California: University of California Press.

Sherman, Jane (1988) Review of Marcia Siegel's book *Days on Earth: The Dance of Doris Humphrey* in *Dance Chronicle*, V. 11, N. 3.

Siegel, Marcia B. (1992) "A Ballet's Best Friend," *Dance Ink*, V. 3, N. 3., Fall, pp. 22–29.

Siegel, Marcia B. (1990) "A Conversation with Merce Cunningham," *Dance Ink*, V. 1, N. 1, May/June, pp. 5–10.

Siegel, Marcia B. (1992) "An Audience of One," *Dance Ink*, V. 3, N. 2, Summer, pp. 26–8.

Siegel, Marcia B. (1972) *At the Vanishing Point (A Critic Looks At Dance)*, New York: Saturday Review Press.

Siegel, Marcia B. (1989) "Dance Criticism," *Dance Critics Association News*, Spring.

Siegel, Marcia B. (1987) *Days On Earth – The Dance of Doris Humphrey*, Yale University Press.

Siegel, Marcia B. (1981) "Education of a Dance Critic": The Bonsai and the Lumberjack" in *Dance Scope*, V. 15, N. 1.

Siegel, Marcia B. (1983) "Edwin Denby: An Appreciation," *Ballet News*, V. 5, N. 4, Oct.

Siegel, Marcia B. (1993) "Marthology," *Hudson Review*, Spring, pps. 183–188.

Siegel, Marcia B. (1993) "Math, Mac, and the Music," *Dance Ink*, V. 4, N. 2, Summer, pp. 20–23.

Siegel, Marcia B. (1979) *The Shapes of Change (Images of American Dance)*, Boston: Houghton Mifflin, reprinted, 1985.

Siegel, Marcia (1991) *The Tail of the Dragon (New Dance: 1976–1982)*, Durham & London: Duke University Press.

Siegel, Marcia B. (1977) *Watching the Dance Go By*, Houghton Mifflin.

Sinclair, Stephen (1976) "Dance Critics on Your Toes; What Makes a Good Dance Critic and How Do You Train One?," *The Cultural Post (Washinton Post)*, Issue 8, November/December.

Snell, Michael (1971) "Cunningham and the Critics" in *Ballet Review*, pps. 16–39.

Sontag, Susan (1987) *Against Interpretation*, London: Andre Deutsch Ltd.

Sorell, Walter (1963) "In Defense of the Future," *Dance Observer*, V. 30, N. 6, June/July, pps. 85–6.

Sorell, Walter (1965) "To be a Critic," *Dance Scope*, V. 1, No. 1, Winter.

Stauffer, Donald A. (1941) *The Intent of the Critic*, Princeton University Press.

Steinberg, Cobbett (ed) (1980) *The Dance Anthology*, New American Library: Plume Books.

Stokes, Adrian (1934) *Tonight the Ballet*, London: Faber & Faber.

Stolnitz, Jerome (1960) *Aesthetics and Philosophy of Art Criticism*, Boston: Houghton-Mifflin.

Stuart, Charles (1951) "Fifty Years of Music Criticism" in *Tempo Quarterly Review of Modern Music*, Spring.

Sutton, Walter and Foster, Richard (eds) (1963) *Modern Criticism: Theory and Practice*, New York: Odyssey Press.

Taplin, Diana (1979) "On Critics and Criticism of Dance" in *New Directions in Dance*, ed., D. Taplin, Oxford: Pergamon Press.

Taplin, Theodores Diana (1982) "Towards Mode and Method in Dance Criticism: Description" in *Dance Spectrum: Critical and Philosophical Enquiry*, ed., D. Taplin, Waterloo: Otium Press.

Terry, Walter (1956) "Interview With John Martin," *Dance Magazine*, January.

Tucker, Ken (1981) "On the Beach with the Children of Frank O'Hara" in *Voice Literary Supplement*, October.

Valéry, Paul (1951) *Dance and the Soul*, trans. Dorothy Bussy, London: John Lehmann.

Valéry, Paul (1964) "Philosophy of the Dance," *Aesthetics*, trans. Ralph Manheim (Vol. 13 of The Collected Works) Patheon Books, Random House: New York.

Van Camp, Julie (1980) "Anti-geneticism and Critical Practice in Dance," *Dance Research Journal*, V. 13, N. 1, Fall.

Van Vechten, Carl (1974) *The Dance Writings of Carl Van Vechten*, ed., Paul Padgette, New York: Dance Horizons Press.

Volynsky, Akin (1971) "The Book of Exultation," *Dance Scope*, V. 5, N. 2, Spring.

Waring, James (1965) "About Dancing, or Dancing I Like and Why," *Dance Magazine*, February.

Waring, James (1967) "Five Essays on Dancing," *Ballet Review*, V. 2, No. 1.

Wilde, Oscar (1976) "The Critic as Artist," *The Portable Oscar Wilde*, ed., Aldington, New York: Penguin Books.

# INDEX

This book is part of a series. The publisher will accept continuation orders which may be cancelled at any time and which provide for automatic billing and shipping of each title in the series upon publication. Please write for details.